BASIC QUESTIONS IN THEOLOGY

WOLFHART PANNENBERG

BASIC QUESTIONS IN THEOLOGY

Collected Essays
Volume I

Translated by George H. Kehm

THE WESTMINSTER PRESS
PHILADELPHIA

This book is a translation by George H. Kehm of pages 1-201 of
Grundfragen systematischer Theologie published in 1967 by
Vandenhoeck & Ruprecht in Göttingen, West Germany.

The text of the first part of chapter 2 is a reprint of the essay
"Redemptive Event and History," translated by Shirley Guthrie,
that appears in *Essays on Old Testament Hermeneutics,* ed. by
Claus Westermann (E. T. ed. by James L. Mays) © 1963 M. E.
Bratcher, and is used with the permission of the publisher,
John Knox Press.

Chapter 4 is adapted from Paul J. Achtemeier's translation of
"Hermeneutics and Universal History" by Wolfhart Pannenberg.
Copyright © 1967 J. C. B. Mohr (Paul Siebeck). Reprinted by
permission of Harper & Row, Publishers, Inc.

Published by The Westminster Press ®
Philadelphia, Pennsylvania

PRINTED IN THE UNITED STATES OF AMERICA
9 8 7 6 5 4 3 2 1

Library of Congress Cataloging in Publication Data

Pannenberg, Wolfhart, 1928–
    Basic questions in theology.

    Translation of Grundfragen systematischer Theologie.
    Reprint. Originally published: Philadelphia :
Fortress Press, [1970-1971]
    Includes bibliographical references.
    1. Theology, Doctrinal—Addresses, essays, lectures.
I. Title.
    BT80.P3413   1983   230'.044   82-15984
    ISBN 0-664-24466-1 (pbk. : v. 1)

V.1
C.2

42,670

CONTENTS

ABBREVIATIONS

BC   *The Book of Concord: The Confessions of the Evangelical Lutheran Church.* Translated and edited by Theodore G. Tappert in collaboration with Jaroslav Pelikan, Robert H. Fischer, and Arthur C. Piepkorn, Philadelphia: Fortress Press, 1959.

CD   Barth, Karl. *Church Dogmatics.* Edited by G. W. Bromiley and T. F. Torrance. 12 vols. Edinburgh: T. & T. Clark, 1936–62.

EvTh   *Evangelische Theologie*

KuD   *Kerygma und Dogma*

RGG³   *Die Religion in Geschichte und Gegenwart.* Edited by K. Galling. 3d ed. Tübingen, 1957–65.

WA   Luther, Martin. *Werke, Kritische Gesamtausgabe.* Weimar 1883–.

ZThK   *Zeitschrift für Theologie und Kirche.*

TRANSLATOR'S PREFACE

THE preparation of this translation has been both eased and complicated by the abundance of translations of German theological works and the variety of their translators in recent years. Three of the essays in this volume have previously appeared in English translation, either in whole or in part. This, of course, was of great help since it made it possible for me to compare my version with these others, which led to greater accuracy and clarity in the version that finally emerged. I am indebted to Shirley C. Guthrie, Jr, whose translation (except for footnotes) of most of the first part of "Redemptive Event and History"[1] (below, pp. 15–38) has been used as it originally appeared; and to Paul J. Achtemeier, whose translation of "Hermeneutic and Universal History"[2] (below, pp. 96–136), has been adapted for this volume. A version of "The Crisis of the Scripture Principle," similar to but not identical with the version appearing here, which was published in *Dialog* 2 (1963) – no translator named – was also consulted.

In adapting the latter two translations several serious distortions of meaning have been corrected. Stylistic changes have been made in the interests of clarity and smoother reading (although in a work of this sort, whose complex themes and critical form necessarily place great demands upon the reader, there is often very little that can be done to satisfy these interests). A significant number of revisions were made to achieve greater precision and, as far as possible, some standardization of the English equivalents for current technical and quasi-technical

---

[1] In Claus Westermann (ed.), *Essays on Old Testament Hermeneutics* (Richmond: John Knox Press, 1963), pp. 314–35.

[2] In Wolfhart Pannenberg *et al.*, *History and Hermeneutic*, Journal for Theology and the Church 4 (New York: Harper Torchbooks, 1967), pp. 122–52.

terms in German theological literature. It is on this latter point that the plethora of translations and translators was somewhat disconcerting. Some decisions had to be made.

Here I am greatly indebted to James M. Robinson. I accepted his renderings of the following terms: *"Seiendes"* as "beings"[3] (not "entities" [Macquarrie and E. Robinson[4]] or "essents" [Manheim[5]]); *"existenzial"* and *"existential"* as "existentialist"[6]; *"Geschichtlichkeit"* as "historicness"[7] (not "historicality" [Macquarrie and E. Robinson[8]] or "historicity"); *"Hermeneutik"* as "hermeneutic"[9] not "hermeneutics"); *"Überlieferungsgeschichte"* as "history of the transmission of traditions."[10]

The main reason for these preferences can be given in brief, although much more could be said in defense of each choice. "Entities" ordinarily includes anything whatever, even merely logical objects, a disadvantage noted by Macquarrie and Robinson themselves.[11] It thus fails to connote the ontological status intended by *Seiendes*, which is retained in "beings." Also, "beings" brings out better the contrast and relationship between *das Seiende* and *das Sein* ("Being"),[12] which is crucial for Heidegger and also seems to figure in Pannenberg's usage. "Essents," besides sounding too much like "essences" (thus seeming not to

[3] James M. Robinson and John B. Cobb, Jr (eds.), *The Later Heidegger and Theology*, New Frontiers in Theology 1 (New York: Harper and Row, 1963), pp. ix–xii.

[4] Martin Heidegger, *Being and Time*, tr. John Macquarrie and Edward Robinson (London: SCM Press and New York: Harper and Row, 1962), p. 22, n. 1.

[5] Martin Heidegger, *An Introduction to Metaphysics*, tr. Ralph Manheim (New Haven: Yale University Press, 1959), pp. viiif.

[6] Robinson and Cobb, *Later Heidegger*, pp. ixf.

[7] Cf. Robinson's translation of the opening paragraph of Pannenberg's "Redemptive Event and History" in James M. Robinson and John B. Cobb, Jr (eds.), *Theology as History*, New Frontiers in Theology 3 (New York: Harper and Row, 1967), pp. 14ff.

[8] Heidegger, *Being and Time*, p. 31, n. 2.

[9] James M. Robinson and John B. Cobb, Jr (eds.), *The New Hermeneutic*, New Frontiers in Theology 2 (New York: Harper and Row, 1964), pp. ixf.

[10] Robinson and Cobb, *Theology as History*, pp. ixf.

[11] Heidegger, *Being and Time*, p. 22, n. 1.

[12] Robinson and Cobb, *Later Heidegger*, p. x.

entail existence, contrary to *Seiendes*), seems to be an unnecessary neologism. The meaning of *existenzial* has been determined by its contrast to *existenziell*. The latter may be defined as "that which has to do with the individual's own unique situation and responsibility."[13] The former has to do with an understanding of the structures of human existence such as Heidegger's phenomenological ontology of *Dasein* has produced.[14] Pannenberg uses *existential* mostly with reference to Bultmann's conception of *"existentiale Interpretation."* It is clear that what Bultmann means by this term is an *"existenziale"* interpretation which employs the kind of analysis of human existence Heidegger has developed, and not an interpretation an individual makes out of his own understanding of his particular situation. Hence, "existentialist interpretation," suggesting a theoretical mode of interpretation, is more appropriate than "existential interpretation," which might be taken as meaning the actual, personal interpretation an individual makes in a concrete situation.

"Historicness" picks up better than the other terms the contrast between *historisch* and *geschichtlich* (now commonly rendered "historical" and "historic," respectively).[15] "Historicality" obviously looks as if it were more closely related to "historical" than "historic," even though it is supposed to stand for *Geschichtlichkeit*. Therefore, it seems less preferable than "historicness," which clearly shows that it is related to what "historic" stands for. "Historicity" has long been used in theological literature to designate an event which has been verified by historical research.[16] It is therefore unsuitable for

---

[13] So Schubert Ogden in his introduction to Rudolf Bultmann, *Existence and Faith*, ed. and tr. Schubert M. Ogden (New York: Meridian Books, Inc. and London: Hodder and Stoughton, 1960), p. 7.

[14] Robinson and Cobb, *Later Heidegger*, pp. ixf.

[15] Cf. *ibid.*, p. xi; also Martin Kähler, *The So-called Historical Jesus and the Historic, Biblical Christ*, ed. and tr. Carl E. Braaten (Philadelphia: Fortress Press, 1964), p. 21 (note the presence of the distinction already in the translation of the title). Pannenberg's distinction between *Historie* and *Geschichte* (below, pp. 61f.) seems to tally with Robinson's and Braaten's.

[16] Cf. James M. Robinson, *A New Quest for the Historical Jesus* (London: SCM Press and Naperville, Ill.: Alec R. Allenson, 1959), p. 26.

Geschichtlichkeit, which refers to a fundamental structure of human existence, and not to something as an objective occurrence.

"Hermeneutic," in the singular, was preferred to the plural, "hermeneutics," because it signifies a difference in the character of the modern form of the discipline called *"Hermeneutik"* as compared to the older form of this discipline. Whereas it had been conceived as dealing with the principles of textual exegesis, the newer conception regards it as a comprehensive theory of understanding, including analysis of the ontological conditions of understanding.[17] Such a radical change in the character of a discipline warrants at least a somewhat different name to identify its new form.

The arguments favoring the seemingly cumbersome translation of *Überlieferungsgeschichte* as "the history of the transmission of tradition" are stated by Robinson[18] and need not be repeated here. The most important consideration favoring this translation is the fact that the German term refers as much to the process of transmission as to the context ("the tradition") being passed on.

The term *Aussage* has been rendered both "assertion" and "statement," depending upon the context. "Assertion" was used particularly in the essay "Hermeneutic and Universal History." The usage of the term was governed there by Gadamer's and Ebeling's critiques of conceptions of the process of understanding dominated by the *Aussage.* While their usage was not explicitly dependent upon Heidegger's phenomenological analysis of *Aussage,*[19] the context of Gadamer's discussion, at least, indicates that he had Heidegger's polemic against objectifying modes of thought and speech in mind, and possibly, also, Heidegger's treatment of *Aussage* as a "derivative mode of interpretation." Hence, following Macquarrie and Robinson's rendering of this term in Heidegger, the more restrictive term, "assertion,"

[17] Cf. Robinson and Cobb, *The New Hermeneutic,* pp. 39–77; also Heinz Kimmerle, "Hermeneutical Theory or Ontological Hermeneutics", in Wolfhart Pannenberg *et al., History and Hermeneutic,* pp. 107–21.

[18] See above, n. 10.

[19] Heidegger, *Being and Time,* pp. 195ff.

was preferred to "statement" where the term stood for a very specific mode of linguistic expression. The adjectival use of this term (e.g., "*Aussagestruktur*") in the same context was translated "predicative structure," however, in order to bring to mind the fact that the underlying problem being dealt with in this context is that of objectifying thought, which tends to hold that the most appropriate way of communicating knowledge of something is to speak of it as a subject to which certain predicates may be assigned. In contexts where the meaning of "*Aussage*" was not determined by this underlying problem (e.g., in "What is a Dogmatic Statement?") the less restrictive translation, "statement," was preferred.

I have chosen to go my own way in translating several terms that are either usually rendered differently or else lacking clear precedents in the translations known to me. The notoriously difficult term "*Sache*" has been translated here "essential content," "objective content," and "matter," depending upon the context. The term "subject matter," often used for *Sache*, was used here for *Sachbereich*, which is in accord with the frequent use of "subject matter" in English to refer to the material made available in a particular branch of study. Pannenberg uses *Sache* as synonymous with what Luther called the *res* or "*hauptsächlicher Inhalt*" ("most important content") of Scripture. Hence, in the context of discussions dealing with the relation between the biblical writings and their *Sache*, or between texts in general and their *Sache*, the translation "essential content" has been used. In relation to the *Sache* of a conversation, where the *Sache* is a third thing in which the two partners share, the translation "objective content" has been used. Where *Sache* designates that with which a *Sachbereich* (= "subject matter") has to do, the most general of the three renderings, "matter," seemed most appropriate.

Pannenberg often uses *Deutung* in a pejorative sense, so that the term tends to stand for an interpretation of the significance of a text or an event that imposes on it the interpreter's horizon of meaning rather than expressing its inherent meaning. Hence, *Deutung* has sometimes been rendered here "way of construing" or "construction," rather than the more commonly seen "interpretation," which has been used here chiefly for "*Auslegung*" or "*Interpretation*."

The most difficult set of terms to translate has been *Zusammenhang* and its cognates. *Zusammenhang* has been frequently rendered here as "continuity," rather than the weaker "relationship" or "connection." However, "continuity" does not convey the sense of being linked by a chain of actual events, which is an important element in what Pannenberg means. "Continuity of meaning" (*Bedeutungszusammenhang*) – which, in fact, is something Bultmann might claim for the relationship between his version of the kerygma and the New Testament witnesses – is often all that is meant by "continuity," whereas, for Pannenberg, genuine continuity of meaning exists only where it is inherent in the *Geschehenszusammenhang* ("nexus of events") in which an event stands. "Nexus of events" was chosen for *Geschehenszusammenhang* as more precise than "constellation of events" or "context of events", since the term "nexus" refers more directly to a *connected series* of events than do terms like "context," "constellation," "configuration," etc.

Finally, *Weltoffenheit* has been rendered "openness beyond the world" (and not "openness to the world") in order to express Pannenberg's interpretation of the phenomenon referred to by this term. For Pannenberg, man's openness to the world includes his ability to question every given content and condition in the world, and to imagine something beyond any given state of affairs. In the last analysis, according to Pannenberg, this capacity of man indicates his inalienable determination for God. While "openness to God" would be too strong, "openness to the world" would be too weak a translation. Hence, "openness beyond the world" was selected as including the correct emphases of the two extremes just mentioned.

Where a standard translation of the text cited by Pannenberg already existed in English, that has been followed except for a few cases in which there was warrant for some change.

Pittsburgh Theological Seminary　　　　　GEORGE H. KEHM

FOREWORD

THESE volumes present several works devoted to the understanding of God. They also make accessible essays on the theological importance of history for the understanding of faith, for hermeneutic, and for the concepts of reason and truth – essays which were scattered about in different periodicals and *Festschriften*, some of which are no longer available. The works that deal with the understanding of God [in Vol. 2] are materially very closely related to the studies dealing with the theology of history. Likewise, the question of the theology of history, in the last analysis, has to do with the one theme of all theology which is, quite properly, built into its name. To say that the revelation of God is not a supernatural event which breaks into history perpendicularly from above but rather that it is the theme of history itself, the power that moves it in its deepest dimension, is to say something about God and his relation to the world. Furthermore, if it is true that only with reference to the *totality* of reality can one speak meaningfully about a revelation of God as the world's creator and lord and that reality (understood as historical) is first constituted as the totality of a single history by the end of all occurrences, then eschatology acquires constitutive significance not only for the question of the knowledge, but also for that of the reality, of God. The fundamental significance of eschatology for the concept of history, which the reader can find formulated here in an article from 1959,[1] was applied to the concept of revelation two years later in the second and third dogmatic theses of *Revelation As History*.[2] The studies of truth, reason, and faith [to appear in Vol. 2] trace the roots of these themes to a relation to the eschatological future. My works on

[1] See below, pp. 35ff.
[2] Wolfhart Pannenberg *et al.*, *Revelation as History*, tr. David Granskou (New York: Macmillan Co., 1969), pp. 131–9.

ethics, particularly political ethics, not included in this volume, expressed the critical relevance of this future for presently existing reality. Likewise, in my book on Christology,[3] the eschatological function of Jesus as the anticipation of God's future forms the key to the central theme of the Incarnation. The foundation of all this must ultimately be sought in the concept of God. Epistemological and ontological, as well as cosmological problems arise here which require more extensive investigation if an eschatologically oriented theology is not merely to add to the succession of examples of a theological rhetoric lacking the necessary conceptual backing.

Originally, I planned to add further footnotes in order to provide a running commentary on the diversified critical response that various of these articles have aroused. This intention could not be carried out under the pressure of other commitments. Therefore, I have limited myself to a few indispensable remarks.

The position I took in my argument against the Göttingen historian, Reinhard Wittram,[4] for the unavoidability of the problem of universal history, seems to me to have been strengthened recently by the judgment of Jürgen Habermas that every historian "implicitly" proceeds in such a way that he anticipates "final states of affairs" [*Endzustände*] under the aspects of praxis. By means of these anticipations "he naturally structures the multiplicity of events into deed-orienting histories." The historian's "expectations hypothetically extend the fragments of the previously existing tradition into the totality of a pre-understood universal history, in the light of which every relevant event can in principle be described as completely as possible for the practical, operational self-understanding in a social world of everyday life [*sozialen Lebenswelt*]."[5]

[3] *Jesus – God and Man*, tr. Lewis L. Wilkins and Duane A. Priebe (Philadelphia: The Westminster Press and London: SCM Press, 1968).

[4] Reinhard Wittram, "Die Verantwortung des evangelischen Historikers in der Gegenwart," in *Im Lichte der Reformation* (Jarhbuch des Evangelischen Bundes 5 [Göttingen 1962]), pp. 26–43, especially pp. 39ff. For my argument, see below p. 160, note 19.

[5] Jürgen Habermas, "Zur Logik der Sozialwissenschaften," *Philosophische*

The emphasis on a meaning inherent in and belonging to events themselves[6] has occasionally been felt to be scarcely compatible with the appeal to the nexus of events [*Geschehenszusammenhang*] in which individual events emerge and through which their meaning is determined.[7] This is indeed a serious objection,[8] and it would be unanswerable but for the fact that the specific meaning of the individual event always anticipates a totality of meaning, so that the advance of events and experiences can clarify and correct such anticipated meanings but cannot be that which first gives meaning to them. By virtue of its transcendent meaning, every event is always more than it would be if considered purely by itself, and can become the object of a hermeneutical process[9] that cannot be concluded so long as history continues. This therefore leaves room for different ways of construing events [*unterschiedliche Deutungen*] on the basis of contrasting anticipations of meaning.

One change in my view on an important question cannot go unmentioned here. In "Redemptive Event and History" it is stated that history is event suspended between promise and fulfillment.[10] This thesis, which was oriented toward the historical writings of the Old Testament, was already modified by me in 1961 since, in the judgment of historical science, the biblical "fulfillments" do not correspond to the promises as perfectly as the dogmatic history of the biblical accounts would have it. The perspective of "the history of the transmission of tradition" took the place of a simple correspondence between promise and fulfillment.[11] At the same time it was also necessary to abandon the idea, common to the Old Testament and the ancient Near East, of an event-producing word, and to replace it with that of

Rundschau, Suppl. vol. 5 (1967), p. 166 with reference to Dilthey; cf. also pp. 180 and 194f. To be sure, Habermas evades (p. 166) the question of the conditions for the possible truth of such anticipations – and, therefore, also the question of the real end of history – and in this way avoids making the transition to an eschatological-theological theme.

[6] See below, pp. 85ff., 197ff.   [7] See below, pp. 71ff.; *passim*.

[8] Klaus Schwarzwäller, *Theologie oder Phänomenologie* (Munich, 1966) p. 111; see also p. 117.

[9] See below, pp. 140ff.; 151ff.; 155, note 17.

[10] See below, pp. 19f.   [11] See below, pp. 81–95.

a hermeneutical process involving the ceaseless revision of the transmitted tradition in the light of new experiences and new expectations of the future.

References to "the apocalyptic concept of history," especially in the second essay, need to be modified and made more precise in the light of new research such as the work of Odil H. Steck.[12] The concept of dogma which is used as the point of departure for the discussion on pp. 182–210, has to be criticized in the light of the detailed arguments of Martin Elze.[13] The reader will find more involved discussion of the criticisms that have arisen in the last few years in the volume edited by James M. Robinson and John B. Cobb, Jr, *Theology as History*.[14] In this connection, I must not fail to mention the excellent presentation of my thought by Carl E. Braaten in his *History and Hermeneutics*.[15]

I am grateful to my assistants, Dr Traugott Koch and Harold Ihmig, for their help in proof-reading the manuscript. I dedicate this book to all those persons without whose faithful efforts through all the years in which these essays took shape my work would not have been possible.

Mainz, August 1967   WOLFHART PANNENBERG

[12] *Israel und das gewaltsame Geschick der Propheten* (Neukirchen-Vluyn, 1967).
[13] "Der Begriff des Dogmas in der Alten Kirche," *ZThK* 61 (1964), 421–438.
[14] Especially pp. 221–76.
[15] Philadelphia: Westminster Press, 1966.

I

THE CRISIS OF THE SCRIPTURE PRINCIPLE

A lecture delivered at various places in the United States during 1963. In an earlier form, it appeared in English (*Dialog*, 2 [1963], 307–13) and in Norwegian (*Norsk Teologisk Tidsskrift*, 66 [1965], 106–15). In a longer form, it appeared under the title "Die Grundlagenkrise der evangelischen Theologie" (in *Radius*, 7 [1962], 7–14), and under the title "Die Fragwürdigkeit der klassischen Universalwissenschaft (Evangelische Theologie)" (in *Die Krise des Zeitalters der Wissenschaften* [Frankfurt, 1963], pp. 173–88). The latter, which was the original version, reproduces a lecture given at a conference of the *Deutschen Instituts für Bildung und Wissen* in Arnsberg on October 18, 1962.

SYSTEMATIC theology always takes place within the tension between two tendencies. On the one hand, it is concerned about the faithfulness of theology itself (and, beyond this, of the Christian church) to its origin, the revelation of God in Jesus Christ as this is attested in Scripture. On the other hand, however, the task of theology goes beyond its special theme and includes all truth whatever. This universality of theology is unavoidably bound up with the fact that it speaks of God. The word "God" is used meaningfully only if one means by it the power that determines everything that exists. Anyone who does not want to revert to a polytheistic or polydaemonistic stage of the phenomenology of religion must think of God as the creator of all things. It belongs to the task of theology to understand all being [*alles Seienden*] in relation to God, so that without God they simply could not be understood. That is what constitutes theology's universality.

A theology that remains conscious of the intellectual obligation that goes along with the use of the word "God" will try in every possible way to relate all truth, and therefore not least of all the knowledge of the extra-theological sciences, to the God of the Bible, and to attain a new understanding of everything by viewing it in the light of this God. That task might seem presumptuous, but it is the non-transferable burden laid upon any responsible speech about God. Certainly theology will never be finished with this task. However, the bearing of its burden constitutes not only theology's need but also its dignity, especially in an intellectual situation otherwise characterized by specialist fragmentation.

A theology that devotes itself to this task can easily be suspected of having lost sight of the particular theme with which Christian theology, in distinction to the other disciplines of our universities, is charged. Does not theology – regardless of whether or not it can thereby appear as a "science" alongside the other sciences – have to do, in any event, with the particular revelation of God in Jesus Christ as this is attested in Scripture? On the other hand, rightly understood, the revelation of God as the revelation of *God* is only borne in mind when all other truth and knowledge is organized around it and appropriated by it. Only in this way can the biblical revelation be understood as the revelation of God, the creator and perfecter of all things.

The fathers of the patristic period and the authors of the great scholastic summas knew something about this. Against this background, it seems misleading to me to suppose that theology would be closer to its own "essential content" [*Sache*] (that is, to the biblical tradition) when it falls back upon a separate province of divine revelations and becomes one science alongside others, as has happened increasingly in the course of the modern period and especially in positive, ecclesiastical theology. Such a concept of theology might have its advantages for the peaceful coexistence of theology with the other faculties of the university. But the universality connected with the idea of God thereby falls into oblivion, and a betrayal of the first commandment threatens to occur in theological thought at this point, concealed by sweet-sounding assurances about theology concentrating on its distinctive task.

From its beginnings, Protestant theology has practised such a self-limitation as a matter of course. This fact is to be explained by the late medieval conditions under which it came into existence, especially by the "Scripture-positivism" [*Schriftpositivismus*] which was characteristic of the times, and not only of the school of William of Ockham. Nevertheless, even within such thematic limitation of the task of theology to the exposition of Scripture, the universality of the theme of theology, which is rooted in the monotheistic idea of God, reasserted its claim again and again. Even a theology that wants only to expound Scripture speaks of the creation of the world, of man, and of God's history with the human race comprising all events from the beginning of the world to its coming end. Such statements claim universality, even if theology no longer methodically investigates their relation to statements made by other sciences about the same themes (i.e., the world, man, and the course of history), believing that it has to do only with the particular aspect of revelation and thus only with the exposition of Scripture, independently of what other sciences can discover about these themes on the basis of their own presuppositions.

Such neglect of its universal task has, however, recoiled upon theology. To be sure, the consequences remained hidden for some time, as long as scientists in other fields felt bound to agree with the Bible and the doctrines of the church. But this feeling was chiefly an after-effect of the enormous intellectual exertions of the Middle Ages. As soon as theology understood itself as only one more positive science, the science of revelation, this heritage was at best only formally employed, but not developed further. Theology then no longer changed along with advances in knowledge in the extra-theological sciences. Thus, despite counter-efforts, theology and the secular sciences became estranged from each other. This development sooner or later had to take its toll on theology precisely because of the inalienable universal tendency anchored in the biblical conception of God. If theology and the secular sciences make different and even opposing statements about the world, man and history, then the question as to which of these statements is to be regarded as true becomes imperative. The answering of such questions in accord with the view of the modern sciences could not but reflect upon the credibility of theology and Holy Scripture itself. The self-evidence of theology as a positive, special science for the separate province of revelation proved to be untenable since in the course of modern history the foundation of such theology, Scripture itself, was assailed by criticism. This happened as a reaction brought about by the new understanding of reality worked out by those special sciences that theology had dismissed from its universal theme.

The dissolution of the traditional doctrine of Scripture constitutes a crisis at the very foundation of modern Protestant theology. In our considerations thus far, we have staked out the horizon within which this process developed. Thus, it is clear from the outset that the dissolution of the Scripture principle is very closely connected to the failure of theology in its universal task, although at first glance Scripture might seem to be only a special theme. The concentration upon Scripture and renunciation of the secular sciences had already set in motion the process that resulted in the dissolution of the Scripture principle.

To begin with, let us consider the peculiarity of the Protestant Scripture principle and its connection with the task of the historical-critical exposition of the biblical writings. For the starting-point of the transformation of the foundations of Protestant theology which has been accomplished under the influence of historical consciousness is to be found here.

Luther and the other reformers shared with the patristic and medieval tradition the conviction that Holy Scripture is the ultimate norm of theological doctrine. The meaning of this conviction, however, had already shifted in the course of the Middle Ages. Up to the fourteenth century, orthodox theology in the West felt no contradiction between Scripture and tradition. Although the priority of literal exegesis of Scripture over all moral and allegorical construction [*Deutung*] had been stressed ever since the Scripture research of the school of St Victor in the twelfth century, there was a strong conviction that, in the last analysis, this literal sense of Scripture had itself to be decided by the teaching office of the church. For the authority of Scripture was based on the belief that the biblical books of the prophets and apostles had been verbally inspired by the Holy Spirit. Who, then, could be better equipped to interpret the literal sense of Scripture than the teaching office of the church, to which the gift of the Holy Spirit had been imparted?

Since the Holy Spirit was considered to have been the real author of the biblical writings and, as such, also their authoritative interpreter, the possibility of a conflict between the literal sense of Scripture and the teaching office of the church was not even thought of prior to the fourteenth century. Nevertheless, the possibility of such a conflict became more likely as the methodical application of specific rules for the interpretation of Scripture was perfected in the doctrinal pursuits of the theological schools. Now it could happen that a doctrinal decision by the church or the pope would contradict the results obtained by theologians expounding the pertinent Scripture passages on the basis of these rules. This is in fact what actually did happen in the fourteenth century when William of Ockham and Marsilius of Padua proclaimed the authority of scientifically interpreted Scripture to be above the teaching authority of the pope.

Luther's corresponding doctrine of the clarity of Scripture is no more than the consequence of the methodical and, to that extent, scientific Scripture research of the Middle Ages. The clarity (or self-evidence) of Scripture meant for Luther that its most important or "essential" content [*Sache*] arises clearly and univocally from its words when they are expounded in accord with sound principles, and that nothing remains in a kind of twilight that would require a special, additional construction [*Deutung*]. It was through the univocal sense of Scripture revealed by literal exegesis that Luther saw himself obliged to carry out the fight against the papal teaching office. Luther was convinced that his own doctrine was identical with the "essential content" [*Sache*] of Scripture as this was concentrated in the person and history of Jesus Christ and unfolded in the dogmas of the church. Luther affirmed the clarity of Scripture precisely for the sake of this central content.

From this perspective, one can understand the importance historical-critical investigation of Scripture did and had to acquire in the history of Protestant theology. For what is today called historical-critical exegesis is, according to its goal, simply the endeavor to understand the biblical writings – the intention and content of their statements – out of themselves. The doctrine of the clarity of Scripture necessarily led to the demand that each theological statement should be based on the historical-critical exposition of Scripture. Nevertheless, the development of historical research led to the dissolution of the Scripture principle in the form Protestant scholasticism had given to it, and thereby brought on the crisis in the foundations of evangelical theology which has become more and more acute during the past century or so.

The modern view of the relation of theology to the biblical writings differs from Luther's in two respects. First, for Luther the literal sense of the Scriptures was still identical with their historical content. For us, on the contrary, these two matters have become separated. The picture of Jesus and his history which the various New Testament writers give us cannot, without further qualification, be regarded as identical with the actual course of events. The second difference is linked to the first. Luther could still identify his own doctrine with the content of the biblical writings, literally understood. For us, on the contrary, it is impossible to overlook the historical distance between every possible theology today and the primitive Christian period. This distance has become the source of our most vexing theological problems.

As I have already said, both aspects are intimately related. Both the distance of the New Testament documents from the events to which they witness and their distance from our present situation were discovered by the application to biblical exegesis of one and the same methodological principle, viz., the fundamental principle that the texts be understood out of themselves and, thus, primarily in relation to their contemporary environment. On the one hand, this principle demanded that the interpreter should avoid uncritically injecting his own thoughts and those of his time into the text. The distance between the intellectual milieu [*Gedankenwelt*] of the text and that of the present is already contained in this principle. On the other hand, this way of viewing the texts also made it possible to discover the different tendencies [*Tendenzen*] of the individual New Testament witnesses which guided them in the composition of their writings. Scrutiny of the various tendencies among the New Testament writers threw the differences between the individual writings into bold relief. Thus, the old conception of the biblical canon, involving a material agreement among the biblical writings free from contradiction, collapsed. It was found necessary to distinguish between the attested events themselves and the tendencies in the reporting of the individual biblical writers.

For our historical consciousness, the "essential content" of Scripture which Luther had in mind, viz., the person and history of Jesus, is no longer to be found in the texts themselves, but must be discovered behind them. Thus, the question arose for theology as to which is now to be considered theologically normative, the biblical texts themselves or the history to be discovered behind them. As is well known today, this problem has been disputed over and over again in Protestant theology. The nineteenth-century quest for the historical Jesus based itself on the history of Jesus, but in such a way that the connection between Jesus and the apostolic proclamation of Christ became obscured. The kerygmatic theology of our century countered this approach by declaring that the historical attempt to go behind the texts was theologically irrelevant, and that the texts are theologically binding only in their witnessing character. Today, it is becoming apparent that this is no solution. For the unified "essential content" of Scripture which, for Luther, was the basis of its authority, is for our historical consciousness no longer to be found in the texts but only behind them, in the figure of Jesus who is attested in the very different writings of the New Testament in very different and incongruous ways.

However, it is important today, in contrast to the approach

taken by the liberal quest for the historical Jesus, to keep in mind the connection between the figure of Jesus and the primitive Christian proclamation of him. The fact that it is so difficult to do this reflects the reaction upon theology, noted at the outset, of modern man's secularized view of himself and his world. Only the resurrection of Jesus, conceived in the framework of the cultural situation of primitive Christianity, renders intelligible the early history of Christian faith up to the confessions of Jesus' true divinity. If the resurrection of Jesus cannot be considered to be a historical event, then the historical aspect of the primitive Christian message and its different forms, both of which have crystallized into the New Testament, fall hopelessly apart. In that case, one can relate these two factors to each other at best in a merely external way, as fact and value-judgment, event and significance. The price one pays, however, is that the community's confession of Christ, conceived as a valuation or construction [*Deutung*], takes on the appearance of subjective arbitrariness and "enthusiasm" [*Schwärmerei*] in relation to the event to which it refers.

The gulf between fact and significance, between history and kerygma, between the history of Jesus and the multiplicity of the New Testament witnesses to it, marks one side of the problem of theology today. On the other side is the equally deep gulf between the intellectual milieu of the New Testament texts and that of our own present age. We have already seen that these two aspects are intimately related. They have their common root in the exegetical principle that the contents of the biblical writings are to be understood first of all solely as their authors intended them to be understood and as their original readers understood them. By setting up this exegetical goal, however, the consciousness of the difference between the present situation of the interpeter and the intellectual world of the biblical texts will be continually deepened. And this must happen if one wants to understand what these texts mean in themselves. The only question is how the gulf created by this method can be bridged. Once it has become conscious of the depth of this gulf, no theology can understand itself any longer as "biblical" in the naive sense, as if it could be materially identical with the conceptions of Paul or John. Nor is it possible to offer Luther's thoughts or those of the confessional writings without further ado as the solution for the problem of theology today, and to proffer a so-called reformation theology in such a sense. For in a changed situation the traditional phrases, even when recited literally, do not mean what they did at the time of their original formulation. An external assimilating of Christian language to the thoughts and manner of speaking of the biblical writings is always an infallible sign that theology has side-stepped its own present problems and thus has failed to accomplish what Paul or John or, in his own way, even Luther each accomplished for his own time.

Theology, perhaps, comes closest to material agreement with the biblical witnesses when it seriously takes up the questions of its own time in order to express in relation to them what the biblical writers attested in the language and conceptual framework of their time. Modern hermeneutic deals with this problem of the "repetition" of the same content in a completely changed situation. The question here is how to span the distance between the texts and the present of the interpreter. The Heidelberg philosopher Gadamer has described this task as that of a "fusion of horizons" [*Horizontverschmelzung*], that is, as an expansion of the intellectual horizon of the interpreter to such an extent that it can also encompass the horizon of the text to be interpreted. Such a fusion of horizons would presuppose the historical difference between our own horizon and that of the text. This difference would be overcome without being effaced. But how can that be accomplished? How can the horizon of our present consciousness be fused with that of the primitive Christian writings without effacing the difference between them and us, without diminishing their historical individuality, and without forcing the thought of the present into the conceptions of a past age?

This is, again, an entirely open question in contemporary theology. Can certain biblical conceptions be abandoned as mythological without thereby losing the "essential content" that they really intended to express? What about the resurrection of Jesus, the Christian hope for the future, and, finally, the very idea of a personal God, in this respect? Can theology express the intention of these conceptions in quite another way, say, by a "non-religious interpretation" of the Christian tradition, as is so often talked about today? Or does not theology then cease to be theology? I think it is very questionable whether a satisfactory solution of the hermeneutical problem can be found in the direction of such alternatives.

The reaction against the biblical tradition on the part of the secular consciousness shaped by the emancipated special sciences manifests itself again in the fact that the hermeneutical difference between our present situation and the biblical texts has reached the proportions of a seemingly unbridgeable chasm. Theology can do justice to this situation only if it succeeds in bringing modern thought again into a more conscious connection with Christian tradition. That, however, cannot be accomplished by returning to the authoritarian forms of thought and life from which modern secular culture has freed itself. Rather, it must be shown to the secular present that its own hope for the future becomes recognizable in the event that was foundational for primitive Christianity, and whose meaning for that time was that the eschatological future of the world and the whole human race has dawned. In view of the historical difference between the modern world and primitive Christianity, participation in that primitive Christian faith is possible, without falling into enthusiastic self-forgetfulness, only on the condition that this difference is itself a moment in the action among men of the future of God which appeared in Jesus. Only in this way will it be possible to understand the future of God which appeared in Jesus at that time as the future that still holds sway in our secular world.

Therefore, the attempt must be made to show which motifs of this primitive Christian faith push beyond the limits of the primitive Christian, the patristic, and the medieval worlds. At the same time, it is just as important to show that these impulses have not been impotent in relation to the realities confronting them, but that they have cleared the way for – even if they did not alone produce – the history of Christianity subsequent to these periods as well as its supersession by secular culture in the modern period. An eschatological faith that did not become involved in the structuring of the world and never acquired effectiveness for the present could only be considered as the impotent expression of a past age's longing to flee from the world, instead of being something that could set our present age into that unrest which protects it from self-complacency in the face of death.

It is, therefore, especially necessary to comprehend theologically the Christian legitimacy of the modern period in contrast to older periods of the history of Christianity. To this end, it will be necessary to work out the Christian motifs and the conditions that have grown out of the history of Christianity which have been operative in the rise and development of modern thought and life. But it will also be necessary to analyze the limits and constrictions of the modern view of reality which, with the modern disengagement from the authoritarian form of Christianity, has set itself up in the place formerly occupied by the Christian faith with its hitherto authoritarian forms of tradition.

In this way, it will be possible to view the present situation together with that of primitive Christianity within that horizon which alone connects them without allowing their differences to disappear, viz., the horizon of the process of history itself. The hermeneutical difference between the transmitted texts and our present time must be both established and annulled by a projection of the history that connects them both. Of course, whether consciousness of the historical connection of the present time with primitive Christianity will at the same time mediate truth that can illuminate and unite our contemporary experience of reality depends upon the weighty question whether reality itself, in its fundamental aspects, is to be understood as historical, and the history of nature and man understood in their unity as the history of God.

The hermeneutical problem of how to span the distance

between the ages, and how text and interpreter can be connected by a common horizon, points to the question of a universal history. But universal-historical thinking has its origin in the biblical idea of God. It was the biblical God who first gave rise to an understanding of the totality of reality as a history of ever new, once-occurring events directed toward a final goal, in contrast to the Greek understanding of the world as a constantly uniform order of events. The universal-historical theme of modern philosophy of history was inherited from Jewish apocalyptic and Christian theology of history. The difficulty of speaking of a goal of history as a whole makes it questionable whether universal history can be understood as a unity without the biblical ideas of God. In any case, the history of historicism shows that the universal-historical horizon of understanding faded away with the disengagement of modern historical thought from the biblical idea of God. To be sure, more recent discussions reveal that historical science has been able neither to dismiss nor to avoid the problem of universal history. Do not even the modern natural sciences tend toward a historical understanding of the totality of reality? It appears that the ultimate horizon of the knowledge of nature is today no longer called "law" or "development," but "the history of nature."

We have looked at the double crisis of the Protestant Scripture principle arising, on the one hand, from historical criticism, and, on the other, from the growing awareness of the hermeneutical problem. The result of this analysis is that theology cannot continue as a special science of divine revelation on the basis of Holy Scripture. Precisely in endeavoring to understand the biblical writings it will be led back to the question of the events they report about, and of the meaning that belongs to them. Theology, however, can understand the meaning of these events as deeds of God only in relation to universal history, because statements about the origin of all events can be defended only with a view to the totality of all events. Thus, even for primitive Christianity, the meaning of the resurrection of Jesus was based on the conviction, held by those contemporaries who lived in apocalyptic expectations, that with this event the end of all things had already arrived. Universal history also enables us to span the distance between the time of the earthly appearance of Jesus and our own time, and thus can furnish the basis for a solution to the hermeneutical problem. The problems of a "Scriptural theology" as a positive science of revelation tend of themselves toward the renewal of the universality of theology in the sense of an all-embracing theology of history.

The breakthrough that is necessary here does not mean, to be sure, a mere revision of the specifically Protestant tradition. The scriptural positivism of Protestant scholasticism has its roots far back in medieval scholasticism. The origins of the "positivism of revelation," underlying the rise of Protestant theology, are to be found in the setting of intrinsic [*prinzipiell*] limits between a realm of supernatural knowledge and a contrasting realm of so-called natural knowledge. This distinction was first made as a matter of principle in the thirteenth century. At that time it was justified to the extent that the Christian tradition was indeed the expression of a way of thinking quite different from the Aristotelian philosophy of that century which confronted it and was then considered to embody the classical completion of "natural" knowledge. If one wanted to recognize Aristotelian philosophy and the Christian tradition as belonging side by side, then one had to arrive at such a distinction and such a coordination of the natural and supernatural realms of knowledge. But, for their parts, neither Aristotelian philosophy nor Christian theology were keen on such a mutual completion. Their coordination may have been, rather, the expression of a compromise of theology with the intellectual might of Aristotelianism.

The historical roots of the loss of universality in theology lie in this compromise. The realm of the natural, which in Thomas Aquinas had been carefully tuned to the supernatural order, could change and become independent, and theology would then become a positive science of revelation. The danger of this situation was that theology, and with it the Christian faith itself, increasingly had to appear superfluous from the standpoint of autonomous "natural" thought, instead of taking every thought captive into the obedience of Christ, as the apostle Paul styled his endeavors in 2 Corinthians 10:5.

Today, the need for a breakthrough to such universality is urgent because the revelational point of departure of scriptural theology itself demands it, since the history of the problem of the Scripture principle leads to the question of universal history. However, the understanding of the unity of all reality as history requires taking up the task of understanding all things in relation to the God of the Bible and, thus, to know the biblical God anew as the creator of the world. For the God of the Bible is the God of history, and the understanding of the world as history is that conception of reality which the biblical understanding of God has disclosed to mankind.

2

REDEMPTIVE EVENT AND HISTORY

The following discussion is a slightly revised version of a lecture given in Wuppertal on January 5, 1959, at a meeting of teachers from the theological schools of Bethel and Wuppertal. It deals, particularly in the first part, with a theme on which a theological circle originally from Heidelberg had worked regularly for seven years. Although I am responsible for the following considerations, many of them could not have been expressed as they are without constant conversations with M. Elze, K. Koch, R. Rendtorff, D. Rössler, and U. Wilckens. This essay first appeared in *KuD* 5 (1959), 218–37 and 259–88. [The English translation, by Shirley C. Guthrie, Jr, of most of the first part of the essay, which appeared in Claus Westermann (ed.), *Essays on Old Testament Hermeneutics* (Richmond: John Knox Press, 1963), pp. 314–335, is reprinted below at the request and with the permission of the publisher. The translation of key terms in this reprinted portion of the essay therefore differs from their translation in the rest of the book – Tr.]

HISTORY is the most comprehensive horizon of Christian theology. All theological questions and answers are meaningful only within the framework of the history which God has with humanity and through humanity with his whole creation – the history moving toward a future still hidden from the world but already revealed in Jesus Christ. This presupposition of Christian theology must be defended today within theology itself on two sides: on the one side, against Bultmann and Gogarten's existential theology which dissolves history into the historicity of existence; on the other side, against the thesis, developed by Martin Kähler in the tradition of redemptive history, that the real content of faith is suprahistorical. This assumption of a suprahistorical kernel of history, which was actually present already in Hofmann's delimitation of a theology of redemptive history (*Heilsgeschichte*) over against ordinary history (*Historie*), and which still lives today especially in the form of Barth's interpretation of the Incarnation as "pre-history" (*Urgeschichte*), necessarily depreciates real history just as does the reduction of history to historicity. Both theological positions, that of pure historicity and that of the suprahistorical ground of faith, have a common extra-theological motive. Their common starting point is to be seen in the fact that critical-historical investigation as the scientific verification of events did not seem to leave any more room for redemptive events. Therefore the theology of redemptive history fled into a harbor supposedly safe from the critical-historical flood tide, the harbor of a suprahistory – or with Barth, of pre-history. For the same reason the theology of existence withdrew from the meaningless and godless course of "objective" history to the experience of the significance of history in the "historicity" of the individual. The historical character of redemptive event must therefore be asserted today in discussion with the theologies of existence and redemptive history, and with the methodological principles of critical-historical investigation.

I. THE ACCESSIBILITY OF REALITY AS HISTORY
THROUGH THE BIBLICAL REVELATION OF GOD

1. It is commonly recognized in contemporary research that Israel occupies a singular position in the history of religion because of its historical consciousness. The people of the ancient Orient also recognized, of course, what we call today "historical event." They even developed a historiography; its significance and basic concepts have recently been pointed out. [1] But they

[1] Mircea Eliade, in his work, *The Myth of the Eternal Return*, tr. Willard R. Trask, Bollingen Series, 46 (New York: Pantheon Books, 1954), has comprehensively shown the uniqueness of Israel's historical understanding of reality. The description above follows his exposition. The fact of this uniqueness has been emphasized by Eduard Meyer (*Geschichte des Altertums* [Stuttgart, ³1958], II, 2, p. 285), and in Old Testament research by Gerhard von Rad and Walther Eichrodt (*Theologische Zeitschrift* 4 [1948], 321ff). Recently, Hartmut Gese has not so much disputed as more clearly defined this uniqueness in his "The Idea of History in the Ancient Near East and the Old Testament" (in James M. Robinson (ed.), *The Bultmann School of Biblical Interpretation: New Directions?*, Journal for Theology and Church 1 [New York: Harper and Row, 1967], pp. 49–64). Gese sees the uniqueness of Israel's historical consciousness not simply in the fact that it holds fast to historical details, or in the fact that these details are understood according

could not find any meaning in that which incessantly changes as such. Human life seemed to be meaningful only insofar as it participated in a pre-temporal divine event which was reported by myth and to which men remained in contact through the cult insofar as in the cult the myth was realized. Man saves himself from the threat of the constant change of history in the security of the changeless mythical primal reality which is reflected in the circular course of earthly history. By way of contrast, Israel is distinguished by the fact that it experienced the reality of its God not in the shadows of a mythical primitive history, but more and more decisively in historical change itself.

The disclosure of history in Israel appears to have different roots than those Mircea Eliade holds responsible. Eliade connects Israel's discovery of a meaning of history with prophetic proclamation: The prophets threatened historical catastrophes as God's punishment for the transgression of the people, and history gained meaning and coherence when these announcements were fulfilled in the historical destiny of Israel (*Eternal Return*, pp. 102ff.). But Eliade's arguments do not touch the real basis of the

to a particular scheme (the sequence of times of prosperity and times of disaster, or the connection between act and consequence), but rather in the fact that history moves from God's promise toward a goal (*ibid.*, p. 62), and that God's covenant is consequently not an archetypal, pre-temporal event but a "historical process' (*ibid.*). Just this last characteristic shows how for Israel the historical process becomes the bearer of meaning, whereas the concept of a pre-temporal covenant of God (*ibid.*, p. 52) or of an archetypal order of the sequence of times allows only those aspects of events to appear meaningful which correspond to the extra-historical archetype, so that history as such has no meaning at all (*ibid.*, pp. 55ff.). The state of the case to which Gese calls attention is thus far in complete agreement with the basic view of Eliade (*Eternal Return*, pp. 141ff.), although the details of Eliade's more phenomenologically than historically oriented description may need revision. It is generally acknowledged today that the conceptions of history outside Israel were caught in a cyclical view of time. This view cannot be refuted simply by pointing out that no mythological, cyclical conceptions are to be found in the historiographic documents of the ancient Orient (Gese, "The Idea of History," p. 49). The historiographic schemes could still have an inner connection with such myths, especially if the participation in archetypal events and relationships, which Gese has pointed out in the historiographical schemes of the ancient Orient, is to be conceived in Eliade's way as a fundamental motif of the cyclical view of time (*Eternal Return*, pp. 85ff., 90ff., 112ff., *passim*.).

Israelitic consciousness of history. It cannot originate with the prophets' proclamation of judgment because the beginnings of Israelitic historical writing, which can be recognized as the characteristic understanding of history for Israel, reach back into the time of David and Solomon.

The presuppositions of the historical consciousness in Israel lie in its concept of God. The reality of God for Israel is not exhausted by his being the origin of the world, that is, of normal, ever self-repeating processes and events. Therefore this God can break into the course of his creation and initiate new events in it in an unpredictable way.[2] The certainty that God again and again performs new acts, that he is a "living God," forms the basis for Israel's understanding of reality as a linear history moving toward a goal. But we have not yet thereby described the structure of this history itself.

Within the reality characterized by the constantly creative work of God, history arises because God makes promises and fulfills these promises. History is event so suspended in tension between promise and fulfillment that through the promise it is irreversibly pointed toward the goal of future fulfillment.

This structure is pregnantly expressed, for instance, in Deuteronomy 7:8ff.;

It is because the Lord loves you, and is keeping the oath which he swore to

---

[2] It is a distinctive feature of the Greek view of God that the nature of the gods is exhausted in the function of grounding the normal order of reality. There is no suspicion of a "hidden form" behind their normal activity which needs special revelation (cf. Walter F. Otto, *Theophania*, Rowohlts deutsche Enzyklopädie 15 [Hamburg, 1956], p. 29; Bruno Snell, *The Discovery of the Mind: The Greek Origins of European Thought*, tr. T. G. Rosenmeyer [New York: Harper Torchbooks, 1953; reprinted 1960], pp. 30ff.). On the other hand, it is characteristic not only for Yahweh but for the gods of the ancient Orient generally that such a "hidden form" of the god behind his normal working is presupposed (Hubert H. Schrade, *Der verborgene Gott* [Stuttgart, 1949], pp. 128ff.; Hermann Kees, *Die Götterglaube im Alten Ägypten* [Leipzig, 1941], p. 346). Is this not the basis for the fact that the ancient Oriental gods intervene very arbitrarily in history and can work also in an extraordinary way to bring about contingently a change from a time of prosperity to a time of disaster (Gese, "Idea of History," pp. 54f.)? Despite their similarity, the gods are different from the "living God" of Israel in that even in their contigent activity they are bound to a higher order (*ibid.*, p. 55).

your fathers, that the Lord has brought you out with a mighty hand, and redeemed you from the house of bondage, from the hand of Pharaoh, king of Egypt. Know therefore that the Lord your God is God, the faithful God who keeps covenant and steadfast love with those who love him and keep his commandments to a thousand generations . . . (RSV)

The goal here of Yahweh's action in history is that he be known – revelation. His action comes from his love, begins with his vow, and aims at the goal that Yahweh will be revealed in his action as he fulfills his vow.[3]

What is here compressed into an especially deep and significant formulation is expressive of the structure of the Israelitic consciousness of history in general. The tension between promise and fulfillment makes history. The development of the Israelitic writing of history is distinguished by the fact that the horizon of this historical consciousness becomes ever wider, the length of time spanned by promise and fulfillment ever more extensive.

The first developed concept of history of this kind in Israel[4] is the account of the succession to David's throne (II Sam. 7 – I Kings 2). It begins with the promise to David through Nathan the prophet, the assurance of the continuation of the Davidic dynasty. Everything connected with what is reported here faces the question of who will be the successor to the throne. How will the promise be fulfilled? It often seems that the promise will be frustrated. Finally the fulfillment comes with Solomon's coronation.

In a much greater framework the Yahwistic history certainly shows a similar structure. After the introductory statement of the pre-history, Genesis 12 opens with the promise to Abraham. The J document ends in the book of Joshua with the fulfillment of the promise through Israel's reclaiming the land.

---

[3] On the basis of 1 Kings 20:13, 28, and especially the sayings of Ezekiel, Walther Zimmerli has established the probability that the formula ". . . that you may know that I am the Lord" points back to a form of prophetic speech (Walther Zimmerli, "Das Wort des göttlichen Selbsterweises," *Mélanges Bibliques rédigés èn l'Honneur de André Robert* [Paris, 1957], pp. 154–64).

[4] The following discussion depends on Gerhard von Rad, "Theologische Geschichtsschreibung im Alten Testament," *Theologische Zeitschrift* 4 (1948), 161ff.; and *Old Testament Theology*, tr. by D. M. G. Stalker (Edinburgh: Oliver and Boyd and New York: Harper and Row, 1962), 1, 334 to the end.

In the Deuteronomic source the promise-fulfillment structure appears in a somewhat different form. Promise alone controls the course of history in the account of the succession to the throne and with the Yahwist. This brings all the more impressively into the open the errors of the men involved: *Dei providentia, hominum confusione.* The D document, on the other hand, attaches a qualification to the promise – the qualification of the fulfillment of the law. Along with the promise, the law comes to be the power which determines the course of history. Here we may see the influence of the prophetic proclamation of judgment. With the qualification of the promise by the law, the author of the D source explains why history has worked out negatively. Because of the ever growing guilt of the people, Israel must lose its monarchy and the land which God had promised and given it. Only on the periphery here does the question perhaps remain – whether God nevertheless will cause his promises to triumph. With the law, therefore, the ever growing sin of the people comes to be a power which determines history alongside the promise.

After the genealogies of the Chronicles had already begun history with Adam, Jewish apocalypticism completed the extension of history so that it covered the whole course of the world from Creation to the end.[5] This extension of the concept of history has two important presuppositions: (1) The fulfillment was no longer (as was still the case with prophets) expected within history and therefore seen as a goal which could be superseded, but it was expected at the end of the whole of world history; (2) as already was the case in the D document, the promise is bound to the law. But for apocalypticism the law is not effective only from the time of its historical proclamation; it is an eternal law which is the unchangeable ground of all world history. An eternal election

---

[5] Cf. on this Dietrich Rössler, *Gesetz und Geschichte: Untersuchungen zur Theologie der jüdischen Apocalyptik und der pharisäischen Orthodoxie*, Wissenschaftliche Monographien zum Alten und Neuen Testament 3 (Neukirchen, 1960, ²1962). For a different point of view, see Martin Noth, "The Understanding of History in Old Testament Apocalyptic," in *The Laws of the Pentateuch and Other Essays*, tr. D. R. Ap-Thomas (Oxford: Basil Blackwell and Philadelphia: Fortress Press, 1967), pp. 194–214, esp. pp. 204ff., 207f., 213ff.

precedes the course of history. The communication of the law through Moses is the saving gift which in the future judgment guarantees to the elect salvation through the promises connected with the fulfillment of the law. Jewish apocalypticism may be distinguished from Parsiism precisely by its connection with the scheme of promise and fulfillment.

Thus Israel not only discovered history as a particular sphere of reality; it finally drew the whole of creation into history. History is reality in its totality.

In light of the Israelitic historical writings, it is amazing that Collingwood in his *The Idea of History* asserts that the quasi-historical elements in the Old Testament are not essentially different from the views of other ancient Oriental literature.[6] According to Collingwood, it was not Israel but the Greek Herodotus who discovered history.[7] This judgment shows that he has something in mind quite different from history in the sense of an understanding of the reality of all existence distinguished by certain characteristics. Collingwood means by history the methodical determination of past events – not *Geschichte* but precisely *Historie*. When I distinguish between history as *Geschichte* and as *Historie*, I understand by *Historie*, as H. Diem puts it,[8] "not the history which happened as such" with its own peculiar structure of reality, "but the *historein* of this history" in the sense of the "becoming-acquainted-with and bringing-into-experience and reporting on that which is experienced." Herodotus became the father of history by critically determining the military activities of his time through questioning eyewitnesses so that he was able to make an informed judgment about what actually happened. His express intention, as the autobiographer of his generation,

---

[6] Collingwood, in *The Idea of History* (London: Oxford University Press, 1946), emphasizes only that the "theocratic" element shows not a particularistic but a universalistic tendency (p. 17). Orientalists have also rejected his description of ancient Oriental historiography (cf. the literature cited by Gese, "Idea of History," p. 50, n. 4).

[7] Collingwood, *History*, p. 17.

[8] Hermann Diem, "The Earthly Jesus and the Christ of Faith," in Carl E. Braaten and Roy A. Harrisville (eds.), *Kerygma and History* (New York and Nashville: Abingdon Press, 1962), pp. 207f.

was to create a literary monument to his time.[9] In comparison with other Greek thinkers, Herodotus thereby founded a new methodical way of reporting on past events, but not a new understanding of reality. In this sense Karl Löwith has emphasized that until Polybius Greek historical writing remains completely on the ground of the cyclical understanding of time.[10] The Greek urge toward the unchangeable betrays also in its philosophical form a connection with the way of life of all religions which seek salvation from the "terrors" of historical change in an imitative participation in the archetypal. And the intention of Herodotus not to let the deeds of men be lost with time[11] suggests comparison with the belief of the ancient Egyptians that mortal man may live on in a monument and thus outlast death. In any case, we see in Herodotus anything but an interest in historical change as such.

2. Judaism and the New Testament also hold fast to the reality of history discovered by Israel. In *The Presence of Eternity*, Bultmann argues against this. He sees a close connection between apocalypticism and dualistic Persian eschatology[12] and makes a sharp contrast between apocalypticism and the Old Testament understanding of history. Eschatology is said to contradict the Old Testament concept of God: The dualism of the doctrine of aeons contradicts the Old Testament doctrine of creation; moreover, in the Old Testament God is thought of as the Ruler not of world history but of the history of Israel.[13] Neither of these arguments of Bultmann's is convincing. The concept of aeons in apocalypticism[14] did not displace faith in creation, but rather the law of God controlled the course of history. Already in the prophets God as the Ruler of history is not limited to Israel. Indeed, the pre-history of J places Israel among the peoples of

---

[9] Collingwood, *History*, pp. 25f.

[10] Karl Löwith, *Meaning in History* (Chicago: University of Chicago Press, 1949), pp. 7f.

[11] *Herodotus*, The Loeb Classical Library (London: William Heinemann and New York: G. B. Putnam's Sons, 1931), I, I, p. 3.

[12] Rudolf Bultmann, *The Presence of Eternity: History and Eschatology* (Edinburgh: University Press and New York: Harper and Brothers, 1957 [British title *History and Eschatology*]), pp. 26ff.

[13] *Ibid.*, p. 28.

[14] On the following, see Rössler, *Gesetz und Geschichte*.

the world. Eschatology is not new in apocalypticism, but only the fact that instead of the inner-historical eschatology of the prophets there is now an eschatology of the end of history. In any case, we cannot accept Bultmann's assertion that "now ... history is understood from the point of view of eschatology, which is a decisive change from the Old Testament conception."[15] On the contrary, we must say that the historical consciousness of Israel was always eschatologically oriented insofar as, on the basis of the promise and beyond all historically experienced fulfillments, Israel expected further fulfillment. It is significant that Bultmann does not consider the connection between the apocalyptic picture of history and the Old Testament scheme of promise-fulfillment. On the basis of this connection, he could have understood the end of history as the goal of fulfillment belonging to history, whereas he maintains that "The end is not the completion of history but its breaking-off . . ." and that apocalypticism means a "dehistorization" of history.[16]

It seems to me that the eschatology of the New Testament stands in contradiction to the structure of the historical consciousness of Israel just as little as does that of apocalyptic eschatology. Bultmann's judgment that in the New Testament "history is swallowed up by eschatology"[17] is closely connected with his concept of Jewish apocalypticism, the profound influence of which he himself emphasizes (except in the Gospel of John). It is true that in contrast with apocalypticism, Jesus made expectancy of future salvation depend no longer on relation to the law but on relation to his person.[18] But otherwise the apocalyptic scheme of

[15] Bultmann, *Presence*, p. 29.
[16] *Ibid.*, pp. 30, 35.
[17] *Ibid.*, p. 37.
[18] On the latter point, see Rudolf Bultmann, *Theology of the New Testament* (New York: Charles Scribner's Sons and London: SCM Press, 1951), 1, 7ff. This remains a characteristic of Jesus' proclamation as a whole for Philipp Vielhauer, too ("Gottesreich und Menschensohn in der Verkündigung Jesu," in *Festschrift Günther Dehn*, ed. Wilhelm Schneemelcher [Neukirchen Kreis Moers, 1957], pp. 51ff.), although Vielhauer does not believe the sayings about the Son of Man (also in Mark 8:38) are authentic. This peculiarity of Jesus' message would stand out even more sharply if Heinz Eduard Tödt (*The Son of Man in the Synoptic Tradition* [London: SCM Press

history is maintained. The anticipation of the eschatological decision in the decision with reference to the person of Jesus does not mean the elimination of the futurity of the end. Yet, without destroying this futurity, Jesus is the anticipated end and not the middle of history.[19] We shall see what consequences the presence of the yet outstanding eschaton in Jesus Christ has for the understanding of history.

Bultmann asserts, "Paul has interpreted the apocalyptic view of history on the basis of his anthropology."[20] "But although the history of the nation and the world has lost interest for Paul, he brings light to another phenomenon, the historicity of man...."[21] The "historicity of man" means that "... he gains his essence in his decisions."[22] This understanding of Pauline theology as anthropology is characteristic also of Bultmann's *Theology of the New Testament*. Günther Bornkamm has protested and convincingly argued that Paul is not concerned only with a new self-understanding but with "a new history and existence," in which I am taken up into the history of Christ.[23] Beyond this it must be emphasized that Paul also held fast to the continuity between the salvation event which happened in Christ and the history of Israel. Bultmann obviously does not know what to do with the main document of this continuity, Romans 9–11. He thinks only that the question of the fulfillment of the promises to Israel creates a "difficulty" for Paul.[24] But why then is Paul in Galatians 3.15ff. so decisively interested in the fact that the faithful are the heirs of the promise to Abraham? The promise-fulfill-

---

and Philadelphia: The Westminster Press, 1965]) is right, against Vielhauer, that the Son of Man sayings (especially in Mark 8:38) are genuine. The above description of the relation of this peculiarity of the message of Jesus to the apocalyptic scheme of history follows Dietrich Rössler.

[19] Rudolf Bultmann, "History of Salvation and History," in *Existence and Faith*, ed. and tr. Schubert M. Ogden (New York: World Publishing Co., Meridian Books, 1960), pp. 226–40 – in contrast to Cullmann's conception.

[20] Bultmann, *Presence*, p. 41.   [21] *Ibid.*, p. 43.   [22] *Ibid.*, p. 44.

[23] Günther Bornkamm, "Myth and Gospel," in *Kerygma and History: A Symposium on the Theology of Rudolf Bultmann*, tr. and ed. by Carl E. Braaten and Roy A. Harrisville (New York and Nashville: Abingdon Press, 1962), p. 192.

[24] Bultmann, *Presence*, p. 42.

ment structure remains constitutive also for Paul. This is shown precisely in Romans 9–11 where Paul, without dealing with its details, discusses, so to speak, the general structure of God's redemptive history only to show how the Gentiles are introduced into the redemptive history whose goal is the salvation of Israel (Rom. 11.11ff.).

Bultmann's crowning witness for the dehistorization of history by eschatology is John, with his renunciation of "apocalyptic eschatology."[25] It is well known that Bultmann comes to this understanding of the Gospel of John by excluding expressions which sound apocalyptic on literary-historical grounds.[26] In case these literary-critical operations should prove valid, one must nevertheless agree with the theological judgment of the "early church" that in Christian theology the renunciation of the goal of history is intolerable. But even apart from these considerations, the Gospel of John thinks of Jesus as the fulfillment of the Old Testament witnesses when it calls them witnesses to the Son (John 5.39).

3. It is of great theological significance that the confession of Israel and that of the community of the new covenant consistently hold fast to the one history of God which binds them together. The connection between the Old and New Testaments is made understandable only by the consciousness of the one history which binds together the eschatological community of Jesus Christ and ancient Israel by means of the bracket of promise and fulfillment. Jesus is the revelation of God only in light of the Old Testament promises. When one takes the title "Christ" together with "Son of Man" and "Lord," he must conclude with van Ruler:

Speaking from a Christian point of view, everything stands or falls with the Messiahship of Jesus. And one can decide about this Messiahship only when the question is raised and answered as to whether Jesus really does the works of God. But one can know what the works of God are only on the basis of the Old Testament.[27]

[25] *Ibid.*, pp. 47ff.
[26] Cf. Rudolf Bultmann, *Das Evangelium des Johannes* (Göttingen, [17]1964), p. 196 (on John 5:28f.), p. 162 (on John 6:40, 54).
[27] Arnold A. van Ruler, *Die christliche Kirche und das Alte Testament*, Beiträge zur evangelischer Theologie 23 (Munich, 1955), p. 70.

However, we must also admit with van Ruler that the "subject matter" of the Old Testament received its "foundation" only in Jesus Christ[28] insofar as in him the promises of the Old Testament are fulfilled – in an unexpected way, of course. But the basis for all further Christological statements about Jesus of Nazareth is formed by the dependence of the meaning of Jesus on the fact that his way is understood in the framework of the history of God with Israel attested by the Old Testament. This dependence must not be degraded to a secondary interpretative statement of a Christology which begins with a doctrine of the Incarnation, much less of a Christology which with Schleiermacher begins with the fact of the Christian community. On the contrary, the meaning of Jesus on the basis of his connection with Israel's history of promise is the only foundation on which the doctrine of the Incarnation is to be judged. We must understand also the New Testament proofs from prophecy in terms of the fundamental meaning of this history for the recognition of Jesus Christ. It will not do, as it happened again and again in the case of Schleiermacher and still happens with Baumgärtel,[29] to dismiss the New Testament arguments from prophecy as nothing but an apologetic against the Jews, relevant only to the New Testament period. The use of prophecy as proof is the sharpest expression of the connection between the meaning of Jesus and the history of God with Israel to which the Old Testament witnesses – even though our present historical consciousness cannot uncritically develop the connection in this form.

One gains the impression from the present discussion of the theological hermeneutics of the Old Testament that the theories we have mentioned about the connection between the Old and New Testaments very often do not do adequate justice to history as the unity which holds the old and new covenants together. This is true when the connection is grounded on other phenomena

[28] *Ibid.*, p. 71.
[29] Friedrich Baumgärtel, *Verheissung; Zur Frage des evangelischen Verständnisses des Alten Testaments* (Gütersloh, 1952), pp. 75ff. Cf. Friedrich Schleiermacher, *The Christian Faith*, tr. H. R. Macintosh and J. S. Stewart from the 2nd German ed. (Edinburgh: T. and T. Clark, 1948), sec. 12, par. 2, pp. 60f.; reissued by Harper Torchbooks, 1963.

than the process of the history of promise. I shall attempt to indicate what I mean by this with respect to Bultmann, Baumgärtel, and the advocacy of a typological exegesis of the Old Testament. It is the merit of Bultmann's essay "Prophecy and Fulfillment"[30] that it seeks the connection between the Old and New Testaments in the factual course of Israel's history. But Bultmann determines this connection in such a way that Old Testament history is a history of failure. According to him, this history has a promissory character precisely because in the failure of the hopes centered around the covenant concept, in the failure of the rule of God and his people, it becomes clear that "the situation of the justified man arises only on the basis of this miscarriage."[31] In answer to this position, Zimmerli has rightly asked whether for the New Testament the hopes and history of Israel are "really only shattered." "Is there not fulfillment here even in the midst of the shattering?"[32] Zimmerli sees clearly that the concept of shattering or failure becomes the means by which Bultmann is able "to elevate the Christ-message purely out of history in existential interpretation."[33] Zimmerli's question whether the concept of a pure brokenness of the history of Israel must not lead to an unhistorical conception of the Christ-event, to a "new Christ-myth,"[34] carries much weight. Of course he does not dispute the fact that the New Testament fulfillment of the Old Testament promises does indeed mean a shattering of the original expectations. But he points out that the prophets themselves bear witness to the freedom of Yahweh to "legitimately interpret his promise through his fulfillment, and the interpretation can be full of surprises even for the prophet himself."[35] The fact that Bultmann finds no continuity with the New Testament is certainly connected with the fact that he does not begin with the promises and their structure which for Israel were the foundation of history, and therefore does not understand the events of the history of Israel in their significance as change, as God's "interpretation"

---

[30] In Westermann (ed.), *Essays*, pp. 50–75.   [31] *Ibid.*, p. 75.
[32] Walther Zimmerli, "Promise and Fulfillment," in Westermann (ed.), *Essays*, p. 119.
[33] *Ibid.*, p. 119.   [34] *Ibid.*, p. 120.   [35] *Ibid.*, p. 107.

of the content of the promises – promises which thus endure precisely in change.

Baumgärtel cannot follow Bultmann's thesis of a total failure.[36] He assumes an enduring "basic promise," the content of which is said to be the promise "I am the Lord thy God." Instead of seeking the significant, revelatory history precisely in the transformation of the content of prophecy, he completely abandons the proof from prophecy as unacceptable to our historical consciousness. Beyond this Baumgärtel sees the meaning of the Old Testament only in the fact that its frustrated "salvation-disaster history" exemplifies the way of man under the law and as such is still relevant also for us. Here Baumgärtel comes close to Bultmann's view of the failure of Israel's history and like Bultmann relates it, in dependence on the Lutheran doctrine of the law, to the way of salvation of the individual. It is clear that the history of Israel has no positive theological significance when it is split up into an illustration of the way of the law, on the one hand, and a general basic promise, on the other. Baumgärtel therefore maintains characteristically that the historicity of Jesus Christ is grounded not on the Old Testament but on the Incarnation.[37] One sees how the historicity of Jesus Christ falls when the history of Israel falls.[38] Von Rad attacks the unhistorical concept of a "basic promise" which makes invisible any positive theological significance of the history of Israel. He characterizes the separation of such a general basic promise from particular historically realized promises and prophecies as a "presumptuous encroachment."[39]

The advocacy of a typological exegesis of the Old Testament is based on a concern to find in the Old and New Testaments not only a common "doctrine" or "spiritual content", but to "regain reference to the facts attested in the New Testament"; that is, to discover the connection between the Testaments in the historical process itself.[40] Therefore one looks in the "history worked by

[36] Baumgärtel, *Verheissung.*
[37] *Ibid.,* p. 113.   [38] Van Ruler, *Die christliche Kirche,* pp. 79ff.
[39] Gerhard von Rad, "Verheissung," *EvTh* 13 (1953), p. 410.
[40] Gerhard von Rad, "Typological Interpretation of the Old Testament," in Westermann, *Essays,* pp. 17–39.

God's Word" to the places where "the Christ-event of the New
Testament is prefigured."[41] But it seems that this emphasis on
typological prefiguration as that which really connects the Testaments tends rather to undermine the important intention of discovering the connection between them in historical facts. Not
that the existence of such analogies is to be contested. Of course
we do find analogies between the acts of God, and also in the
behavior of men in response to the historically acting God. Thus,
for instance, in Romans 4 Paul can describe the meaning of faith
with the example of Abraham. But it is doubtful whether in such
analogies, or in those of Hebrews, we see the real unity of the Old
and New Testaments. Do we not thereby lose the connection
again in a finally unhistórical, purely structural similarity of the
Old Testament type to its New Testament counterpart? It is true
that the typological analogy begins with a relationship which
takes place in history. This is reflected in the way the New Testament counterpart goes beyond its Old Testament prefiguration.
But for the typological consideration does not the course of history which unites type and counterpart emphasize the distinction between them, while the connection is discovered in their
structural correspondence?[42] But then, it is difficult to see why
the Old Testament types should still be relevant for Christians
after the New Testament prototype itself has appeared. So long

[41] *Ibid.*, p. 31.

[42] Hans Walter Wolff, "The Hermeneutics of the Old Testament" (in
Westermann, *Essays*, pp. 160–99), emphasizes that history is the foundation
of typological connections. The analogy is "supported by the historical
relation" (pp. 180f.). This is expressed, however, as the "historical distinction" in the analogy between the old and new covenants (p. 180). But the
historical relation may not be understood as historical difference only.
Precisely the connection between the old and new covenants consists not
only and not primarily in the structural analogy, but also and above all in
the temporal, historical continuity of structurally incomparable events.
Doubtless much would be gained and many a hesitation overcome if the
historical relation, in the sense of the historically demonstrable connection,
too, between the changing contents of the promise in the process of its transformation, were emphasized as that which bears and limits the analogical
correspondences and guards against wild analogizing (cf. Walther Eichrodt,
"Is Typological Exegesis an Appropriate Method?," in Westermann,
Essays, pp. 224–45).

as the connection between the Christ-event and the Old Testament is sought primarily in structural agreements, the primary realization in Christ necessarily depreciates the shadowy preliminary representation in Old Testament history. The Old Testament then becomes only a copious picture book – not only of the history of faith,[43] to be sure, but above all of the Christ-event. Those who advocate typological exegesis would doubtless not intend that the Old Testament should be no longer constitutive for the meaning of the Christ-event but only serve as an illustration of it. Von Rad expressly emphasizes:

> . . . for our knowledge of Christ is incomplete without the witness of the Old Testament. Christ is given to us only through the double witness of the choir of those who await and those who remember.[44]

Nevertheless, the conceptual means of the typological analogy is not adequate to express the qualification of the Christ-event by Old Testament history, since in any case nothing is added to the more perfect of the two compared realities (or more exactly, relations) by the analogy with its prefiguration. It is another question whether the typological trains of thought in the New Testament do not mean more than is expressed by the conceptual means of the typological analogy. One would have to investigate the extent to which in the New Testament typologies the theological emphasis falls precisely on the anti-typical element of the Christ-event, especially as it is clear in Hebrews. The relationship between the anti-typical as such and the Old Testament types – a relationship which can hardly be understood to imply only a difference of degree[45] – is a very important theological prob-

---

[43] Von Rad, "Typological Interpretation," p. 27, so characterizes the view of Althaus (*Die Christliche Wahrheit* [Gütersloh, 1947]. pp. 229, 240). This characterization could be extended to apply to Bultmann and, to some extent, to Baumgärtel, too.

[44] Von Rad, "Typological Interpretation," p. 39; cf. Wolf, "Hermeneutics," p. 187.

[45] Thus, Frederik Torm, *Hermeneutik des Neuen Testaments* (Göttingen, 1930), p. 223; and Leonhard Goppelt, *Typos; Die typologische Deutung des Alten Testaments im Neuen* (Gütersloh, 1939), p. 244. But Paul's "how much more" (Rom. 5:17, for instance) expresses precisely the incomparability of Christ and Adam – the point at which there is not simply a higher degree within a common quality, but at which the analogous relationship of the typological

lem.[46] This relationship will be understandable only as a temporal continuity, not as a purely structural correspondence. It is based on the fact that the promises of God were fulfilled in a different way from that in which they were understood by those who first received them, but in such a way that the promises themselves hold good in the change of their content. The new covenant belongs together with the old because of this historical unity, seen in the continuity of the promises in the change of their content. Only from this point of view does the Old Testament remain an independent basis also for the Christian faith – just because the promise must go before the fulfillment if the fulfillment is to be different from the promise. W. Zimmerli has to date worked most decisively in this direction.[47] Certainly on this foundation one can then establish all kinds of typological connections and structural agreements. But they can never be understood as that which constitutes the connection between the Old and New Testaments. This connection is constituted by the one history which includes both Testaments, the history which is itself grounded in the unity of the God who works here as well as there and remains true to his promises.

4. The critique of an anti-historical interpretation of New Testament eschatology in the second section above has consequences for the evaluation of the Christian theology of history in its relation to the New Testament. The theology of history now appears in principle at least as the legitimate heir of the biblical understanding of reality. This point must be made with reference to the two philosophers who have been especially concerned with this problem, Karl Löwith and Wilhelm Kamlah.

Since Löwith depends exegetically not on Bultmann but on Cullmann, he does not speak of an opposition between eschato-

---

parallels is broken. Cf. Günther Bornkamm, *Das Ende des Gesetzes; Paulusstudien*, I (Munich, 1952), pp. 86ff.

[46] The problems designated by the concept "prophecy" intrude themselves here. Prophecy must be distinguished from typological analogy (as Baumgärtel, in opposition to Goppelt, has rightly emphasized [*Verheissung*, p. 71, n. 63]), but at the same time the former can be connected with the latter (e.g., I Cor. 10:4).

[47] See Westermann, *Essays*, pp. 95ff., 112f.

logy and history, but between the salvation event and history. "Considered in the light of faith, worldly occurrences before and after Christ form no continuous sequence of meaningful events, but only the external framework of redemptive history."[48] The anti-historical result is nevertheless similar to that of Bultmann's thought. Löwith speaks of a "modern overrating of history" as the "consequences of our alienation from the natural theology of antiquity and from the supernatural theology of Christianity."[49] He does not understand that redemptive history is not a supra-history, but because of its universal tendency essentially includes all events. For him Augustine's theology of history is already on a wrong track, although it considers world history only as a "fragmentary reflection of its suprahistorical substance."[50]

Kamlah, who appropriates the Bultmannian school's interpretation of early Christian eschatology, makes an even sharper judgment: "According to the original proclamation, Jewish history was in no way continued but rather broken off by Christ."[51] But already in the writings of Theophilus of Antioch "the turn of the aeons has become the turn of a Christian-historical world process."[52] Kamlah considers this development to be an inevitable withdrawal from early Christian beginnings. In this respect he differs from Bultmann: The abolition of the "system of law" in Jesus' proclamation cannot be realized "as soon as and so long as history continues."[53] Thus the delay of the *parousia* must lead to a new turning to the historical. The breach presupposed here by Kamlah does not exist, however, if one maintains the historical horizon of the New Testament itself as the basic presupposition of the early Christian proclamation.

On this basis, it is also not necessary to think so simply as Löwith that a philosophy of world history in the West is a deviation from its origin in the Jewish-Christian understanding of history. Löwith has pointed out very impressively that Western philosophy of history in its whole development, even in its

---

[48] Löwith, *Meaning in History*, p. 184.
[49] *Ibid.*, p. 176.   [50] *Ibid.*, p. 166.
[51] Wilhelm Kamlah, *Christentum und Geschichtlichkeit* (Stuttgart, [2]1951), pp. 111f.
[52] *Ibid.*   [53] *Ibid.*, p. 25.

deterioration, lives from its Christian origin. The deterioration takes place, however, not in the concept of world history as such, but only in the fact that since the Enlightenment, since Vico and Voltaire, man has been exalted to the place of God as the one who bears history.

5. Biblical faith is not only the temporary, accidental presupposition of the Western consciousness of historical reality, but the origin to which this consciousness remains essentially bound.

When man—first of all in the form of mankind – becomes the center which bears history, this function must finally fall to the individual man as soon as the insight prevails that man exists concretely only as the individual. But when the individual man becomes the point of reference for history, then the unity of history is necessarily dissolved into a multiplicity of aspects of the past. Historicism's relativistic dissolution of the unity of history, therefore, was the consequence of the anthropocentric turn of the philosophy of history. The next step along this road could only be the atrophy of the historical consciousness and historical (or at least universal historical) interest generally.[54] With the historical dissolution of the unity of history came automatically the evaporation of the uniqueness of historical reality – including the historicity of man – over against natural reality. Collingwood emphasizes that the interest of the historian rests on presuppositions of faith which have their deepest root in Christianity. In Christianity there is in fact an interest in the past which cannot be surrendered, because it contains the promise which will be fulfilled in the future. Historical experience of reality is preserved only in the biblical understanding of history, in the biblical faith in the promise. With the loss of this origin the experience of reality as history threatens to disappear today.[55]

---

[54] Is something like this beginning to happen with the orientation of historical interest today around the problem of the present? Cf. Reinhard Wittram, *Das Interesse an der Geschichte* (Göttingen, 1958), pp. 7f.

[55] Though without consistent clarity, Nietzsche already attempted to turn back from historical thinking to the ancient conception of nature. Cf. Karl Löwith, *Nietzsche's Philosophie der ewigen Wiederkehr des Gleichen* (Stuttgart, 1956), pp. 113ff. Löwith himself, following Nietzsche, seems to strive to turn away from history to "natural" thinking (cf. *Meaning in History*, p. 207).

For Dilthey the relativization of all historical phenomena and traditions means at the same time the opportunity for the pure development of the historicity of man. The historicity of human freedom in all its creative origin and peculiar significance becomes visible for the first time when the comprehensive world views and systems, including the philosophies of history, lose their claim to authority. "The last step to the liberation of man is the historical consciousness of the finiteness of every historical appearance and every human or social condition, of the relativity of every sort of faith."[56] The later Dilthey expected as the consequence of this liberation the development of a unitary culture of humanity made possible by the relativization of all particular pasts and traditions.[57] In a peculiar transformation of Dilthey's thought, Heidegger also achieved the historicity of existence by going behind the "vulgar" understanding of history. "... because factual existence breaks up, decaying, into the anxious, it understands its history first of all in a world-historical way."[58] Heidegger's concept of the experience of anxiety and being-unto-death achieves something analogous to the historical relativization of world historical content:[59] the liberation of man to his real historicity in existential freedom.

It is understandable that this philosophical position could be appropriated by Christian theology as in Bultmann. The eschatological proclamation also liberates man from the world, from the powers, from the shells of tradition. One cannot deny that there is a certain similarity between these philosophical ideas and the Christian faith. Dilthey himself was aware of the fact that the historicity of man was discovered by Christianity.[60]

[56] Wilhelm Dilthey, *Gesammelte Schriften* (Leipzig and Stuttgart: B. G. Teubner, 1927: [2]1948), 7, p. 290; cf. 8 ([2]1960), p. 223. See also the excellent characterization by Erich Fülling, *Geschichte als Offenbarung; Studien zur Frage Historismus und Glaube von Herder bis Troeltsch* (Berlin, 1956), pp. 36–61.

[57] Dilthey, *Gesammelte Schriften*, 8, p. 167. Cf. Fülling, *Geschichte*, p. 55.

[58] Martin Heidegger, *Being and Time*, tr. John Macquarrie and Edward Robinson (London: SCM Press and New York: Harper and Row, 1962), p. 441 [based on the 7th German edition, *Sein und Zeit* (Tübingen: Neomarius Verlag, 1953), p. 389].

[59] Heidegger, *Being and Time*, pp. 441ff., 443ff.

[60] Cf. Fülling, *Geschichte*, pp. 57f.

There is of course a limitation to this similarity to the Christian faith. Heidegger agrees with Dilthey that the origin of all history is to be sought in the historicity of man: "Existence does have its 'history' and can have it because historicity constitutes the being of this existing one."[61] It must be asked, however, whether historicity rather is not grounded in the experience of reality as history, just as it is made accessible in the history of promise of God with Israel pointing toward the anticipated fulfillment in Jesus Christ. Dilthey's insight that Christianity discovered historicity certainly points most obviously in this direction, and not to the idea that history is grounded in historicity. If the latter were true, that would mean that "Christianity" itself is understood as the expression of the "historical" freedom of man which itself gives form to his life. But if the historicity of man has its origin in the Jewish-Christian faith, and therefore is bound to the experience of reality as history, then it will hardly survive for very long the destruction of the understanding of reality as historical process. The emancipation of historicity from history, the reversal of the relationship between the two so that history is grounded in the historicity of man[62] – this seems to be the end of the way which began when modern man made man instead of God the one who bears history.[63] When the historicity of man is set up in opposition to the continuity of the course of history, the last possible step is taken along the way which leads to the loss of the experience of history as well as that of historicity.

Bultmann[64] and Ernst Fuchs[65] summarize the criticism of the

[61] Heidegger, *Being and Time*, p. 434.

[62] See also Johannes Körner, *Eschatologie und Geschichte; Eine Untersuchung des Begriffes des Eschatologischen in der Theologie Rudolf Bultmanns*, Theologische Forschung: Wissenschaftliche Beiträge zur kirchlich-evangelischen Lehre, 13, (Hamburg, 1957), pp. 111ff.

[63] G. Krüger, *Geschichte im Denken der Gegenwart* (Frankfurt am Main, 1947), pp. 14ff., provocatively described the "historicness" of existentialist philosophy as the expression of the anthropocentric character of modern thought.

[64] Bultmann, "History of Salvation and History," in *Existence and Faith*, pp. 227ff.; "Prophecy and Fulfillment," in Westermann, *Essays*, pp. 71f.; *Presence of Eternity*, pp. 40ff.

[65] Ernst Fuchs, "Christus das Ende der Geschichte," *EvTh*, 8 (1948/49), pp. 447–61, esp. pp. 454ff.

theology of history with the formula that Christ is the end of history. In Christ the eschaton has already appeared. Therefore it seems that history, at least in the sense of a universal historical process, is finished. Christ is the end of history: That means that for the man who believes in Christ the problem of universal history no longer exists. Now we have already seen that the universal historical framework of apocalypticism remains completely valid for the proclamation of Jesus and the New Testament witnesses. From Bultmann's point of view this must appear as a compromise or as an anachronistic holdover. Bultmann is of course correct in saying that for the whole New Testament the eschatological decision takes place already now in encounter with Jesus or the proclamation of him so that the end of history is already here. But this end is provisionally only anticipated within history. What it means that in the person of Jesus the end of history is already anticipated can itself be understood only within the apocalyptic concept of history. Thus the historical framework remains intact. History is by no means abolished. On the contrary, an understanding of history as a whole is made possible for the first time because the end of history is already present.

The misunderstanding that the anticipated appearance of the end of history in the person of Jesus of Nazareth does away with history seems to have risen from making a false parallel to Paul's statement about Christ as the end of the law (Rom. 10.4). But this parallel is not convincing. Law and history are not comparable for Paul. He is concerned with the question of whether the law or the promise controls history (Rom. 4; Gal. 3). History remains the framework of Paul's questioning and within this framework he asks in opposition to apocalypticism whether it is not the promise rather than the law which plays the decisive role in history. He grants that the law is a controlling factor only in a particular period of history – the period which reaches its end with the coming of Christ.

We have said that the anticipated coming of the end of history in the midst of history, far from doing away with history, actually forms the basis from which history as a whole becomes understandable. This does not make possible, however, an oversight over the drama of world history as from a stage box. Second Corinthians 5.7 applies here: "We walk by faith and not by sight" (RSV). Jesus Christ, the end of history, is not available to us as the principle of a "Christologically" grounded total view of world history. Christ's Resurrection, the daybreak of the eschaton, is for our understanding a light which blinds as Paul was blinded on the Damascus road. Even the New Testament witnesses, however powerfully they attempted to express as clearly as possible the reality of this event, could only stammer of it, each in his own way, all of them together in a right contradictory way. Also our participation in this event, the hope of our own resurrection, is still hidden under the experience of the cross. No one can make the eschaton into a key to calculate the course of history, because it is present to us in such a mysterious, overpowering, incomprehensible way. We know only that everything earthly must pass through the cross. The coming of the end of time has broken through all conceptions of the promise of God; indeed, in the event of the Resurrection, it has broken through everything we can conceive of. Therefore we are made receptive to the command of Jesus not to calculate the end (Luke 17.21, 23ff.). The Father alone knows the hour (Matt. 24.36). Thus the freedom of the pure futurity of God is preserved, and thereby also the independence of man, from supposed laws of the course of history.

Does this mean, then, that a theology of history is after all impossible? Not at all. It is one thing to renounce from the very beginning every universal conception of history. It is something quite different if the total view of reality as history which moves from promise to fulfillment is broken open as it were from within. This happens first of all through the unexpected way in which God fulfills his promise, but then through the fact that this fulfillment, the end of history in Jesus Christ, had provisionally already come – and yet precisely thereby is deprived of all comprehension. We can say what such an outbreak of the incomprehensibility of the eschaton in history means only in the framework of a universal historical understanding of the reality in which this outbreak occurs, just because through it the universal historical scheme itself is forced open. Also the sending and history of the eschatological community in the world can be understood only from this point of view.

II. THE HISTORY OF GOD AND
HISTORICAL-CRITICAL RESEARCH

It is usual today to regard historical research and the history of the promises of God as belonging to two completely different spiritual planes. Historical research seems to be essentially a method for discovering and reconstructing past events of our choosing under the guidance of contemporary experience of reality. In contrast to this, the history reported by the biblical witnesses is a sequence of events that happen but once, and which are superior to ordinary criteria and therefore cannot be measured by them.

For the time being, we may leave open the question of the extent to which this kind of contrast is correct. More will be said about this later. In any case, neither history nor theology can be satisfied with such a separation. A general collapse of historical method must result if there exists alongside it another, more fruitful way to certainty about past events, or if this other method were to be declared to be the right historical method. But even from the side of theology, the exclusion of the distinctive biblical history from the realm of historical method is out of the question. The history of God from which faith lives bears witness to the one true God only because the symphony of all human life finds its fulfillment in it. This is expressed in the universal-historical tendency in the Israelite historical consciousness. The exclusive claim of the God of Israel to be the only true God finally becomes effective in this tendency. For this reason, no genuine Christian theology can be satisfied to see the work of historical research as an inquiry on another spiritual plane. Rather, if historical inquiry is not to be rejected as an expression of the untruth in which sinful man lives,[66]

[66] So Erwin Reisner, "Hermeneutik und historische Vernunft," *ZThK* 49

then its truth must be related in some way to the history of God.

1. The Anthropocentrism of Historical Criticism

A fundamental antithesis between the world views of historical method and the biblical history of God can be found in the anthropocentricity of the historical-critical procedure, which seems apt to exclude all transcendent reality as a matter of course.

The profile of the origins of historical-critical research in the cultural history of modern times is undoubtedly marked by anthropocentricity. Vico saw, against Descartes, that historical knowledge is the most reliable we can obtain, since historical events are produced by men and therefore can be reconstructed by the historian by analogy with the universally human, in which the historian also participates. Vico thereby provided the philosophical basis for what the commentaries of the Bollandists had already practiced.[67] But were not the anti-Christian implications of this methodological anthropocentrism obvious by the

---

(1952), 227–35, against Gerhard Ebeling's instructive way of formulating the question in "The Significance of the Critical Historical Method for Church and Theology in Protestantism," in *Word and Faith*, tr. James W. Leitch (London: SCM Press and Philadelphia: Fortress Press, 1963), pp. 17–61. Reisner, who has already presented the same interpretation in his essay, *Offenbarungsglaube und historische Wissenschaft* (Der Anfang 3; Berlin, 1947), draws the radical conclusion that the latter can be completely rejected on the grounds of what he takes to be the difference between the biblical understanding of history and the principles of historical research. Reisner can avoid a docetic abridgement of the Incarnation (*ZThK* 49 [1952], 225ff.) only by opposing the tradition, as an organic, living relationship to the past, to the allegedly disintegrating "analysis" which necessarily precedes a critical reconstruction (*ibid.*, pp. 229f.). However, it is impossible to see why the tradition as the mode of man's relation to God should be absolutely true, while historical criticism should always be in the wrong from the outset, not only in contrast to God but also in contrast to the tradition, no matter how rank tradition's growth may be. In order to find this thesis illuminating, one must share with Reisner an aversion, rooted in the biologistic world view of E. Dacque, from "analytical" thought (*ratio*) and a predilection for the "organic."

[67] Collingwood, *History*, pp. 62ff.

time of Voltaire, at the latest? Is it an accident that the secularization of the Christian consciousness of history through the
elevation of man to the status of the bearer of historical progress
runs parallel to the development of modern historical criticism
with its anthropocentrism?

It must be said here, against all the prejudgments that lie
close at hand, that the principles of historical research do not
have to be essentially and unavoidably imprisoned within an
anthropocentric world view. On the contrary, tendencies of such
a world view hamper the progress of historical research. To be
sure, the connection in cultural history between the development
of historical method and the rise of modern anthropocentric
philosophies of history cannot be dismissed by remarking, for
instance, that this was only a matter of the accidental conditions
involved in the origin of historical method. For there is indeed
an anthropocentric element in the very structure of the methodological principles of historical criticism. The question is only
whether this methodologically essential element must be
bound up with an anthropocentric world view.

The summary of the principles of historical research in Ernst
Troeltsch's famous essay, "Über historische und dogmatische
Methode in der Theologie," offers a convenient way to open up
the discussion of this problem.[68] According to Troeltsch, historical method rests on the "application of analogy," which includes "the fundamental homogeneity [*Gleichartigkeit*] of all
historical events,"[69] as well as on the presupposition of a universal correlation, the "reciprocity of all manifestations of spiritual-
historical life."[70]

The basic thesis of the universal correspondence of all historical phenomena does not have a primarily anthropocentric
structure. That every historical process is reciprocally connected
to events in its environment entirely forbids theological study of
history from taking the biblical witnesses and the events
attested by them in isolation by themselves. Israel's testimonies
of faith, as historical documents, are to be understood only

---

[68] Ernst Troeltsch, *Gesammelte Schriften* (Tübingen, 1913), 2, pp. 729–53,
esp. 731ff.   [69] *Ibid.*, p. 732.   [70] *Ibid.*, p. 733.

against the background of the ancient Near Eastern world, and
the writings of primitive Christianity only in connection with
Judaism and Hellenism.[71] The basic principle of the universal
correspondence of all historical phenomena rules out any
attempt to delimit redemptive history as a realm of a different
kind from the rest of history, which is not to be viewed in
reciprocity with its historical environment, and in which the
rules pertaining to ordinary events are invalid. Still, this is not
necessarily an expression of an anthropocentric, immanentist
way of thinking. The conception of a redemptive history
severed from ordinary history, as in Hofmann's view[72] or in the
sense of Barth's "primal history,"[73] is hardly acceptable on
theological grounds, and is judged not to be so in the first
instance because of historical presuppositions. It belongs to the
full meaning of the Incarnation that God's redemptive deed
took place within the universal correlative connections of
human history and not in a ghetto of redemptive history, or
in a primal history belonging to a dimension which is "oblique"

[71] Georg Wehrung believes it is necessary to defend the autonomy of the
individual against the principle of correspondence (*Geschichte und Glaube;
Eine Besinnung auf die Grundsätze theologische Denkens* [Gütersloh, 1933], pp.
108ff.). But is not Troeltsch's view correct in maintaining against this that
the individual always receives his historical significance first of all from the
matrix of relations in which he stands? Even if "solitary figures" were ever
so important in history, and "the personal decision of the great ones uphold
everything" (*ibid.*, p. 113), they still cannot be isolated from their historical
context.

[72] Ernst-Wilhelm Wendebourg, "Die heilsgeschichtliche Theologie des J.
Chr. K. v. Hofmanns in ihrem Verhältnis zur romantischen Weltan-
schauung," *ZThK* 52 (1955), 64–104, makes it possible to see clearly the
many-sided complex of problems in Hofmann's position, especially by the
instructive comparison with Ranke (pp. 70ff.).

[73] Donald M. Baillie felt tempted to say in response to the early theology of
Barth that "it does not take the Incarnation quite seriously" (*God Was in
Christ* [London: Faber and Faber and New York: Charles Scribner's Sons,
1948], p. 48). This temptation has still not been properly dispelled by the
emphatic theology of Incarnation in the *Church Dogmatics*, since its christological statements refer to a time which is, as it were, above history. Barth's
surmounting of the homogeneous concepts of time and history used in historical research by means of a scheme of hierarchically graded "times of the
Word of God" is penetratingly presented by Hermann Diem (*Dogmatics*,
pp. 52ff., 95ff.).

to ordinary history (and intersects it only at that notorious mathematical point which is without extension on the intersected plane) if, indeed, it has not remained in an archetypal realm above the plane of history.

The principle of universal correlation carries with it the acceptance of causal relations between historical phenomena. Whether such relations are demonstrable in this case or that is a separate question. In any case, however, corresponding phenomena ordinarily allow one to suppose causal and relational connections between them or with some third factor. The most useful form of the concept of development, namely, in the most general sense, that historical formations are not "from the first once-and-for-all-time" finished entities,[74] is associated with the causal character of the universal correspondence. Perhaps it would be clearer at this point to speak of universal changeability instead of development. For every interpretation of history in its totality as de-velopment in the strict sense, namely, as the unfolding of a germ-like tendency, an entelechy, must be judged to be an expression of an immanentist world view which will not do justice to the openness to the future on the part of everything real. An interpretation of the whole of history by means of the idea of development or any idea of an underlying teleology[75] at all, conflicts with the contingency of individual events and is therefore unacceptable on theological as well as historical grounds.[76] The possibility still remains, however, undisturbed by this criticism, of pointing out developmental unities of

[74] Georg Wobbermin, "Geschichte und Historie in der Religionswissenschaft," 2nd. supp. vol. to *ZThK* 21 (1911), p. 15, has rightly designated the concept of development in this neutral sense as belonging to "the essence of history."

[75] Troeltsch eventually undertook this in a grand style, though with many corrections (see, from his early period, "Geschichte und Metaphysik," *ZThK* 8 [1898], pp. 33ff.; and from his later period, above all, *Der Historismus und seine Probleme*, vol. 3 of *Gesammelte Schriften* [Tübingen, 1922], pp. 221–693, esp. pp. 656f.). Troeltsch can make room for contingency only by refusing to allow everything in history to be determined by "historical-developmental idealism."

[76] This explains the reserve of contemporary historians toward the strict concept of development. Reinhard Wittram, in a characteristic manner, will allow it only as a metaphor (*Das Interesse*, p. 45).

limited range within the historical process, which are nevertheless supported and modified on all sides by contingent events.[77]

Thus, the principle of universal correlation by itself provides no basis for an essential opposition between historical method and a theological understanding of history.[78] Only a misuse of the causal principle, which would be historically questionable, too, for the construction of a total explanation of history would necessarily give rise to a conflict at this point.[79] The really critical point for the relation of historical method to theology lies, then, less with historical correlation than with the principle of analogy in historical understanding, which is the root of the comparative method.[80]

As a methodological principle of historical research, analogy means that something difficult to understand, comparatively opaque, is to be conceived and understood by the investigator in terms of what lies closer to him.

Analogy with what happens before our eyes and what is given within ourselves is the key to criticism. Illusions, displacements, myth formation, fraud,

[77] Thus, Friedrich Meinecke, following Herder, allows the concept of development only for the inner unfolding of a temporary individual totality, without including in it changes in the affected individuality itself. Such changes appear as "miracles" in relation to the latter (*Die Entstehung des Historismus* [Munich and Berlin, ²1946], pp. 373ff.).

[78] Hans Emil Weber, *Bibelglaube und historisch-kritische Schriftforschung* (Gütersloh, 1913), also saw no fundamental theological objection to the axiom of the universal correlation of all historical appearances (*ibid.*, pp. 29ff.). However, Weber's thesis that a supernatural causality, too, could and must be admitted into the universal correspondence is in conflict with the historical principle of analogy discussed below and, in addition, implies a false representation of the divine causality as analogous to intraworldly causation.

[79] Otto Kirn strikingly rejected such an absolutization of causal lawfulness, which leads into the vicinity of the dogma of development: "If one formulates the law of causality in such a way that every historical manifestation must be explicable on the basis of the empirically ascertainable total situation of society, then one excludes from the start the originality and novelty which the Christian faith claims for the revelation of God" (*Glaube und Geschichte* [Leipzig, 1900], p. 40).

[80] A survey of the development and application of comparative methods in various cultural disciplines is provided by Erich Rothacker, *Logik und Systematik der Geisteswissenschaften* (Munich, 1926; reissued Bonn, 1948), pp. 92–109.

and party spirit, as we see them before our own eyes, are the means whereby we can recognize similar things in what tradition hands down. Agreement with normal, ordinary, repeatedly attested modes of occurrence and conditions as we know them is the mark of probability for the occurrences that the critic can either acknowledge really to have happened or leave on one side. The observation of analogies between past occurrences of the same sort makes it possible to ascribe probability to them and to interpret the one that is unknown from what is known of the other.[81]

There is obviously an anthropocentric structure in the way in which analogizing deliberations proceed from what lies closest to the investigator's current state of knowledge. This structure is fundamental for the methodological value of analogy as a means of knowing. Only because something about the unknown can be concluded from what is already known can analogy prove its power of disclosure. More difficult to answer is the question of how the nearer, already known entity, on which the analogy is based, is itself constituted. The assumption that lies closest to hand, which goes back to empiricism and was still determinative for the neo-Kantian philosophers of history, Rickert and Simmel, namely, that analogical conclusions ultimately start from present sense experience, has been disputed for good reasons by Dilthey, Cassirer, and, in dependence upon them, Fritz Kaufmann.[82] The priority of the phenomena of expression over all introspective psychology was rightly stressed. The possibilities of life come into view far more clearly in their outward expressions, in the conduct of man, than they do for introspection, no matter how penetrating it might be. Therefore, self-knowledge is gained only by observation of one's own history, not by introspection.[83] The analogies with which the historian understands the content of the tradition as an expression of possible human behavior always arise out of an already given world of expressions in which the historian is at home, and

[81] Troeltsch, "Historische und dogmatische Methode," *Gesammelte Schriften* 2, p. 732.

[82] Fritz Kaufmann, *Geschichtsphilosophie der Gegenwart* (Berlin, 1931), pp. 48f.

[83] It is useful to remember that this central insight of Dilthey's was created out of the heritage of German idealism. It points back to Schleiermacher's hermeneutic and not finally to Hegel's doctrine of the self-knowledge of the spirit through its objectifications.

never from a value-free sense experience. This fact does not change anything about the anthropocentric character of the understanding of strange worlds of expression that moves forward under the guidance of analogy. Therefore, when H. E. Weber objected to the use of the scheme of analogy in historical thought for its "one-sided orientation to contemporary sense experience," he was, in Dilthey's sense, perfectly right. Nevertheless, when one criticizes, with Weber, "the methodological principle of starting with what lies nearest at hand as an expression of the idea of immanence,"[84] then one must be clear that in this form the criticism applies to the analogy principle of historical research generally, and not only to its misuse. For universal analogy should serve not merely to guarantee the unity of historical phenomena, as Weber appears to have presupposed, but also as a means of advancing knowledge. It can do that, however, only if it moves forward on the basis of certain footholds (not necessarily unconditioned by present sense experience), from a fact which had already been illuminated with respect to the thing in question during the process of knowing, to the structure of something which had remained in the dark until then.

A constriction of historical-critical inquiry, in the sense of domination by a biased world view, first occurs when, instead of pointing out analogies from case to case, one postulates a fundamental homogeneity [*Gleichartigkeit*] of all reality with the current range of experience and research. Troeltsch took this step beyond the purely methodological anthropocentrism of the historical conclusion from analogy. He spoke of an "omnipotence of analogy." This includes a "fundamental homogeneity of all historical events, which, to be sure, does not amount to identity, but rather allows all possible room for distinctions, although in general [it] presupposes each time a core of homogeneity in common, from which the differences can be grasped

[84] H. E. Weber, *Bibelglaube*, p. 69. Similarly, already, Martin Kähler, *The So-called Historical Jesus and the Historic, Biblical Christ*, ed. and tr. Carl E. Braaten (Philadelphia: Fortress Press, 1964), pp. 52f.; the English translation is based on the first two essays of the second German ed., *Der Sogennante historische Jesus und der geschichtliche, biblische Christus* (Leipzig, 1896).

and felt."[85] If this sentence said no more than that one might expect always to find this or that similarity between events in this world despite all their dissimilarity, there would be nothing to say against it. However, its meaning is that all differences should be comprehended in a uniform, universal homogeneity. In this form, the postulate of the homogeneity of all events leads to a constriction of the historical question itself. The cognitive power of analogy depends upon the fact that it teaches us to see contents of the same kind *in nonhomogeneous* things [*das Gleichartige im Ungleichartigen*]. If the historian keeps his eye on the nonexchangeable individuality and contingency of an event, then he will see that he is dealing with nonhomogeneous things, which cannot be contained without remainder in any analogy.[86] Provided that historical science is occupied above all with the particularity and uniqueness of phenomena, its interests must therefore be focused more upon the ever peculiar, nonhomogeneous features, rather than the common ones first obtruded by analogies. It was in this sense that Eduard Meyer, in 1902, turned against not only the efforts of the positivistic historians who sought to discover "laws" in history analogous to the natural sciences, but also against an exaggerated interest in the typical at the expense of the individual.[87] The particularity of phenomena, on which genuine historical interests must be focused, threatened to be leveled by a one-sided orientation toward the typical, and historiography became constructivistic. Meyer's argument has lost hardly any of its actuality today:

The need for comprehending the typical in history has become universal.

[85] Troeltsch, "Historische und dogmatische Methode," *Gesammelte Schriften* 2, p. 732.

[86] This point was made emphatically by Eduard Meyer in debate with specialists in history (see n. 87). On the theological side, Otto Kirn (*Glaube*, p. 40) and Georg Wehrung (*Geschichte*, pp. 102ff.) have expressed themselves in a similar way.

[87] Eduard Meyer, "Zur Theorie und Methodik der Geschichte," in *Kleine Schriften* (Halle, 1910 [²1924]), 1, pp. 29ff., 8f., 28. History writing "is also engaged with typical forms, to be sure, but predominantly and in the first instance with the varieties" (*Geschichte des Altertums* [1884], vol. 1, sec. 16, p. 30).

The question about the typical course of the historical process has, in a certain sense, taken over the position held a century ago by the principle of individuality.[88]

In theology, this interest has been expressed chiefly in Lundensian motif-research and in the Uppsala school of Old Testament research. The leveling of historical particularity, brought about by one-sided emphasis on the typical and analogous, threatens to elevate the postulate of the homogeneity of all events to the status of a principle. A similar leveling of the particularity of historical phenomena is also approximated by the attempt to understand historical processes as simply expressions of typical possible modes of existence, following Dilthey's "understanding psychology" [*verstehende Psychologie*] or Heidegger's existentialist analysis.

Nothing that has been said disputes the cognitive power of analogy in historical study. But this power is greater, the more sharply the limitation of the analogy is recognized in each case. Historical method has always enjoyed its greatest triumphs where it could exhibit concrete common possession, and never where it engaged in absolutizing extrapolations of analogies.

The most fruitful possibility opened up by the discovery of historical analogies consists in the fact that it allows more precise comprehension of the ever-present concrete limitation of what is held in common, the particularity that is present in every case in the phenomena being compared.[89] A genuine extension of knowledge takes place in this way. The fundamental anthropological disposition of being able to transcend any given content, the power of concrete negation, is expressed in ability to evaluate discovered analogies right up to their limits.

---

[88] Reinhard Wittram, *Das Interesse*, p. 54 (with reference to the essays by Th. Schieder and B. Zittel in *Studium Generale* 5 [1952]). Wittram himself rates interest in "content as such" higher as it seeks "to understand the astonishing phenomena themselves;" here schemes of typification such as the genetic-causal explanation come into the picture only as auxiliary means (pp. 57f.). A systematic survey of the different forms of typifying modes of observation is given by Fritz Kaufmann (*Geschichtsphilosophie*, pp. 71–109 ["Geschichtliche Typenlehre"]).

[89] So, Rothacker, *Logik*, p. 102. Troeltsch himself could later express himself similarly (*Historismus*, pp. 190ff.).

Theology must take a burning interest in this side of historical work. It is characteristic of the activity of the transcendent God, whose essence is not adequately expressed in any cosmic order but remains free from every such order, that it constantly gives rise to something new in reality, something never before present. For this reason, theology is interested primarily in the individual, particular, and contingent. In the revelatory history, the theological stress falls not least upon the new, upon that which is peculiar to the particular event within the contexts of the history and the promises in which it belongs. For this reason, it is especially important for the historical research carried out within Christian theology that analogies between historical events should not be one-sidedly employed as expressions of homogeneity, but rather used to determine in each case the degree and limits of an analogy. In this way, precisely by uncovering analogies, it will be possible to trace the individual and characteristic features of the events from which the biblical witnesses stem, and also the particularity of the different forms of theological statement in these witnesses, in the context of the biblical tradition itself and in relation to alien material from the history of religions. One can get a clear picture of the state of the case by looking at the way analogy was used in research in the history of religions around the turn of the century, and comparing that to the way it is used today in historical theology. Then, the particularity of the biblical witnesses seemed to disappear behind the parallels from the history of religion. Today, these parallels are the means whereby the particularity of the kerygmatic intention of the biblical witnesses in their transformation of the material they appropriate and have in common with other sources is made visible in a precise way.

If the analogies discovered are employed in full knowledge of the limits of their validity, then they can hardly serve as criteria for the reality of an event affirmed in the tradition, as Troeltsch formulated the matter in the passage quoted above (p. 44, n. 81). That a reported event bursts analogies with otherwise usual or repeatedly attested events is still no ground for disputing its facticity.[90] It is another matter when positive analogies to forms of tradition (such as myths and even legends) relating to unreal objects, phenomena referring to states of consciousness (like visions) may be found in the historical sources. In such cases historical understanding guided by analogy can lead to a negative judgment about the reality of the occurrences reported in the tradition. Such a judgment will be rendered not because of the unusualness of something reported about, but rather because it exhibits a positive analogy to some form of consciousness which has no objective referent [*Realgehalt*].

In conclusion, we return once more to the anthropological character of historical analogy. It is an indication of an unalterable peculiarity of all human knowledge and consciousness that they immediately arrange everything experienced and known around the experiencing ego as their center. But the anthropological character of historical analogy is broken where, by means of such analogies, the more precise comprehension of the

[90] Does not the postulate of the fundamental homogeneity of all events usually form the chief argument against the historicity of the resurrection of Jesus, for example? But if that is so, does not the opinion, which has come to be regarded as virtually self-evident, that the resurrection of Jesus cannot be a historical event, rest on a remarkably weak foundation? Only the particular characteristics of the reports about it make it possible to judge the historicity of the resurrection, not the prejudgment that every event must be fundamentally of the same kind as every other. Characteristic of the influence of this prejudgment in contemporary theological discussion is the way in which Friedrich Mildenberger ("Kerygmatische Historie?" *EvTh* 18 [1958], pp. 419–24) accuses Hans Freiherr von Campenhausen's book, *Der Ablauf der Osterereignisse und das leere Grab* (Heidelberg, 1952; [2]1958) of having illegitimately confused the historical and the kerygmatic because Campenhausen, as a *historian*, risked reckoning with the *possibility* of the resurrection as an explanation for the empty tomb (the emptiness of which Campenhausen believed probable on historical grounds). Mildenberger holds up the authority of an assertion of von Sybel's from the year 1864, according to which "absolute lawfulness in development" is a presupposition of historical research ("Keryg. Hist.?" p. 421). "It will be difficult to refute this statement," he says (*ibid.*). Mildenberger obviously regards as superfluous critical discussion of the above-mentioned argument of Eduard Meyer against every postulate of laws in history, or of the acknowledgment of the contingency of individual events on the part of contemporary natural science.

nonhomogeneous, resistant, alien reality is striven for. To this extent the methodological anthropocentrism of historiography can remain free of the picture of history belonging to an anthropocentric world view.

2. The Monopoly of Historical Method for Historical Knowledge

The fact that something eludes this or that particular analogy by no means demonstrates that it is entirely without analogy. However, to the extent that a datum of tradition bursts the known possibilities of comparison, it remains opaque even for the historian who, among all men, is equipped with extraordinary eyepieces for what has been. He cannot dispute its reality out of hand, Some analogy must be available even for this purpose, namely, a full analogy with some form of consciousness not related to an objective referent. But where analogy ends, there ends with it the possibility of progressively bringing into relief the particular characteristics in contrast to the common ones, and also the process of further deepening understanding. The historian is not the only one confronted by this limit. It is not a matter of a specific barrier that confronts only one among many possible ways of viewing a historical object, so that some kind of "suprahistorical" viewpoint could step in at this "gap" in order to expand our knowledge beyond what is accessible to the historian. On the contrary, the limits of the cognitive power of historical analogy are the limits of possible knowledge of the past generally. In no case is theology, for instance, in the position of being able to say what was actually the case regarding contents which remain opaque to the historian.[91]

[91] Not even historical intuition can open up a second, independent way to what has happened, alongside historical investigation of the particulars. To be sure, the fundamental importance of intuition for all comprehension of past occurrences in their interrelationships, especially for the historian's outline of the course of history, is indisputable. Troeltsch had already vigorously stressed this (*Historismus*, pp. 172, 179). But intuition always needs confirmation by detailed historical observation. Therefore, one can hardly agree with Paul Althaus' statements about the independent certainty that comes

The theologian, like every other man, is referred to the guidance of analogy for his knowledge. The process of pointing out analogies and bringing the particular into relief in view of the concrete, common features always takes place "from below," from the observer's peculiar experiential basis – his everyday world, life-relationships, and contemporary generation – or from this basis broadened by tradition and scientific endeavors. Only along this way "from below" is it possible to shed light on dark matters. The naïve consciousness, however, makes use of analogies in a far more uninhibited way than a scientist might deem justified. Thus, the imagistic world of myth grew up in the form of analogical constructs which, nevertheless, could not stand up to a strict, scientific test of their applicability. The beginning of scientific reflection among the Greeks coincides with the beginning of a reflective and critical use of analogical transference by Empedocles, on the one hand, and Socrates, on the other.[92] This diversified use of analogies (and their respective determination of the element of particularity in each case)

about through intuitive contact with a past fragment of a life (*Fact and Faith in the Kerygma Today*, tr. David Cairns [Philadelphia: Muhlenberg Press, 1959], p. 69). Althaus' concept of intuition is certainly superior to the causal inference from the experience of faith practiced by the old Erlangen school and Kähler. But intuition does not offer an "immediate pre-scientific relationship to past history, spanning centuries and millennia, *which carries in itself absolute certainty about this past life*" (*ibid.*, p. 69; italics mine). Rather, intuition attains its highest possible certainty only when it is confirmed by detailed historical observation. The great work of Georg Wehrung had already left this state of the case insufficiently clear. Although he connected "revelational-historical knowledge" (*Geschichte*, pp. 126ff.), guided by "pneumatic intuition" (*ibid.*, p. 132), closely to "knowledge of the history of religions," and on no account wanted to make it independent of the latter (*ibid.*, pp. 146f.), nevertheless the distinction between a revelational-historical pathway to knowledge and the pathway used in the history of religions closely approximates the assumption of the independent certainty of the former (*ibid.*, p. 131: "Here, if anywhere, is a reality which is known [*Erkennen*] by recognition [*Anerkennen*]"). No matter how it may be grounded, intuition does not constitute a special kind of historical knowledge, but rather a fundamental moment of all historical knowledge insofar as it can be verified by historical investigation of the particulars. The last section of this essay will attempt to explain this further in dependence upon Collingwood.

[92] I hope shortly to establish these assertions in greater detail in a work on the concept of analogy.

in prescientific and scientific thought explains why even where the historian utters a *non liquet* [it is not evident], a great many representations are still possible of the event which remains opaque to the historian. However, such representations do not provide a basis for knowledge of what really happened. They tend more to level down the particularity of the matter in question, which eludes all analogies. This is true of supernaturalistic hypotheses on principle, as well as for unfounded naturalistic attempts at explanation. Here, as well as there, the result is a fantastic transgression of the finitude of the possibilities of human knowledge. Science achieves its success, however, precisely in that, and to the extent that, it remains keenly aware of the finitude of every step it takes. For only in this way will it be possible, among other things, to take further steps. Thus, science reduces the fantastic analogies of naïve thought to those which have been confirmed by critical testing. This means, with regard to knowledge of past happenings, that historical science is the procedure of reducing all sorts of prolific, even redemptive-, supra-, and primal-historical representations of events to those which have been confirmed as reliable.

One could object at this point, in order to rescue a redemptive history which is independent of scientifically established history, that the theological view of history does not proceed "from below," from analogies with whatever experience lies closest to us, but rather "from above," from the side of God. Thus, Hans Emil Weber called special attention to the significance of a type of analogical thought, undertaken in order to have a believing view of history, which is not established "by one-sided orientation toward contemporary sense experience."[93] Karl Barth formulates statements about the redemptive event by means of analogies based on the concept of the revelation of God. The first thing to be said to this is that all analogies "from above to below" already presuppose the construction of a concept of God by means of an analogy "from below" – even if one wanted to subscribe to an innate idea of God. Such a concept of God certainly does not yet correspond to the God of revela-

[93] Weber, *Bibelglaube*, pp. 68f.

tion. But we cannot either think or speak about the God of revelation except through a concept gained in such a way. This concept of God will become a proper concept of a theology based on revelation only – and this is the second thing that must be noticed here – by the correction and transformation it undergoes in its application to the God of Israel: that is, by its referral to the history in which the character of this God first disclosed itself step by step, then finally and with ultimate validity in the presence of the eschaton in the fate of Jesus of Nazareth. True knowledge of God is obtained from this history for the first time, and therefore cannot be presupposed as something that makes it possible to grasp this knowledge.[94] It is this history which first corrects the preliminary (and distorted) representations of God – indeed, even Israel's representations of its God! Thus, all statements about the redemptive event remain bound to analogies "from below," whose applicability is subject to the procedures of historical criticism.

3. The Theological Problem of Historical Clarification of the Basis of Faith

If we do not have to reckon with a second way to reliable knowledge of the past alongside that of historical-critical research, and if, on the other hand, the Christian faith lives from a real past event, then the consequence (which has a threatening appearance for many) follows that for us the object of faith as such cannot remain untouched by the results of historical-critical research.

[94] One should not object that a "hermeneutical circle" exists here. That knowledge and understanding are not to be characterized as purely passive reception, but something made possible by interests and questioning as well as a pre-understanding of the thing in question, is indisputable, to be sure. But no circle that always turns back on itself is involved here. Rather, we have a movement to deepened insight: a movement that is completed by correction of the initial statement of the question and of the pre-understanding from the side of the thing to be understood and by the formation of ever new, more suitable constructs. If one loses sight of this movement, then appeal to the hermeneutical circle can lead all too easily to the rejection of all questions concerning what is the condition and what is conditioned in the process of knowledge.

This consequence was viewed as ruinous by the two theologians whose discussions have determined the debates about the significance of the historical Jesus for faith since the turn of the century, Martin Kähler and Wilhelm Herrmann. Herrmann emphasized that all results of historical research always have the character of mere probability and therefore do not offer a sufficient basis for the certainty of faith.[95] Herrmann's guiding interest on this matter was not far removed from that of his antipode, Martin Kähler, in his demand for an "invulnerable area" of historical and doctrinal content "on which faith is grounded without thereby being dependent upon scientific investigation; since it could accept the results of these investigations always on the basis of authority only . . .'[96] Both arguments contain the demand that faith base itself, in Herrmann's words, on something completely certain,[97] in order that it need not be accepted simply on the basis of authority (which Herrmann saw as the ·characteristically Roman Catholic understanding of faith), but can be something everyone can catch sight of through his own experience.

Both arguments have been satisfactorily answered in the ensuing discussions with their proponents up to the time shortly after the end of World War I. Against the ostensible lack of certainty in the results of historical research, Otto Kirn remarked: "A historical conclusion can be regarded as certain when . . . despite the fact that it is not removed from all possibility of attack, it is nevertheless in agreement with all the known facts."[98] This paraphrases the only kind of certainty

---

[95] Wilhelm Herrmann, "Der geschichtliche Christus der Grund unseres Glaubens," *ZThK* 2 (1892): "What the learned man has before him, something that is a historical problem and can by much effort be made merely probable, does not have the power to establish faith" (p. 253). Cf. W. Herrmann, *The Communion of the Christian with God*, tr. J. Sandys Stanyon, revised, enlarged and altered in accordance with the fourth German ed. by R. W. Stewart (New York: G. P. Putnam's Sons, ³1915), p. 226. Wehrung, too, takes over this argument (*Geschichte*, p. 83).

[96] Kähler, *Der sogenannte historische Jesus* (²1908), p. 147 [not in English translation].   [97] Herrmann, "Der geschichtliche Christus," p. 237.

[98] O. Kirn, *Glaube*, p. 59. Beyond this justified assertion of Kirn's, one must also say that Herrmann constantly confused two different modes of

that can obtain about a past fact. Anyone who wants to have more here, will get less: that is, he will have to bypass the historical fact as such. This was what actually happened in the case of Herrmann as well as Kähler: the former, with his thesis about the "inner life" of Jesus, and the latter, with his formula about the Christ of proclamation. Both bypassed the historical facticity of the past event in their investigations, and therefore fell prey to the fatal consequence of making faith rest, in actuality, upon itself instead of, as both intended, being built upon a historical foundation (to use Herrmann's terms again). The "inner life" of Jesus appears to a contemporary observer as an unhistorical projection back onto the New Testament witnesses of Herrmann's ethical formulation of the question. The problem of the kerygma theology of Kähler[99] was already exposed by Herrmann's assertion that the apostolic proclamation could

---

certainty in his arguments; certainty about a historical fact, and the certainty of trust. Only the latter belongs properly to the certainty of faith. It is true that this presupposes the historical facticity of the object of faith, but for its part it is first established, even demanded, by the particular character of this object, namely, its promissory character. The unconditionedness with which this promise confronts the hearer is by no means compromised by the fact that the event which bears this promise, like every other past event, can be known only with the kind of certainty described by Kirn.

[99] Kähler, *Der sogenannte historische Jesus* ([2]1896), p. 112 [not in English translation; but see p. 95 in the trans. by Braaten for a similar passage]. Kähler goes so far as to draw the conclusion of the historicity of Christ from the effectiveness in us of the Christ preached by the apostles. We win "assurance that they show the historical Jesus to us because we find in them again the effective Christ." Kähler starts from the perception that the effects emanating from a person belong to his historicness (*So-called Historical Jesus*, p. 63). This insight puts him at the very peak of contemporaneous investigation into the foundations of historical science. Eduard Meyer answered the question of which among the plethora of occurrences handed down from the past properly has the significance of a historical event as follows: "historical is . . . what is or has been effective" (*Kleine Schriften*, 1, 36). Gogarten still gives a similar answer: ". . . precisely that is history which is kept in remembrance" (*ZThK* 50 [1953], p. 342). However, an illegitimate reversal of this insight is indicated when the experience of effectiveness is made into an authoritative epistemological principle for knowledge of historicity. This reversal occurs not only in Kähler but in Wilhelm Herrman, too, who stands very close to his competitor in this respect (*Communion of the Christian*, pp. 113f., 84f.).

"not by itself guard against the doubt that we might want to ground our faith on something that is, perhaps, not historical fact at all but a product of faith."[100]

The reference of the Christian faith to history unavoidably carries with it the demand that the believer must not try to save himself from historical-critical questions by means of some "invulnerable area" – otherwise it will lose its historical basis. The believer cannot want to prohibit any historical question, no matter how it be fashioned. To do so would already tacitly admit that he had lost confidence that his faith was grounded in an actual past event. The believer can only trust that the facticity of the event on which he bases himself will continually be upheld throughout the progress of historical research. The history of critical-historical investigation of the biblical witnesses, especially of the New Testament, by no means gives the appearance of discouraging such confidence.[101]

The second argument, that faith loses its independence by being bound to the results of historical research and thus subjected to the authority of science, exhibits a peculiarly neo-Protestant (or, if you like, pietistic) character from start to finish. It supposes that faith is built only on what the self has experienced for itself, whether this be a natural-ethical experience, as in the case of Herrmann, or a supernatural-spiritual experience, as in the case of Kähler. Be that as it may, the unusual unanimity in the rejection of authoritarian constraint is right to the extent that a blind faith in authority always sets up a human authority in the place of God. But historical science by no means claims to be the kind of authority that demands blind subjection. It invites every competent person to make his own test of its results. Still, as Troeltsch rightly emphasized, where someone cannot himself carry out such a test, the certainty of the ground of faith is not relegated to the status of a more or less arbitrary hypothesis of an individual teacher, but rather it

[100] Herrmann, "Der geschichtliche Christus," p. 253.

[101] Cf. Ernst Troeltsch's famous prediction in 1911: "The sensational disavowals will disappear when one works objectively with these things" (*Die Bedeutung der Geschichtlichkeit Jesu für den Glauben* [Tübingen, 1911], p. 40).

shares in the "general feeling of historical reliability that is created by the mark of scientific research."[102]

The great service of Ernst Troeltsch is that he made the attempt to understand the historical Jesus as the ground of faith in a time when all the way down the line theology had surrendered the historical truth of this ground, which Ritschl had still upheld. It is true that Troeltsch did not succeed in solving the problem of the absoluteness of Christianity that had been posed since the time of Hegel, or rather, Christian Wolff. Nor could he, working with the historical categories of his "historical-developmental idealism." Therefore he could not find in the historical Jesus a revelation of God, but only the introduction into history of a Christian idea and the cult-symbol of the Christian religious community. These results were not exactly calculated to excite enthusiasm among the theologians – and for good reason. The distinction, which Troeltsch took over from Biedermann,[103] between the person of Jesus and the Christian principle introduced into history by him, cannot but lead to the severance of the ground of faith from history. But was it the case, therefore, that the task of seeking the ground of faith in the historical Jesus was simply a false pursuit? Why did no one beside Troeltsch step into the breach? Why did the other theologians capitulate before historical relativism by surrendering the field of history to it?

We saw in the first part of this study that historical relativism was the consistent end-result of the displacement of God by man as the bearer of history. On the basis of this relativism, and without having revised the presupposition just mentioned, not even a Troeltsch could find a once-for-all, ultimate revelation of God in history. It is hardly an accident that the most significant pupil of Troeltsch, the systematic theologian, was one of the first to draw from this situation the radical consequence of a complete withdrawal of the theology from history.[104]

---

[102] Troeltsch, *Geschichtlichkeit Jesu*, pp. 34f.

[103] *Ibid.*, pp. 23ff.; cf. "Geschichte und Metaphysik," pp. 56ff.

[104] Gogarten wrote in his early work, "Mystik und Offenbarung," "It has been proved plainly and emphatically enough that from a strictly historical

And like Gogarten, so Barth judged also: "As far as the eye can see, there is nothing in history as such on which faith could ground itself." History is revelation only as "primal history,"[105] that is, history viewed in the light of its "nonhistorical radiance.[106] The thesis that, in the realm of the historically ascertainable, nothing of a divine revelation is to be encountered, found its star witness, next to Nietzsche, in Kierkegaard,[107] and thereby in Lessing's maxim that accidental truths of history cannot provide a proof for eternal truths of reason.[108]

viewpoint the absolute revelation of God at one point within the endless interrelationships of finite things is an absurdity. In view of this fact there are only two possibilities. Either one gives up the claim to the absoluteness of the revelation attested in the Bible, and sets the historical facts which it affirms into universal history and explains them out of its continuities; or one affirms the claim to absoluteness, in which case that to which this claim applies is not simply an uninvestigable phenomenon from the general historical viewpoint (which could still behave as if it had some inkling of such a thing), but rather a vacuum in which not only it but all human thought finds its breath taken away so that it can say neither one thing nor another about this, except to acknowledge something fundamentally other, something fundamentally new in history" (in *Die religiöse Entscheidung* [Jena, 1921], p. 62). See also Emil Brunner, "Geschichte oder Offenbarung?" *ZThK* 6 (1925), pp. 266–78 and the rejoinder by Horst Stephan, *ibid.*, pp. 278–85.

[105] Karl Barth, *Die Christliche Dogmatik in Entwurf* (Munich, 1927), p. 237.

[106] Karl Barth, *The Epistle to the Romans*, tr. Edwyn C. Hoskyns (London: Oxford University Press, 1933), p. 145. Barth speaks here, with Nietzsche and Overbeck, of the "nonhistorical or rather, the Primal History which conditions all history" (p. 140).

[107] Søren Kierkegaard, *Philosophical Fragments*, tr. David F. Swenson, revised and commentary tr. by Howard V. Hong (Princeton: Princeton University Press, 1962), ch. 4, sec. 4 of Interlude, pp. 97ff.; *Concluding Unscientific Postscript*, tr. David F. Swenson (Princeton: Princeton University Press, 1941), Book 2, part 4, ch. 4, sec. 2, B, §2, pp. 508ff. Kierkegaard would not need to have found a contradiction between the approximative character of historical knowledge and the foundation of eternal blessedness in a historical fact if he had considered more closely the character of this (no matter in what ways, or with whatever reservation, nevertheless known) fact as promise.

[108] S. Kierkegaard, *Postscript*, Book 2, ch. 2, §3, pp. 86ff. Cf. Hermann Diem, *Dogmatics*, pp. 9f. But is Lessing's division between reason and history really so unshakably valid? Do not his "accidental truths of history" arise only when one abstracts what has happened out of its referential context and considers it as an isolated individual? And is it not an illusion to find in reason a source of truths which are removed from and superior to all historical conditioning?

The widespread disinterest of dialectical theology and the movements that have issued from it in the question of the historically comprehensible foundation of faith antecedent to the primitive Christian kerygma has recently encountered opposition. It is interesting to note that this opposition has fastened on to Kähler just as much as did the radicalizing of kerygma theology by Gogarten and Bultmann.[109] To be sure, Kähler emphasized that Christian faith does not arise "out of the mere reports of historical facts; rather must these have added to them testimony to their supernatural value, and these statements will become an effective testimony only through believing participation in their objects."[110] Conversely, however, faith is still "not to be separated from the simple, rational comprehension of historical information, and has in this the means of testing its objectivity."[111] It would "convey an unjustified claim if the historical in it were to be viewed as a matter of indifference."[112] Only "in the contents of this history" is there offered "more than a historically shifting content, but a permanent, universally valid content," which, of course, is visible only through believing participation in its objects. This "living union of the permanent-universal and the historical in an effective-present" Kähler calls the "suprahistorical."[113]

Along the lines of Kähler, Ernst Kinder, Walter Künneth and others, as well as Paul Althaus, have recently, in debates with Gogarten and Bultmann, given prominence to the significance of the historical as the *conditio sine qua non* of faith, without, however, finding the revelation of God in the historically

---

[109] Paul Althaus, *Fact and Faith*, p. 19.
[110] Martin Kähler, *Die Wissenschaft der christlichen Lehre*, second rev. ed. (Leipzig, 1893), p. 21.   [111] *Ibid.*, p. 16.   [112] *Ibid.*, p. 12.
[113] *Ibid.*, p. 13. Cf. *The So-called Historical Jesus*, p. 47. A certain unclarity arises from the fact that Kähler, elsewhere in this book, described the "suprahistorical," so understood, as "the truly historic element" [*wahrhaft Geschichtliche*] (p. 63). The essential point of difference and correlation between the historical and suprahistorical is thereby rendered less clearly than it is in *Wissenschaft der christlichen Lehre*. Wehrung (*Geschichte*, pp. 358ff.) also follows Kähler's scheme in the use of the concept of the "suprahistorical."

ascertainable itself. Thus, Künneth writes: "Revelation is therefore always more than history, not only history, but not without history."[114] Althaus' formulation is as follows:

The revelatory character of the history of Jesus is not known by means of historical reflexion or historical reasoning. But on the other hand, it is not known *without these*.[115]

Ernst Kinder diverges somewhat in speaking of "supernatural factual realities" which "disclose themselves" to faith "by virtue of the fiducial assurance," but for which there is "no need of fearing *a posteriori* any historical judgment and of trying to avoid it."[116]

Gogarten has pointed out the difficulties facing such a distinction between historically ascertainable (or at least *a posteriori* verifiable) events, on the one hand, and their faith-establishing revelational and redemptive significance, on the other. Faith is not able to establish the unity of the historical and the suprahistorical. "It would accept this unity only if it were itself founded upon it."[117] One can hardly shut his eyes to Gogarten's argument on this point. That suprahistorical significance must belong to the historical itself, granted that the latter is to be the basis of faith. If the really decisive matter, the revelatory and redemptive significance of the fate [*Geschick*] of Jesus of Nazareth, can be seen only by faith and is in principle closed to rational investigation of this event, then it is impossible to see how the historicity of the pure facts should be able to protect faith against the reproach that it rests upon illusion and caprice. The intention of these Lutheran theologians to affirm the priority of the historical reality of the redemptive event over

[114] Walter Künneth, "Bultmann's Philosophy and the Reality of Salvation," in Braaten and Harrisville, *Kerygma and History*, p. 107.

[115] P. Althaus, *Fact and Faith*, p. 34. In this sense Althaus had already in 1923 fought against dialectical theology for the indispensability of the historical for faith in Christ ("Theologie und Geschichte," *Zeitschrift für systematische Theologie*, 1 (1923), pp. 741–86, esp. 763ff.).

[116] Ernst Kinder, "Historical Criticism and Demythologizing," in Braaten and Harrisville, *Kerygma and History*, pp. 73f.

[117] Friedrich Gogarten, *Demythologizing and History*, tr. Neville Horton Smith (London: SCM Press and New York: Charles Scribner's Sons, 1955), p. 45.

faith and the kerygma can be maintained only if faith derives entirely from this history and has its basis in it. Even the very fact that God is revealed in the fate of Jesus belongs to this event itself and is not seen in the event because faith has somehow first projected it there. Only if the revelatory significance is enclosed in the events themselves will one be able to speak here of Incarnation, an entrance of God into our mode of existence. But then it will be impossible *in principle* to reject out of hand the idea that historical investigation of this event, even in its particularity, could and must discover its revelatory character. Of course, whether historical research *in fact* succeeds in un-covering the character of the fate of Jesus of Nazareth as the revelation of God, or· by what it might *in fact* be somehow hindered in this, is an entirely different question.

It seems to me that Luther's concept of an "outer clarity" of Scripture[118] points in a direction similar to that of the idea that the history of Jesus, at which the historian's inquiry is aimed, includes the revelation of God in itself and, thus, can be grasped in its uniqueness precisely as history only if it is seen as this revelation, since this constitutes its particularity. The two are only similar in direction, however, since Luther was still unable to make the distinction which is unavoidable today between the witness of Scripture and an event attested by it. For him, history, the witness of Scripture, and doctrine still coincided.[119] At a

---

[118] *Martin Luther on "The Bondage of the Will*," tr. J. I. Packer and O. R. Johnston (London: James Clarke and Co., 1957), pp. 70–4, 123–36 (*WA* 18, pp. 606, l. 1–609, l. 14; pp. 652, l. 23–661, l. 28). On this point see the sum-mary by H. J. Iwand in the note to Suppl. Vol. I of the Munich edition of Luther's works (³1940), pp. 317–19. A searching interpretation of the thought of Luther is provided by Rudolf Hermann, *Von der Klarheit der Heiligen Schrift: Untersuchungen und Erörterungen über Luthers Lehre von der Schrift in De servo arbitrio* (Berlin, 1958).

[119] This point is illuminated by the fact that Luther, in line with the medieval doctrine of the fourfold sense of Scripture, straightway designates the literal interpretation of Scripture as historical. Cf. the documentation in Reinhold Seeberg, *Lehrbuch der Dogmengeschichte* (Graz, ⁵1953), 4/1, p. 411, as well as Fritz Hahn, "Die heilige Schrift als Problem der Auslegung bei Luther," *EvTh* 10 (1950/51), pp. 407ff., esp. pp. 418f.; and, above all, Gerhard Ebeling, "Die Anfänge von Luthers Hermeneutik," *ZThK* 48 (1951), 172–230, esp. 182f., 220f.

time when "tendency criticism" was yet unknown and the critical task of the historian, apart from the beginnings of textual criticism, was limited to judging the alternatives with respect to the reliability of a tradition, it could not have been otherwise than that the report of a source that had once become accepted would coincide in substance with the historically ascertained course of events. One may not silently assume the presence in Luther's statements about Scripture of the modern, fundamental distinction between a report and the actual course of events it depicts.

The outer clarity of Scripture in Luther's sense means that its essential content can be set forth from its words with universally evident and materially incontrovertible certainty. The essential content of Scripture (its *res*) is summed up in Christ.[120] This may be characterized in greater detail by such things as the dogma of the Trinity, Christology, etc.[121] Despite some obscure formulations, Scripture is completely unambiguous with reference to this, its *res*.[122] Luther did not thereby distinguish between the meaning of scriptural statements and their truth. The clarity of the *res scripturae* [the essential content of Scripture] obviously applied to the structure of meaning as well as to the truth of its statements. Nor did this clarity exist for believers only; it pertained to every man. Luther insisted that the content of Scripture is open to all the world.[123] In his

---

[120] *Bondage of the Will*, p. 71 (=*WA* 18, p. 609, l. 29).

[121] *Bondage of the Will*, pp. 71, 73 (=*WA* 18, p. 609, ll. 26ff.; p. 608, ll. 6f.).

[122] *Bondage of the Will*, pp. 71, 125, 129 (=*WA* 18, p. 606, ll. 30ff.; p. 653, l. 30; p. 656, l. 11); and in the famous formulation, "*ut sit ipsa per sese certissima, facillima, apertissima, sui ipsius interpres*" [in order that it might be of itself most certain, easy to understand, and reliable, interpreting itself (*WA* 18, p. 606, l. 34; cf. p. 609, ll. 13f. – tr. mine). This statement occurs in Luther's *Defense and Explanation of All the Articles of Dr. Martin Luther Which Were Unjustly Condemned by the Roman Bull*. Vol. 32 of Luther's *Works* (Philadelphia: Fortress Press, 1958), in which this work appears, is based on the German text of 1521, which does not contain the important phrase "interpreting itself." Pannenberg's citation is from the original Latin version of this work (1520), which does contain this phrase. – Tr.].

[123] "*Manifestissime toti mundo declarata*" (*WA* 18, p. 606, l. 34; cf. p. 609, ll. 13f.); "brought forth into the clearest light and proclaimed to the whole world" (*Bondage of the Will*, p. 74; cf. p. 71).

opposition to the pope and the enthusiasts he deliberately avoided appealing to the Holy Spirit for the purpose of establishing the content of Scripture.[124] Luther directed his thesis about the outer clarity of Scripture particularly against the idea that Scripture needed an additional factor besides its literal sense in order for its content to become evident. The inner clarity about the *res* of Scripture which leads to personal certainty,[125] as well as its correlative inner judgment,[126] are, at any rate, not to be had without the Holy Spirit. In contrast to this, however, the external judgment of the content of Scripture made possible by its outer clarity is the special charge of the office of preaching. But this permits the *res* of Scripture to be presented validly not only for believers, but also for unbelievers.[127] Not even its opponents could effectively contradict it, since in the light of the universal judgment of reason[128] their

[124] "*Neque illos probo qui refugium suum ponunt in iactantia spiritus*" (*WA* 18, p. 653, l. 2); "I do not applaud those who take refuge in bragging about the Spirit" (*Bondage of the Will*, p. 124). This delimitation of Luther's should serve as a warning against handing out as Luther's meaning, without further explanation, the idea that "one who has the Holy Spirit can really understand" the Scriptures. This formulation of Reinhold Seeberg's (*Dogmengeschichte*, 4/1, p. 411) is influenced by the Erlangen regeneration-theology, and expresses a one-sided view of Luther's conception. The statements of Luther to which Seeberg appeals to support this formulation (*WA* 18, p. 609) speak only of a necessity of the Holy Spirit for comprehending the *inner* clarity of Scripture, just as do Luther's statements at the other place (*WA* 12, pp. 438f.) to which Seeberg refers. To be sure, Luther can elsewhere speak of the Holy Spirit as a condition for a correct understanding of Scripture without limiting this function of the Spirit to the *inner* clarity. But this occurs under the presupposition mentioned in p. 64, n. 129, which first brings out the full complexity of Luther's position. Where this is not noticed, and such statements of Luther's are summarized without further differentiation in formulations like "correct interpretation of Scripture demands the Holy Spirit" (so Hahn, "Die heilige Schrift," p. 413), then Luther's delimitation against the Scripture interpretation of the enthusiasts is placed in greatest jeopardy.

[125] *Bondage of the Will*, p. 73 (=*WA* 18, p. 609, l. 5).

[126] *Bondage of the Will*, p. 124 (=*WA* 18, p. 653, ll. 14ff.).

[127] "*Non modo pro nobis ipsis, sed et pro aliis et propter aliorum salutem*" (*WA* 18, p. 653, l. 23); "and now not only for ourselves only, but also for the benefit and salvation of others" (*Bondage of the Will*, p. 125).

[128] "*Communis tamen sensus iudicio*" (*WA* 18, p. 656, ll. 39f.); "the judgment of common sense" (*Bondage of the Will*, p. 130).

objections have no force! Luther explains the fact that the
content of Scripture does in fact meet with general resistance by
saying simply that the Devil has so blinded men that they no
longer see the facts that lie manifest before them.[129]

The uniqueness of faith in contrast to mere knowledge of facts
is not at all endangered by the idea of the outer clarity of
Scripture.[130] Faith is not something like a compensation of

[129] *Bondage of the Will*, pp. 71, 73, 131ff. (= *WA* 18, p. 607, ll. 9ff.; p. 609,
l. 3; p. 658, ll. 18ff.). Cf. Hermann, *Von der Klarheit*, pp. 82ff. The blindness
caused by Satan now operates in such a way that man, despite the outer
clarity of Scripture, actually fails to see its content if he is not illuminated by
the Holy Spirit ("*cor humanum sic esse Satanae potentia oppressum, ut nisi spiritu
Dei mirabiliter suscitetur, per sese nec ea videre possit nec audire, quae in ipsos oculos
et in aures manifeste impingunt, ut palpari possint manu*" [*WA* 18, p. 658, ll. 24f. on
Isa. 6:10] [(The human heart) is so bound by the power of Satan that, unless
it be wondrously quickened by the Spirit of God, it cannot of itself see or hear
things which strike upon the ear and eye so manifestly that they could
almost be touched by hand (*Bondage of the Will*, p. 132).]). Thus, the Holy
Spirit is not demanded for the understanding of Scripture because its truths,
in and of themselves, are inaccessible to reason or are not yet convincing, so
that the Holy Spirit must step in as an additional source of certainty. Rather,
the sole reason that a specific influence of the Spirit is indispensable for the
understanding of Scripture is that Satan has blinded man. It is demanded
accidentally – and always, in actuality, to be sure – but is not constitutive for
conceiving and establishing the inherent meaning and truth of scriptural
statements. The Holy Spirit, therefore, does not *supplement* reason, but rather
frees it for its natural function. This corresponds to the result obtained by
Bernard Lohse in his circumspect study of the positive meaning of reason in
Luther's thought: reason is "freed for its authentic naturalness in obedience
to Christ" (*Ratio und Fides: Eine Untersuchung uber die ratio in der Theologie
Luthers* [Göttingen, 1958], p. 113). This viewpoint explains those statements
of Luther's about the indispensability of the Holy Spirit for understanding
Scripture which only seem to contradict the thesis about the outer clarity of
Scripture. This viewpoint also explains Luther's insistence upon the Spirit's
being enclosed in the Word and never allowing it to stand autonomously
alongside the Word, despite references to the Spirit as a condition for knowledge of Scripture (Karl Holl, "Luthers Bedeutung für den Fortschrift der
Auslegungskunst," in *Gesammelte Aufsätze zur Kirchengeschichte* [Tübingen,
1921], 1, pp. 426f.). The Holy Spirit, thus, may not after all be brought into an
exegetical and historical argument in a supplementary way and claimed to be
inwardly constitutive for knowledge of the content and truth of the Word.

[130] It is characteristic that the Augsburg Confession, precisely by detach-
ing justifying faith from the mere *notitia historiae* [knowledge of history]
which the godless and the Devil also possess, at the same time provides a
positive relationship between the two, treating justification as the *effectus*

subjective conviction to make up for defective knowledge. If that were the case every advance in knowledge would certainly help to make faith superfluous. But faith is actually trust in God's promise, and this trust is not rendered superfluous by knowledge of this promise; on the contrary, it is made possible by it for the first time. Believing trust directs itself toward the future fulfillment of the sure promise on which it is grounded. Faith is characterized as *fides non apparentium* [faith in what is unseen] only because it directs itself toward what is coming (and toward the coming, effective, invisible God). This eschatological orientation, its temporal distance from fulfillment, is the reason that faith differs from sight (II Cor. 5.7). Nevertheless, the promise on which it is based must also be certain from the standpoint of reason to the degree of certainty that may reasonably be expected in relation to such things. The certainty of the knowledge of this promise as a presupposition of faith is, of course, to be distinguished from what is properly "the certainty of faith" [*Glaubensgewissheit*], which is based on the promise and is bound up in its future fulfillment. Therefore, on the one hand,

---

historiae [effect of the history] (*BC*, p. 44). This tendency is expressed in a more differentiated way in Apology IV, 51: "So it is not enough to believe that Christ was born, suffered and was raised unless we add this article, *the purpose of the history*, 'the forgiveness of sins' " (*Itaque non satis est credere, quod Christus natus, passus, resuscitatus sit, nisi addimus et hunc articulum, qui est causa finalis historiae, remissionem peccatorum* [*BC*, p. 114; italics mine]). A separation of the *fides iustificans* [justifying faith] from the *notitia historiae* [knowledge of (the) history] such as Gogarten effects (*The Reality of Faith*, tr. Carl Michalson et al. [London: SCM Press and Philadelphia: Westminster Press, 1957], pp. 137f.), is as impossible for the Augsburg Confession and for the Apology as it is for Luther (e.g., *WA* 27, p. 105). E. Buder ("Fides iustificans und fides historiae," *EvTh* 13 (1953): 67ff., esp. 72f.) stands the facts on their heads when he makes "*Tatsachen glauben*" [belief in facts] the "*Frucht*" [fruit] of the *fides iustificans*. The Augsburg Confession (art. 20), says just the opposite quite explicitly. Justifying faith presupposes the *notitia historiae* just as surely as in its character as *trust* in the apprehended promises it must be sharply distinguished from this. In this sense, Luther could say in his lectures on Romans that *fides informis* [unformed faith] is not so much faith as the object to which faith is directed (*WA* 56, pp. 172f. [*Luther: Lectures on Romans*, tr. and ed. Wilhelm Pauck, Library of Christian Classics 15 (London: SCM Press and Philadelphia: Westminster Press, 1961), p. 18. – TR.]).

the character of our knowledge of the past event from which the promise has been issued as probability can no more injure faith's trustful certainty, than can, on the other hand, the distinctiveness of faith be supplanted by such knowledge of the promise.

4. Revelatory History as a Problem of Historical Method

Despite all the theological misgivings that would appear to exclude knowledge of the revelatory character of the event on which faith is grounded, the question whether without such knowledge the historical foundation of faith would drop right out from under its feet and faith be turned into enthusiasm, has so far proven capable of intruding itself again and again. In the light of this question, it seems to be theologically impossible to dismiss the demand that the revelatory character of the redemptive event must be contained in this event itself as the historian portrays it. The requirement hereby directed toward the historian stands no less in the way of this postulate than the offense the theologian can take at this point. Given the thesis that revelation is contained in a historical event of the past, and that there is no other mode of access to a past event than historical research, would it not be the case that the burden of proof that God had revealed himself in Jesus of Nazareth would fall upon the historian? This requirement, which a few decades ago in the era of positivistic theories of science would have been simply scandalous, can in fact hardly be avoided.

Of course, no one should expect that historical research, working with a small segment of past happening, could defend statements about God's revelation in history. In connection with this assertion, the question of the extent to which the historian as such may make any sort of statement about God can remain open for the time being. A small segment of history such as the historian usually has in view because of the need to limit his material, does not in any case provide sufficient basis for meaningfully raising the question of whether a God has revealed himself here in contrast to all other occurrences in nature and in human history. In order to raise this question it is obviously requisite that one should have history as a whole in view, corresponding to the universality of God, whose revelation is the object of inquiry. Only on the assumption of a universal-historical horizon can there be such an inquiry.

This fact corresponds to the theological assertion that the person of Jesus is the revelation of God not in isolation by itself, but only in the historical interrelationships in which Jesus' fate took place.[131] Here lies the error of Wilhelm Herrmann and of Schleiermacher, too, viz., of seeking the revelation of God in the isolated person of Jesus.[132] Against this attempt, the theology of redemptive history is right, despite its otherwise serious deficiencies, in its recognition that Jesus' connection with the history of Israel is fundamental to his revelatory significance. In this regard, connection with Israel refers to the history of Israel as well as to knowledge of its history, as it found a last and, for the preaching of Jesus, foundational expression in apocalyptic. Both – the history and the consciousness of the deeds of God in history – belong inseparably together. This insight, which Noth and von Rad have expressed in a fundamental way, must be made even more vigorously fruitful for the understanding of the significance of the history and theology of Israel for the whole range of theological investigation. Jesus is the revealer of God in relation to the history of Israel understood in this way. The New Testament proofs from prophecy depend upon this. But for the non-Jews, the continuity of Jesus with the Old Testament does not suffice to allow them to recognize the revelation of God in him. There must be added to this the appropriation of Hellenistic thought, especially the philosophical question of the true form of the deity revered in Greek religion, which was extended beyond Hellenism and applied in a logically consistent way to the various other religions. The appropriation of Hellenistic thought, which had been determined by this

[131] See above, pp. 21ff.

[132] This is also the contention of Rudolf Hermann, *Christentum und Geschichte bei Wilhelm Herrmann* (University of Göttingen dissertation, 1914), pp. 129f., who shows that such isolation causes the once-occurring particularity of the person of Jesus to evaporate completely (pp. 121ff.).

question, took place in the Jewish missionary theology and in the New Testament in connection with Gnosticism and also with popular philosophy. In this way Hellenistic thought was broken, at least in the New Testament, but by a kind of criticism that appropriated it at the same time.[133] Only in this way could the universal claim of the God of Israel attain binding validity for non-Jews.[134] Only in this way, therefore, could the revelation of God in Jesus of Nazareth, the fulfiller of the history of Israel, also be convincing to the heathen as the revelation of the one true God. We will see shortly that the philosophical question of God is also significant for the possibility of historical knowledge of revelatory history.

I said above that only on the presupposition of a universal-historical horizon can one meaningfully raise the question as to whether God has revealed himself at one or another place in history. The central question for debate between history and theology arises here: how is the conception of a unity of history possible?

It will be difficult for historical thought to renounce the presupposition of a unity of history. The philosophical presuppositions which everyone who undertakes historical research brings with him are not limited to a specific understanding of human existence, but always also include models of courses of events. Since everything in history stands under over-arching continuities, no particular unitary event can be definitively understood from within itself. Nor is it so certain that even a whole culture, which is widely taken to be the smallest field of historical study that can be understood from within itself,[135]

[133] This situation, which is fundamental for the whole question of the relationship of theology to the thought of man before faith is set forth most clearly in Rudolf Bultmann's essay, "Points of Contact and Conflict," in *Essays: Philosophical and Theological*, tr. James C. G. Grieg (London: SCM Press and New York: The Macmillan Co., 1955), pp. 133–50.

[134] This point is stated and demonstrated more fully in my essay, "The Appropriation of the Philosophical Concept of God as a Dogmatic Problem of Early Christian Theology": forthcoming in Vol. 2.

[135] So, for instance, Arnold Toynbee, *Civilization on Trial* (London and New York: Oxford University Press, 1946), p. 9. On the origin and dissemination of theories of cultural cycles, cf. Rothacker, *Logik*, pp. 99ff.

is isolable from the process of historical conditioning; it is not as self-contained as many proponents of theories of cultural wholes suppose. This can be seen precisely in western history, which, viewed from beyond the borders of its interwoven cultures, appears to have a strong inner unity. It is the horizon of world history which first makes it possible to appreciate the full significance of an individual event. "Without world history there is no meaning of history."[136] This is especially clear in relation to the problem of historical periodization. Only a world-historical viewpoint can provide an adequate basis for a division of the course of history into periods.[137]

[136] R. Wittram, *Das Interesse*, p. 135. Wittram, who devotes a whole chapter to this problem (pp. 122–36), even believes that world history "exceeds the measure of man." Nevertheless, there exists a "certainty that there is a world history – which is just why science cannot cease to search for it" (p. 136). The most profound difficulty of this problem, for Wittram, stems from the fact that although "the end of world history is absolutely not an object of historical science, the question about it is decisive for our conception of history" (p. 135). Certainly no man now knows the end of history in its future coming to pass. But cannot the question whether the end of history in the person of the God who brings it about has already appeared in Jesus be of concern to the historian, too? In any case, an understanding of history as a whole would thereby be made possible for the first time.

Recently, Herman Heimpel (in a lecture entitled "Der Versuch mit dem Vergangenheit zu leben," published in the *Frankfurter Allgemeine Zeitung*, March 25, 1959) has advocated the view that a world history has become possible today for the first time because of the way in which all parts of the world have been drawn together in the present age. Heimpel connects his conviction on this point to a farsighted statement of Jacob Burckhardt. Karl Jaspers and H. Freyer have expressed similar thoughts. Wittram (pp. 130ff.) criticizes this theory in a very instructive manner. He himself is inclined toward Gogarten's heuristic conception that not only the consciousness of world history but also the forces "that have transformed all previous history into world history" (p. 133) stem from the Christian faith. One will not go astray in seeking for one root of these forces in the connection between historicness and universality which is characteristic of the Christian idea of God and is fundamental for the Christian missionary mandate. Further illumination is certainly required, as Wittram emphasizes, as to how, under the aegis of these forces, that impulse of the modern spirit arose without which it is impossible to understand modern culture and technology – the two things, in Heimpel's view, responsible for setting the task of world history.

[137] For this reason, Collingwood finds a thoroughgoing periodizing of history to be the result of Christian historiography (*History*, p. 50). The

The inescapable question of world history and the task of historical periodization point to the fact to which Collingwood has called attention, namely, that research into the particulars of history always presupposes an outline of the whole of history in relation to which the material that has been handed down by tradition is to be interrogated. As in a criminal investigation the most diverse details can be indications for or against the chief investigator's conjectured account of the deed, and for this reason can suddenly gain a significance that had not been anticipated, so, according to Collingwood, the documents accessible to the modern historian are indications for or against the historian's spontaneously projected model of the event.[138] All reported details, which are always to be understood as expressions of the view of the reporter, obtain historical significance only through relationship with the conception of the course of history which the historian brings with him. Depending on the findings concerning the particulars, this conception will be confirmed, modified, or else abandoned as inadequate in order to make room for a new one.

Collingwood is justified in thinking that the influence of positivism upon historical research can be broken only by this theory of historical knowledge. Research does not begin by gathering the greatest possible number of details in a random

---

multi-levelled problem of historical periodization is illustrated by P. E. Hübinger with the example of the arrangement of the late ancient period ("Spätantike und frühen Mittelalter," *Deutsche Vierteljahrschrift für Literaturwissenschaft und Geistesgeschichte* 26 [1952], pp. 1–48).

[138] Collingwood, *History*, pp. 226ff., 275ff. One should also note the important discussion of the autonomy of the historical imagination (pp. 234ff.). The meaning of historical intuition, whose theological relevance Wehrung and Althaus have highlighted (see above, n. 91), and also something of the similarly oriented thought of Kähler (nn. 99 and 110–12) and Kinder (n. 116), receive their due within the framework of this conception of historical knowledge. Collingwood avoids the problematical assumption that intuition is an independent source of historical knowledge alongside historical observation of the particulars. By referring the imagination to verification by detailed investigation, he avoids the danger of a dualism between the two, such as is expressed in theology in the dualism between the revelatory-historical and historical-critical formulations of the question.

manner, in order then to take the second step of exhibiting the laws governing them. Rather, a conjecture about the relationships, the historical circumstances, guides one's interest from the beginning. According to Collingwood, the positivistic procedure of gathering isolated bits of information rests upon an abstraction: the findings must be stripped of their peculiar referential relationships, while these relationships can come to light only if the historian applies to them a model of the course of events. On this point, as Collingwood shows, even Rickert sought to free historical research from the influence of positivism. He had indeed directed historical research toward the singular and individually given, in opposition to the natural sciences, but he had thereby only canceled the second step of the positivistic procedure, the search for laws. The first step, the collection of observations of particulars, he let stand as the first task of history. Only subsequently were the particulars to be related to values and in this way brought into relationship with each other. For Collingwood, on the other hand, it is not the individual as such, but the connection of individual events with each other (which is specifically different from the connections comprehended in natural scientific law) that is the real object of the historian, and the historian begins his work with it immediately.[139]

The spontaneity of the historical imagination stands so much in the foreground of interest in Collingwood that he appears not to have devoted enough attention to another, related question, viz., the question of the cognitive value of the historical projection. To the extent that the projection of a historical course of events is verifiable by its agreement with the available findings on the particulars, it is obviously no mere individually conditioned perspective in the consciousness of the historian but rather a recounting of the event itself in its own context. To be sure, the historian with his own historical location belongs together with the effects of the event he is investigating. But despite this "subjective conditioning" of his viewpoint, he

---

[139] Collingwood, *History*, pp. 168f. (on Rickert); pp. 130ff. (criticism of positivism).

cannot change his picture of the course of history in any way he pleases without thereby surrendering the cognitive value of his historical projection. If the historian does not want to lose sight of his own involvement in the event he describes, but on the other hand also does not want to surrender the cognitive claim of his historical projection, then he can only interpret this projection as a spontaneous reproduction of a previously given unity of history, which, to be sure, only becomes conscious of itself in this reproductive act.

The theological fruitfulness of Collingwood's historical epistemology is easy to see. It is most evident in relation to the question of the conditions that have to be satisfied by the historian's pre-projection of a unity of history if it is to do justice to the uniqueness of historical events. *One* such condition presses for recognition above all the others: a projection of the course of events must be so constructed that it does not exclude the contingency of the historical.

This demand sounds almost self-evident. Contingency and individuality are indeed fundamental characteristics of the historical. Still, it has proven extremely diffcult to uphold the unity of history in acknowledging this demand.[140]

First of all, the idea of a teleology, immanent in the events and determining the whole course of history, i.e., the idea of development in the strict sense, must be set aside. So long as one understands the unity of history as a developmental unity, the contingency of events must be neglected. Therefore, the way to a metaphysics of history which was tried by as recent a scholar as Troeltsch, is impassable.

Furthermore, the unity of history can never be portrayed in a purely morphological way. Whether, with Dilthey, one takes as

[140] It is only too easy to sacrifice the contingency of events in favor of a conception of the unity of history. The justifiable fears of Kierkegaard about an obliteration of individual existence by the "universal," and of Gogarten about a threatened blanketing of the openness of man for the future by a philosophy of history that anticipates it, are aroused at this point. It is in the face of the question raised by these thinkers that every projection of the unity of history will have to prove that it has not betrayed the peculiar contingency of historical events.

the basis for ordering the manifoldness of history a psychological typology of the possible forms of expression of human life, or, with Spengler and Toynbee, develops a view which employs a cultural morphology oriented toward analogies in the rising and passing of cultures, the genuinely historical is always to be sought in precisely the variations and modifications of the typical. Common morphological traits can, therefore, make possible a certain panoramic view and encourage the comparative mode of observation, but they cannot express the specific unity of history.[141] This must be conceived as an all-embracing unity that nevertheless does not obscure the contingent.

Karl Jaspers sets out on such a path. He leaves the beginning and end of history undetermined, and tries to establish its unity around a center which he believes can be empirically displayed. All previous history was only preparatory for it, and it remains the measure of all subsequent history. But, upon closer inspection, the 'axial period' between 800 and 200 BC, in which Jaspers finds in different cultures over the whole earth the breakthrough to the human values and attitudes which are still valid today, does not form such a self-contained and, from the standpoint of its spiritual profile, clearly delimited unity in contrast to previous cultures, as he thinks. Nor does it form such a final measure of everything afterward that its place could not be taken by a natural center of history, as Jaspers himself sees. Jaspers deliberately constructs his outline as a secularization of the Christian view of Jesus as the axis of history.[142] But by

---

[141] Troeltsch (*Historismus*, p. 520) had already argued against Dilthey in a similar fashion.

[142] Karl Jaspers, *The Origin and Goal of History*, tr. Michael Bulloch (New Haven: Yale University Press, 1953), p. 1. Jaspers holds that the Christian view of history is philosophically unacceptable. The Christian faith is taken to be "only one faith, not the faith of mankind. This view of universal history therefore suffers from the defect that it can only be valid for believing Christians. But even in the West, Christians have not tied their empirical conceptions of history to their faith. An article of faith is not an article of empirical insight into the real course of history. For Christians, sacred history was separated from profane history as being different in its meaning" (*ibid.*). The last assertion is completely inconsistent with the universality of the biblical concept of God, and luckily was not advocated in this form even

transporting this structure onto the "axial period" the properties necessary for its significance for the philosophy of history are lost. The inner unity of the person of Jesus of Nazareth and especially his eschatological significance as the presence of the end of history by which alone Jesus Christ becomes the final measure of all subsequent history, cannot be transported to a period of human history.

Perhaps the unity of history can be conceived only in a way that shows that the contingency of events and their continuity have a common root. Then the protection of the unity of history would no longer have to be gained at the expense of losing contingency. This condition seems to be fulfilled if one understands the unity of mankind as the root of the unity of history, which nevertheless always brings forth new, contingent life-expressions of its individuals. But even this way is barred. If one thinks of the unity of mankind in the sense of a biological unity of the species, or as a unity of a stream of life, one does not yet have a historical unity. However, if one understands it as the unity of a historical process, it becomes problematical because the human spirit always exists only as an individual and for the individual.

The futility of all these attempts can be taken as an indication that the unity of history has its ground in something transcending history. The God who by the transcendence of his freedom[143]

---

by the theology of redemptive history. It has been shown above that the event upon which faith is founded must, at least in principle, be accessible to "empirical insight." A Christian will find empirically confirmed even the fact that Jesus Christ is the "axis" of history because the end of history has already appeared in him. He will trust that the course of history will further strengthen his conviction. And there will be a day when the empirical confirmation of the Christian knowledge of Jesus Christ as the fulfillment of history will be acknowledged by all men, either joyfully or against their will. It already has validity for all men, however; the validity of the mission of the church depends upon this.

[143] Cf. on this formulation my article, "The Appropriation of the Philosophical Concept of God as a Dogmatic Problem of Early Christian Theology" (forthcoming in vol. 2). One can also speak, with Gerhard Stammler, of "in-scendence" [*Inszendenz*] (*KuD* 3 [1957], p. 17). But "in-scendence" or, still more clearly, "condescendence" [*Kondeszendenz*], or the language of God's coming, all presuppose a "trans" as the starting point of the move-

is the origin of contingency in the world, is also the ground of
the unity which comprises the contingencies as history. Thus,
history does not exclude the contingency of the events bound
together in it. It seems that only the origin of the contingency
of events can, by virtue of its unity, also be the origin of its
continuity without injuring its contingency. However, the unity
of history does not consist merely in its transcendent origin.
Events are not only contingent in relation to each other, but
they also cohere among each other. This indwelling connection
between them is grounded in the transcendent unity of God,
which manifests itself as faithfulness. If, however, the connection
of events is grounded in the faithfulness of the free God, then we
do not have to conceive a continuity of something enduring
from the past into the future after the manner, say, of a development. Rather, we have to think of events which are in themselves contingent, as being at the same time linked backward
and referred to what has happened.[144] By means of such

ment expressed, and therefore cannot be described as pure opposites of
transcendence. In any case, there is no room for doubt that the idea of a
transcendence frozen in the distant beyond is alien to the Christian conception of God.

[144] This backward linking does not occur in human history as a relationship of spiritless facts, but rather along with the participation of men. For
this reason, it has a correlate on the side of human conduct: the responsibility of man for the heritage handed down to him as he stands before the
future, before the "coming God" (cf. the profound "Anmerkungen zur
theologischen Auffassung des Zeitproblems," by Carl H. Ratschow, *ZThK*
51 (1954), pp. 360–87, esp. p. 376), who through his coming at once creates
something contingent and at the same time refers to what has happened
previously. On the basis of the responsibility corresponding to the coming of
God, man always reaches back again to his past and holds fast to it even in
new situations. To this extent, Bultmann and Gogarten have been right in
bringing together the continuity of history and the responsibility of man
(Gogarten, *Was ist Christentum?* p. 14; Bultmann, *The Presence of Eternity*,
pp. 143f.). They have thereby, following Heidegger, raised in a new way the
question of the essence of historical connections, justly rejecting all models of
historical continuity oriented solely by the idea of causality. Nevertheless,
man can only return responsibly to his heritage because he receives the
instruction to do so through what he has been confronted with by the coming
God. The responsibility to which he is directed in a given case is transmitted
from thence, and thereby also the continuity of history. Thus, while the
responsibility of man certainly shares in the maintenance of the continuity

backward linking the continuity of history is constantly re-established. This is the way in which the faithfulness of God expresses itself. Only in this way, as a backward-reaching incorporation of the contingently new into what has been, but not the reverse, as a predetermining mastery and its effect, can the primary connection of history be conceived without losing its contingency. The fact that the continuity of events is always visible only in retrospect points in this same direction.[145]

Since only the concept of God makes it possible to conceive the unity of history in a way that maintains the peculiar characteristics of the historical, it should really be indispensable for the historian. A radical humanism, which would understand all events as nothing but life-expressions of man, must lose sight of the specifically historical. To say this does not speak for any supernaturalism, which would be unacceptable to the critical reason of the historian, since by asserting transcendental incursions it would cut short historical research into inner-worldly causes and analogies. The God who works in the contingency of events and at the same time creates their continuity can at first be only a problem for the historian as he sets about his work. How God works and how he has created the continuity of history again and again can only be taught by history itself. For long stretches of historical investigation into the details of individual events, these questions will at first go unanswered and remain in suspension, and be significant only as questions. Even-

of history, it may not provide the proper basis of this. Such an assumption would only lead to the dissolution of the unity of history into intersecting realizations of human existence.

[145] The alleged founding of the continuity of events by the contingent member linking itself to the past is illuminating only when it is seen as valid for natural events and not only for human history. This conception must be confirmed by an understanding of natural laws as specific expressions of the faithfulness of God. The presupposition for this would be that nature, too, is to be understood as history. This conception is theologically sound, since a distinction between nature and history is alien to the biblical writings (cf. also Ratschow, "Anmerkungen z. theol. Auffassung d. Zeitproblems," pp. 376f.). It corresponds also to the facts of natural science (cf. the statement by Carl Friedrich von Weizsäcker on the significance of the second law of thermodynamics in *The History of Nature*, tr. Fred D. Wieck [Chicago: The University of Chicago Press, 1940], pp. 8ff.).

tually, however, especially in the field of the history of religions, it will be impossible to miss hearing them. For as man fails to account for the uniqueness of individual religious experiences when he tries to understand them as merely a function of other psychological phenomena, construing them as objectifications of psychological tensions, so does he also fail to account for the uniqueness of the changes in religions in their history when he takes them to be merely functions of other, perhaps sociological, changes. The history of religions is the place where the question about the deity that effects these changes is most directly raised. And this question will cast its light backward upon all the rest of history that occurs in living relationship to the major and minor religions. In this connection, the historian will have to take a stand on the question of the deity of the God of Israel in contrast to the gods of other religions. He will not be able to approach this problem with any criterion fundamentally different from what the Greeks employed in asking about the true form of the divine. But he will encounter material in the history of Israel and of primitive Christianity which will defy measurement by this criterion, which annuls it and nevertheless is confirmed by it. And these discoveries, too, will shed their light upon all other events.

The more exact form of the continuity of history grounded in the unity of God can, thus, only be discovered in contact with historical research, and not through some anticipatory logic of the Absolute. Within the limits of this essay it cannot be shown in detail that and how in relation to such questions the Israelite-Christian understanding of God is alone able to prove adequate for the foundation of the continuity of reality as history; that and how Israel's understanding of its history as revelatory history represents, in fact, the condition of the possibility of regarding the continuity of history as grounded in the unity of God; that and how Jesus of Nazareth is the end of the still unconcluded history, and just for this reason is for us (as those who still wander along the way) the inexhaustible center of meaning. That efforts to discover the continuity of reality that is grounded in God lead to such results is not to be judged as a theological-Christian perspective external to the historical material itself, and which could be played off against some other perspective as being of equal historical value. On the contrary, it is the only appropriate view of historical reality. This claim will appear less astonishing, perhaps, if one considers that it was Israel's history of God and the fate of Jesus which first disclosed to man the understanding of the world as history.

Such a theology of history distinguishes itself from the usual sort of redemptive-historical thinking by the fact that it wants to be in principle historically verifiable. This does not mean that it would allow itself to be directly read off of any kind of historical details. In the sense of Collingwood's exposition, such a thing cannot be expected for any historical projection. In any case, the theological understanding of history cannot meet the positivistic demand that the continuities be derivable from the observations of the particulars. Were this to be acknowledged as the only legitimate formulation of the historical question, then theology could only emigrate to the field of a supra- or primal history. This situation has been fundamentally changed by Collingwood's proof that this positivistic demand is inappropriate to the historical object as such. A verification through subsequent testing by observation of the particulars may unreservedly be expected of a theological projection of history. Its ability to take into account all known historical details would be the positive criterion of its truth; the proof that without its specific assertions the accessible information would not be at all or would be only incompletely explicable, can be used as a negative criterion.

The double task of verification just indicated extends fundamentally to all accessible phenomena. To be sure, every historical interest involves a selection. This is not conditioned only by the individuality of the historian. The theological interest as such has a selective tendency. It favors the selection that leads directly to the eschatological fate of Jesus or to events that refer back to it. But the selective tendency undergoes a correction within the theological conception of history by the universal claim of the God of Israel to be the only God of all man, and by the definitive use made by Jesus of Nazareth of the authority of this God. It thereby becomes imperative to discover as far as possible the links between all other events and this one in order to know the universality of the God of Israel and his revelation in Jesus of Nazareth as verified.

The consideration, demanded by the universality of the biblical God, of all events and continuities of whatever kind in a theological conception of reality as history, corresponds, conversely, to the confidence that every event in the world stands in the service of the Creator of all things. From this there follows the rule that the investigation of history should orient itself as closely as possible to these occurrences, and not in some way begin immediately to speculate about God's providence. If God were not the Creator, then he could accomplish his will in the world by naked miracles alone, by excluding all the other powers operative in history. Nevertheless, his will does not occur at the expense of human activity, but precisely through the experience, plans, and deeds of men, despite and in their sinful perversion. By grasping God's works in such indirectness that it seeks the connections between events in concrete, inner-worldly circumstances, without explaining away the novel, more or less analogy-less aspects of the events, theological history writing bears witness to God as the Creator of the world.[146] Proper theological research into history must absorb the truth of the humanistic tendency toward an "immanent" understanding of events. It may not supplant detailed historical investigation by supranaturalistic hypotheses.[147]

---

[146] I am grateful to a seminar conducted jointly with Hans Walter Wolff in the summer of 1959 for, among many other things, the reference to the significance of the change that occurred in the Israelite understanding of history through the transition from saga to historical writing in the narrower sense, e.g., in the narration of the accession of David and especially in that of the succession to his throne. Here, Yahweh does not act in competition with human acts, as in the book of Judges. Rather, he uses human suffering, plans and deeds as means for accomplishing his will without directly intervening in events himself. Was not the still young belief in the creation of the world by Yahweh the presupposition for the formation of this sort of history writing?

[147] Collingwood levels against the Christian historiography of the Middle Ages the charge that it had little interest in the details of human events

From the universality of the biblical God there emanates a drive to unlimited expansion of historical research. The Christian faith must seek its intellectual confirmation in this just as it was necessary for the ancient church to lay claim to Greek philosophy for its witness to the universal deity of the Father of Jesus Christ.

---

because of its being carried out along the lines of the idea of the divine providence. For this reason, too, this historiography developed little sense for a critical historical method (*History*, pp. 54ff.). It is to be suspected that the theological point of departure for such a detour is the fact that the mysterious character of the eschatological revelation of God in Jesus Christ, which makes it unsuitable as a speculative key to world history (cf. *KuD* 5 [1959], p. 237; above, pp. 100ff.), was not properly observed.

3

KERYGMA AND HISTORY

First appeared in Rolf Rendtorff and Klaus Koch (eds.), *Studien zur Theologie der alttestamentlichen Überlieferung; Festschrift Gerhard von Rad* (Neukirchen: Neukirchener Verlag der Buchhandlung des Erziehungsvereins, 1961), pp. 129–40.

IN ORDER to gain clarity about the place von Rad's *Old Testament Theology* occupies in the whole spectrum of contemporary theological dialogue beyond the boundaries of the special discipline of Old Testament study, one cannot ignore its connection with the history and present preoccupations of kerygma theology.

It is no longer possible today to overlook the totality of kerygma theology as a phenomenon in the history of theology, since we ourselves are still involved in it. The work of Martin Kähler is certainly to be regarded as its most important root. To be sure, its later, radical form had not yet appeared in Kähler. The famous sentence from his book, *The So-called Historical Jesus and the Historic, Biblical Christ*, that "the real Christ is the Christ who is preached,"[1] may, of course, be designated as the theme of kerygma theology, particularly of the antihistorical front it set up against the life-of-Jesus movement of the nineteenth century. But, after all, Kähler did not want to abandon the question of the actual facts of Jesus' career as unimportant. On the contrary, he believed the Christ of proclamation was the

[1] Martin Kähler, *The So-called Historical Jesus and the Historic, Biblical Christ*, ed. and tr. Carl E. Braaten (Philadelphia: Fortress Press, 1964), p. 66.

truly historic Jesus. Only in this sense can one understand Kähler's statement that the substance of Christian doctrine is "not history, such as that of primitive Christianity, the plan of salvation, or something of that sort, but rather the content of the continuing preaching, in which the historic element is set forth in its immediate significance for every present time."[2]

The thought of Kähler has acquired its great and continuing significance less through the direct effect of his writings than through the fact that the different tendencies prevalent in the theological situation during the first half of the twentieth century happened to coincide with his insights, e.g., the rise of form-critical method in New Testament research. Even Wilhelm Herrmann, whose position ran counter to Kähler's in many respects, could arrive at a formulation similar to Kähler's on the basic question of the relationship between the primitive Christian kerygma and Jesus. Since the thing that matters is that in relation to the person of Jesus we have, "an experience that can be produced in no man by external force," but which frees one who has been overcome by it from every attempt at historical comprehension, Herrmann, too, thought it made sense to claim that we know "the Person of Jesus only in the preaching of the disciples who believed in him."[3] Above all, the renewal of the dogmatic theme of "the Word of God," which had long

---

[2] Martin Kähler, *Die Wissenschaft der christlichen Lehre*, second rev. ed. (Leipzig, 1893), sec. 44, 1a. Johannes Wirsching, in his "Offenbarung und Geschichte: Studien zur theologiegeschichtlichen Stellung und systematischen Grundlegung der Theologie Martin Kählers" (dissertation, University of Heidelberg, 1960), pp. 25ff., rightly emphasizes that Kähler's retention of a historical basis for faith and of the concept of the redemptive history prevented him from becoming a kerygma theologian in the modern, radical sense.

[3] Wilhelm Herrmann, *The Communion of the Christian with God*, tr. J. Sandys Stanton, revised, enlarged and altered in accordance with the fourth German ed. by R. W. Stewart (New York: G. P. Putnam's Son's, [3]1915), pp. 113f. The difference between this and Kähler is, of course, immediately evident in the fact that the person of Jesus, for Herrmann, is never simply identical with the Christ "of the whole New Testament"; so Kähler, *Der sogenannte historische Jesus und der geschichtliche, biblische Christus* (Leipzig, 1892), p. 41, *passim* (not expressly stated in *So-called Historical Jesus*, but cf. p. 72).

been submerged in the doctrine of inspiration, gave powerful impetus to kerygma theology. Kähler himself played an important part in this renewal, which stemmed from Erlangen Lutheranism and was championed particularly by Ludwig Ihmels. The decisive insight behind this development was that the "Word of God" was not only the written word of the Bible (as the older doctrine of inspiration had it) but primarily the preached Word, the Scripture being understood as the written residue of this. The effect of this insight was strengthened by the twenty years of the Luther renaissance. All these tendencies flowed into the eruption of the so-called dialectical theology insofar as it wanted to be essentially a"theology of the Word of God." Dialectical theology itself is to be understood as a particular and, in fact, most important manifestation of the many-sided movement of kerygma theology. It is no accident that Barth's doctrine of the Word of God takes the proclamation as its point of departure. Nevertheless, the purest and, so to speak, classical expression of kerygma theology is found in Rudolf Bultmann. His theology, however, also brings into sharpest focus the problem of its basic tendency.

Kerygma theology stressed the character of the biblical writings as witness against two other mutually supportive ways of dealing with historical material: the quest for general truths, on the one hand, and a particular form of historical research, on the other. It might seem surprising that these two viewpoints are related to each other, since history essentially deals with once-occurring matters. Here, however, the form of historical investigation involved is one that bases its judgments on the postulate of the homogeneity of all reality. Even in the most singular phenomena of the past it can discover, in the last analysis, only realities of the same sort as are experienced in the present. The biblical writings, on the other hand, insofar as they have the character of witnesses, do not deal with general religious truths – or with any other kind of general truths – which would be accessible at other times, but rather with very definite, most particular events which they attest to be acts of God, indeed, of the biblical God who is completely without analogy.

Historical investigation around 1900 seems to have devoted little attention to this particularity. It studied the biblical writings as documents of human religiosity, starting out from analogies with man's former and, above all, contemporary experience of himself and the world. It could not seriously speak of particular deeds of a particular God who disclosed himself only here. It could not have been otherwise on the basis of the methodological self-understanding of historical science as formulated, for instance, by Ernst Troeltsch. Much today depends upon whether one sees that this understanding of historical method is not identical with historical research generally, but only a time-bound and, in many respects, constricted and one-sided conception of the task and foundations of historical research, which still consists essentially in a methodical inquiry into the real circumstances of some past events. Today, this insight has been forced upon historical method by its own inner problems, as perhaps enigmatically resounds through the catchword "pre-understanding."

Progress in the basic questions of historical thinking is possible only if one sees the true nature of historical research and does not behave as if the formulation of historical method by Troeltsch somehow defined for all time in prototypical fashion the essence of historical thought. Kerygma theology, however, saw itself in contrast to just this particular and time-bound form of historical thought and developed itself in opposition to it. It was discovered that the intention of a historical question construed along these lines bypassed the intention of the biblical texts and failed to catch sight of their real content as witness to the deeds of God. This failure became almost crassly evident in the case of the nineteenth-century life-of-Jesus research. There was no possible bridge from the man Jesus, whose biography and religion was the object of this research, and the apostolic witness to him as the Christ. This was the point at which Kähler began his attack, and his intuitive insight that the Gospels were witnesses to the risen Christ and not biographical reports was later confirmed step by step through form-critical research. The problem of the historical Jesus brought to light in an exemplary way something that was for the most part valid for the rest of the biblical writings. Where they are read as merely documents of secular events and human religiosity, their genuine content, which is precisely their witness to the deeds of God, remains untapped. Kerygma theology, in discovering this, was perfectly correct over against the historical practice and methodology of its time.

Kerygma theology's opposition to the contemporaneous historiography, however, led it, in its further development, to lose sight of the historical basis of the biblical witnesses. As proclamation of "God's Word," these witnesses do not stand in isolation, as sheer assertions, but rather speak of events in which God has acted or will act and whose language is heard through the biblical witness insofar as this formulates the inherent meaning of these events. Can these events be judged to have really occurred even from our standpoint? That would indeed be the presupposition for the testimony of the biblical writings having any binding validity for us. But precisely this question was rejected ever more vigorously by kerygma theology in the course of its development, and even branded outright as a mark of unbelief. Faith must be satisfied with the kerygma and may not seek false security by inquiring behind the kerygma for the event attested by it. The life-interest of faith in the reliability of its historical basis was obscured by this sort of glib prejudgment, and people became blind to the perplexity that spread throughout the Christian congregations on this matter. The Word alone with its sheer *claim* to truth, taken abstractly by itself, is not yet sufficient ground for faith. The message of Jesus itself required historical legitimation, a confirmation by God himself. And it received it, too, through the resurrection of the Crucified from the dead.

The loss of history, just pointed out, had not yet happened in Kähler. A real event as the foundation of faith remained indispensable for him. The Christian faith is "not to be separated from the simply reasonable interpretation of historical information and has in this the means of proving its objectivity." In any case, Kähler immediately continued:

In this information, however, the reports about the historical fact are always accompanied by a testimony to its revelatory value, which is supplementary to it and exists precisely for faith alone.[4]

The whole problem is already contained in this distinction. Is not the "revelatory value" related to the "fact" as something added from outside? Does not this argument accept all too uncritically the neo-Kantian distinction between being and value? Does not the meaning of an event belong to the event itself insofar as it is to be understood only within its own historical context [*Geschehenszusammenhang*]?[5] If, on the other hand, Kähler's separation (and the external linkage presupposed by this separation) is correct, then the possibility arises that the "revelatory value" can stand upon itself as witness, and the historical "fact" whose value it is supposed to refer to would no longer need to have any special interest devoted to it. Such a way of rendering the kerygma autonomous over against its historical correlate later succeeded under the influence of form-critical research. A curious process: precisely by making the biblical witnesses to Christ itself the object of historical investigation, taking the Gospel texts as expressions of the primitive Christ-kerygma, the event to which they bore witness remained in the dark, from a historical perspective. In every stratum of the text one always found again yet another testimony of the Christian community, and never made direct contact with Jesus himself and his fate, hardly even with his own words. In this situation the question about the historical Jesus seemed – as long as one persisted in doing nothing but analyzing the texts – to be a hopeless undertaking. But a significant change in

---

[4] Kähler, *Wissenschaft*, sec. 16, cf. 17f., 45.

[5] I am happy to find myself in agreement with Heinrich Ott (*Die Frage nach dem historischen Jesus und die Ontologie der Geschichte* [Theologische Studien 62; Zürich, 1960], pp. 12ff., 21) in this criticism of the positivistic division between "fact" and "valuation" (or "significance"), which I expressed in *KuD* 5 (1959), p. 282 (above, pp. 7of.), following Collingwood. Still, Ott does not seem to me to have taken sufficiently into account the fact that the unity of fact and meaning is already given in the nexus of events [*Geschehenszusammenhang*] in any given instance.

historical interest now took place, not without the stimulation of existentialist philosophy, to be sure. One now searched the Gospels less for documents of any kind of event in the career of Jesus, and much more for primitive Christianity's interpretation of human existence. The historical basis of the kerygma, however, remained an open question. The systematic construction and justification of this position was accomplished by Bultmann. Consistently with this position, Bultmann had to depart from the view of Scripture as redemptive history which Kähler had still presupposed. For Bultmann, not history but eschatology is the origin of the New Testament kerygma. What has to be accomplished is the uncovering of the eschatological understanding of existence. For this purpose what matters is not the "what" but the "that" of the shock that gave rise to the primitive Christian Easter-faith and thereby to the kerygma of the earliest congregation.

It is characteristic of the progress of kerygma theology that in achieving the autonomy of the kerygma over against its historical basis, its development has been oriented entirely toward the problems of New Testament research. Since the historical basis of the New Testament kerygma is concentrated in a single event, the resurrection of Jesus, the attempt could be made to set this event in opposition to all other history as an eschatological event, since it seemed to be entirely inaccessible to the then current understanding of historical reality, and all the more so as the preaching of Jesus can itself be understood only as eschatological.[6] In Old Testament studies, on the other hand, it is in no way possible to eliminate the reference of Israel's testimonies of faith back to a continuous, Yahweh-effected history. Thus, it is no accident that precisely from the side of Old Testament research tendencies have appeared which counterbalance the loss of history in kerygma theology. Herein lies the

[6] The circumstance just mentioned made it possible for a new quest for the historical Jesus to arise in the form of an attempt to find support for the eschatological self-understanding of primitive Christianity in Jesus himself. This new quest, likewise, knew how to circumvent the historical question of the fate of Jesus by confining itself to the understanding of human existence contained in his message.

overall significance of von Rad's *Old Testament Theology*. Someone has said of this work that in it "kerygma theology has
invaded the field of the Old Testament in full force."[7] It is
certainly true that the tendencies of kerygma theology have
been incorporated into the way von Rad formulates the problems he deals with in this book. But precisely for this reason this
book can prepare the way for a genuine corrective, from the
side of the theme of the Old Testament, of the one-sidedness of
kerygma theology, insofar as Jesus himself and also primitive
Christianity must now be understood in connection with the
history of the transmission of the tradition of Israel, in which
so-called ancient Judaism also belongs. The method hammered
out by von Rad, perhaps more in the execution than in its
programmatic formulation, signifies that the isolation of the
kerygma from history will be overcome.

The point of departure for von Rad's whole exposition is the
perception

that in principle Israel's faith is grounded in a theology of history. It regards
itself as based upon historical facts, and as shaped and re-shaped by facts in
which it saw the hand of God at work.[8]

To be sure, Israel's interpretation of particular crucial events
and its projections of the whole of the divine history it experienced in them, which gradually became more and more comprehensive, do not square with today's historical-critical picture
of the history of Israel and the ancient Near East. Von Rad has
called attention to this tension and added that only Israel's
understanding of the history of this period as the redemptive
history of Yahweh with his people, and not the historical-
critical picture of this history, can be the object of Old Testament theology.[9] This explanation has evoked violent opposition.
Von Rad was seen as surrendering "real" history, whose course

[7] Franz Hesse, "Kerygma oder geschichtliche Wirklichkeit?," *ZThK* 57
(1960), 21.
[8] Gerhard von Rad, *Old Testament Theology*, tr. D. M. G. Stalker (Edinburgh: Oliver and Boyd and New York: Harper and Row, 1962), I, p. 106.
[9] *Ibid.*, p. 114.

is visible to our historical inquiry, in favor of Israel's representations of its history which our historical knowledge has shown to be incorrect in many respects. In other words, von Rad was thought to be demanding a sacrifice of the intellect.[10]

Von Rad, however, defended himself against the charge that the real historical course of Israel's history was of no consequence in his view.[11] His whole procedure of trying to understand the rise and transformation of the Israelite traditions from within the historical situation of that time, as this appears to our historical view, certainly justifies his reply. Historical-critical knowledge of the history of Israel is everywhere presupposed where von Rad set about working out the intentions of the different witnesses. Even in his fully developed interpretations, historical understanding is involved right down to every last detail. For this reason, it is impossible to set von Rad's conception into opposition with historical-critical exposition of the history of Israel like, for example, that of Martin Noth. Even if, perhaps, some of his basic formulations can be construed in a way that supports this misunderstanding, still, in view of the execution of his conception, there can be no room for doubt on this point. On the other hand, von Rad rightly insists against his critics that one may not abandon the historical testimony of Israel in favor of the picture of the history of Israel our historiography has produced.[12] When Hesse formulates the thesis, "for us as Christian theologians the real course of the history of Israel . . . is much more important than the representations Israel developed about the course of its history,"[13] must one not, with von Rad, designate such a dichotomy between real history and interpreted history as "untenable"?[14] When Hesse wants to allow Israel's historical depictions themselves validity *only* as "testimony to the peculiar character of the faith of the Old

---

[10] Hesse, "Kerygma o. g. Wirklichkeit?," pp. 25f.

[11] Gerhard von Rad, *Theologie des Alten Testaments* (Munich, 1960), 2, p. 8 [not in English tr.]; against Hesse, "Die Erforschung der Geschichte Israels als theologische Aufgabe," *KuD* 4 (1958), 8.

[12] von Rad, *Theologie des Alten Testaments*, 2, p. 11.

[13] Hesse, "Kerygma o. g. Wirklichkeit?," p. 24.

[14] von Rad, *Theologie des Alten Testaments*, 2, 9.

Testament narrators,"[15] then that is obviously too little, since they were dealing not with subjective impressions of the external events which were of no consequence for the course of history itself, but rather with inexpungeable moments of the historical process itself.

The historical process – and this means the one course of events with which historiographical inquiry has also to do – is essentially a process of the transmission of tradition. All political events – in fact, even natural events – that play into it gain their meaning and significance only by virtue of their relation to the traditions in which the human society that is affected by them lives. To be sure, this happens for the most part in such a way that they call into question the previous forms of tradition and provide an impetus for their transformation and reconstruction. It is precisely this sort of process that von Rad exhibits in detail. He does not assert the normative validity of a single Israelite picture of history, but shows the changes of the traditions in which Israel lived. The unity of its history and its historical consciousness emerges in this very process, which is again and again reflected within itself. Since Israel lived from specific events which were transmitted, preeminently in the election tradition, for remembrance by the next generation, it was necessary to expound these events again and again as binding upon each successive generation. At the very least, the coming redemptive event was represented by analogy with the past, as in the case of the prophets. In that von Rad retraces the history of Israel through close association with its traditions, he has been the one who has been able to bring their unity into view in the reciprocal interpenetration "of the political, economic, and especially the spiritual history of Israel," which Hesse also seeks, following Justus Köberle.[16] Von Rad no longer has anything to do with an "inner" and an "outer" history existing side by side,[17] because in the structure of the process of the trans-

---

[15] Hesse, "Die Erforschung," p. 17; cf. "Kerygma o. g. Wirklichkeit?," p. 25.
[16] Hesse, "Die Erforschung," p. 9.
[17] *Ibid.* and p. 15.

mission of tradition he has grasped the point of concrete unity which bifurcates into divergent moments only from an abstract way of looking at it. Does not Hesse lose sight of this unity, in spite of his intention, when he affirms a history of God with Israel *in contradistinction* to "Israel's representations of what happened" as the real redemptive history?[18]

By his conception of the history of Israel as a process of tradition, von Rad distinguishes himself not only from the usual juxtaposition of "inner" and "outer" history, i.e., from most of the older historical expositions, but also from the older theology of redemptive history. The latter had all too hastily lifted out of the Old Testament witnesses a unified unfolding of redemptive history and in this sense constructed an "objective history of redemption." This effort could not succeed without pious harmonization of Old Testament statements with each other, and, at the same time, such a treatment could not but lead to a supranaturalistic, unhistorical construction of history. Perhaps the most magnificent achievement of von Rad's tradition-historical viewpoint is that it avoids these dangers while nevertheless allowing the theological substance of the theology of redemptive history to be preserved. The Old Testament witnesses find expression in the entire conflict-laden variety of their diverse intentions and perspective. An extraordinary advance has been accomplished in this respect even in comparison with Procksch's *Theologie des Alten Testaments*. By precise observation of the uniqueness of the different texts, von Rad finds room to sketch each of them as "distinctive contemporanizations and actualizations of the redemptive facts,"[19] i.e., as efforts of the Old Testament witnesses to disclose the foundational redemptive event to each new generation as effective and valid even in their particular situation. The kerygmatic character of the history of tradition finds expression in this way. The astonishing thing about this is that close attention to the differentiable kerygmatic contemporanizations and actualizations of the supportive "redemptive facts" leads to a consistent utilization of

---

[18] *Ibid.*, pp. 10f.
[19] von Rad, *Theologie des Alten Testaments*, p. 6 [tr. mine – Tr.].

scientific-historical interpretation of the text such as was previously unheard of in an interpretation of the history of Israel determined by the point of view of redemptive history.

It can be asked whether the continuity of the historical process is not left in the dark beyond the multiplicity of perspectives and the variations of the traditions of Israel among the individual witnesses. It is indeed the case that von Rad has not once made the whole process of the transmission the object of a special, comprehensive view. But the aspects of such a view have already been provided everywhere in the detailed expositions. That which links the different witnesses together is to be found precisely in the process of the history of the transmission of traditions, insofar as each of them in their different situations refers back to a few foundational traditions, and these in turn coalesce in a meaningful way in the process of their actualization. A decisive turn in this process occurred in the prophetic movement, since here it was no longer the already completed redemptive deed, but a future saving act of God surpassing everything that had gone before, which drew all interest to itself. But even this turn did not occur abruptly. Rather, it stood in agreement with the older traditions not only with respect to their content, insofar as the future was portrayed entirely according to analogies taken from earlier deeds of God, but also with respect to form, since the older election traditions had already been transmitted as fulfillments of promises. This viewpoint is by no means limited to the Old Testament. Even the post-canonical Jewish literature, the emergence of Jesus, and the primitive Christian history of tradition may be understood as actualizations of the Old Testament tradition. In all these cases the process of "actualization" is always occasioned by an event of novel character, and succeeds amid the acceptance of new images, as was already the way in the Old Testament. Thus, von Rad's approach opens up the possibility of a "biblical theology" which would by no means need to remain suspended in a schematic typologizing, but could rather unfold the problems of the late Jewish and early Christian history of tradition with the same differentiation von Rad showed in treating the becoming and transformation of the historical and prophetic traditions of Israel. In this way one would overcome in principle a kerygma theology isolated from history and oriented to a point-like saving event abstracted from the tradition-determined form in which it is portrayed. Furthermore, the history of redemption would have to be understood as the history of the transmission of tradition even from the standpoint of dogmatics. Special consideration would, of course, have to be given to the dialectic of the tradition – which, because of the fact that it provides the language used to speak of the future, expected, new redemptive deed, always brings with it the danger of not being able to do justice to this in its newness – precisely in view of the history of Jesus.

We conclude by returning to the question of the relation between a kerygma theology so understood and the historical-critical conception of the history of Israel. Are they really as different as von Rad states in his introductory remarks to the two volumes? The impression created by the whole work is that in negotiating the path he set out on he has gone beyond such cleavages. The magisterial character and consistency in the interpretation of historical details is precisely what characterizes this work. The history of the transmission of tradition, including the origins of the traditions and the concrete occasions of their changes, is itself treated as a historical object, and can hardly be treated in any other way. It is just the history of the transmission of tradition that has to be seen as a deeper concept of history generally. But does not talk about an act of God designate a limit which a historical statement is forbidden to transgress? Von Rad is especially cautious on this point in his concrete statements, and these remain preponderantly at the borders of the interpretation of the Israelite testimonies of faith. But is it perhaps permissible, even here, to make historically responsible statements about the process of the history of the transmission of tradition in Israel and about the individual moments in it? Perhaps this is the place where we must drop certain specific prejudgments about the limits of the historical understanding of reality which have become almost universally accepted as valid since the time of Troeltsch.[20] Perhaps only

[20] Of course, God can be spoken of only in relation to the whole of reality because, since the critical question of Greek philosophy about the true form of the divine, only one who was the author of all things and all events could seriously be called God. The historian is in the habit of seldom asking about the whole of reality, only doing so when he raises the question of universal history. Coupled with this is the special difficulty of how the historian could be able to speak about an act of God. In his work he always presupposes, of course, some understanding of reality as a whole. But still, the intention of his investigation must be designated as primarily individualizing, not generalizing. Nevertheless, this thesis of Rickert's, designed to delimit history from the natural sciences, is forgetful of the fact that individuality does not directly belong to a historical detail, but is visible only to the extent that it may be viewed within a nexus of events. Our question is very closely related to this point, since to speak of a deed of God with regard to an individual event means to judge it in its concrete relation to the occurrences of its nearer and farther connections and to history as a whole. Not every event permits these relations to become visible in the same way. It is the particularity of the event of Jesus that through it for the first time the totality of reality was constituted as a whole, whereas all other occurrences have a relation to the whole of reality only through their relation to this unique occurrence. In the case of Jesus, the relation to the whole of reality is established by the eschatological character of his message, his claims, and his fate (which, for their part, are to be understood only on the basis of the Israelite understanding of history). For history receives its wholeness for the first time precisely by the fact that the end of history – which had occurred in an anticipatory form in the claim and fate of Jesus – comes into view. The eschatological character of the claim and fate of Jesus is the ground of the statements about a deed of God in him, whereby, to be sure, the meaning of the word "God" and its indispensability for an understanding of reality as a whole (and, above all, of man himself) is already presupposed. Since, however, the way of Jesus is wholly grounded in the history of the transmission of Israel's tradition, and since the God of Israel was his God, so that the history of Jesus cannot be understood by itself but only in the context of the history of this tradition, one may therefore in retrospect perceive a deed of the true God even in the history of Israel. Then, the witnesses of Israel can themselves be questioned in genuine objectivity, certainly not on the basis of some modern criteria or even, without qualification, New Testament criteria (although it is from the New Testament that the events of the history of Israel come into view as deeds of God), but rather always only in relation to the situation of the witness in question in the history of the transmission of tradition. But whether objective or not, the testimony to a specific deed of God is always to be understood as (positively or negatively) a reference point for all later understanding of this and further acts of God, and as such belongs, as an inalienable member, to the history of God with Israel.

Not even the historian can fundamentally dispute the possibility of statements of such a kind because they do not intend another, supernatural then will the full scope of von Rad's method of analyzing the history of the transmission of tradition become visible.

---

reality, but refer, rather, to the event that the historian himself investigates. To be sure, such statements would refer the event to the totality of reality and especially to the event of Jesus because in him, as the eschatological reality, reality conceived as history acquires its wholeness. The historian will be led along this way by his own problems since, in spite of his primary interest in this or that particular event, he will always be unable to determine its peculiar character except by means of its nearer and farther connections. In attempting such determinations, he anticipates, in one way or another, insights about reality as a whole, the problem of which is the special theme of the philosopher or systematic theologian. Why, then, should not such anticipations take place in the form of the historian speaking about a deed of God in a specific event?

4

HERMENEUTIC AND UNIVERSAL HISTORY

Originally published as "Hermeneutik und Universalgeschichte," *ZThK* 60 (1963), pp. 90–121. A translation by Paul J. Achtemeier appeared in Wolfhart Pannenberg *et al.*, *History and Hermeneutic*, Journal for Theology and Church 4 (New York: Harper Torchbooks, 1967), pp. 122–52.

I

THE EARLY Protestant doctrine of the clarity of Scripture, by means of which Luther made the authority of Scripture independent of interpretation by an ecclesiastical teaching office, has become problematical in modern times in two respects. For Luther and early Protestantism, the literal sense (*sensus literalis*) of the biblical writings passed at the same time for the historical sense (*sensus historicus*); and, on the other hand, his own conception of the doctrine of the Gospel (*doctrina evangelii*) coincided with the content of Scripture understood literally (*ad litteram*). Since that time, however, a gulf has opened up between the literal meaning of the biblical writings and the historical course of events to which they refer, on the one hand; and, on the other hand, the distance separating our period and any possible theology today from the time of primitive Christianity and the various theological conceptions of the New Testament witnesses can no longer be overlooked.

With respect to the difference between the biblical texts and the events to which they point, we have to do with the central problem of historical study. With respect to the distance between primitive Christianity and our age, we have to do with the central problem of hermeneutic. The two are closely related and probably form a single theme. Whether or not that is actually the case should be clarified in the course of our reflections. In any event, both gaps – the one between the biblical texts and the events of the history of Jesus and his community, which henceforth have to be sought out by going behind the texts; as well as the other one between the biblical writings, as witnesses of an age long past, and our own present age – have arisen from one and the same methodological requirement, namely, the principle that the biblical texts are to be interpreted in accordance with the intention of their authors, and thus with reference to the situation in which they were written. This requirement was occasionally expressed as early as the sixteenth century by Matthias Flacius and Joachim Camerarius. It was J. S. Semler (1725–91), however, who, after the attempts of Grotius and Lightfoot, succeeded in winning general recognition for the principle within theological exegesis. This development in turn opened up the possibility of noting the various *tendencies* within the biblical writings in their portrayal and interpretation of the Christ-event and its consequences. This "tendency criticism" [*Tendenzkritik*], which was methodically elaborated for the first time by F. C. Baur, forced one to go behind the text to form a picture of the actual course of events. In that way, the proper content of Scripture (its *res*), the actual history of Jesus, was separated from the biblical texts as something to be sought out behind them. The same methodological requirement that led to this result, viz., the requirement that the texts be interpreted relative to the time of their origin, also produced an awareness of the distance between the intellectual milieu of the New Testament writings and the spirit of the age contemporaneous with any given interpreter. This consciousness gave rise in the eighteenth century to the special hermeneutical problem of the modern era, the task of achieving an understanding that spans the historical distance between primitive Christianity and the present time.

The distinction between going behind the texts by means of historical investigation and building hermeneutical bridges from them to some present time can claim no more than limited validity. Upon deeper consideration, these two prove to be aspects of a single theme. Nor is it easy to tell whether the totality that embraces both should be called hermeneutic or history. Modern historical investigation, which inquires after what lies behind the texts, has itself arisen in connection with the tasks of interpreting texts. To this extent it seems as if the hermeneutical theme includes historical inquiry as a subordinate element. On the other hand, historical inquiry goes beyond the text, nevertheless, since it asks about what lies behind it, and it even includes the specifically hermeneutical theme in itself insofar as the event sought in inquiring behind the texts does not manifest itself for what it really is when taken as an isolated fact, but does so only within universal continuities of events and of meanings, i.e., only within the horizon of universal history, which, incidentally, also embraces the present era of the investigator. This latter point is often overlooked, and can also be neglected, to a certain extent, in dealing with history. Of course, every event has its peculiar character and meaning only within the nexus of events to which it belongs from the very beginning. But this is at first a matter of the proximate environment of the event and not immediately of universal history. This observation is correct insofar as it may suffice, for the understanding of average events and figures, to see them within the horizon of their epoch and life-setting. This life-setting and this epoch, however, have their meaning only within more comprehensive continuities. Even significant individual occurrences and historical figures require for their evaluation a view of the broader continuities that extend beyond their narrower life-setting and epoch. The more significant an occurrence or a figure is, the more comprehensive must be the nexus of events to which one has to relate it in order to do justice to its true significance, at least in an appropriate way. It is to such notable occurrences and figures, in turn, that the remaining events of an epoch are referred. To that extent, we can justify in a general way our assertion that the event sought for in inquiring behind the texts reveals its true visage only within universal continuities of events and of meaning. To that extent, however, the historical quest, as a quest for universal history, includes on its part the specifically hermeneutical theme, namely, the relationship of a text (or event) of the past to the present age of the interpreter.

Thus, there proves to be a certain competition between the hermeneutical and universal-historical ways of looking at things. Both have to do with texts. Both arrive at the interpreter's present on the basis of the text, and draw the interpreter into the interpretation of the text. However, the hermeneutical outlook apparently moves solely between the past text and the present interpreter, whereas the universal-historical outlook first goes back behind the text, and considers the essential content [*Sache*], i.e., the event being inquired into behind the text,[1] in its universal-historical context of meaning, including also the interpreter's own present era. The universal-historical approach thus makes a detour, the detour of going behind the text to the underlying event which the text attests, in order to build a bridge to the era contemporaneous with the interpreter (or historian).

The competition between hermeneutic and universal-historical methods can nevertheless also signify a convergence; for the correct resolution of both tasks must actually lead to the same results. In the course of its struggles with the text it is dealing with, the hermeneutic endeavor would have to take the step behind the text back to the essential content it expresses, because that is demanded by the intention of the texts themselves in that, for example, they say something about an event distinct from themselves and so point away from themselves to this event. To that extent, understanding of the text itself, namely, of its assertion, necessarily leads to the movement back

[1] The essential content stated by a text is not, of course, always a specific event. That is only the case with texts that speak of occurrences and persons, as well as of their significance. The essential content of a text can also be a mathematical truth, a natural entity, a technical construction, or a philosophical idea. The fact that all these contents are for their part also historically conditioned is another question and can occupy us only marginally. With regard to the biblical texts, however, we have to do in every case with testimonies to specific events and their inherent meaning. The inquiry which presses behind them to their essential content will to that extent be a quest for the actual course of events, and will thus be historical.

behind the text, and thus, in our case, to the properly historical formulation of the question of the relationship of its theme to the time of the investigator, since when one investigates a historical object, that object is always already viewed from the perspective of the present time. The historian may forget this in his drive for "objectivity" and in his passionate quest to know "how it really happened." As a result of this passion, historical discussions easily fall under the suspicion (viewed from the standpoint of the hermeneutical task) that the things being spoken about have been placed at a distance from the speakers themselves as something that is simply over and done with. If it were actually the case that the historical outlook, because it objectified the past, destroyed the living relationship of the present with what has been handed down by tradition, then the problem of the historical distance which is always created anew by historical thinking could only be overcome on an entirely different intellectual basis. But as a universal-historical conception of events, historical investigation cannot represent the events it seeks to reconstruct in going behind their texts as something merely past, but, on the contrary, must grasp them in the continuity of meaning in which they stand, which connects them with the present age of the historian. Insofar as historical work always implies the problem of universal history, it by no means deals with the dead remains of the past, as is sometimes asserted, as though the post of the historian were comparable to that of the caretaker of a cemetery.[2]

II

The insight concerning the relationship between historical and hermeneutical problems has recently been advanced by the

[2] So, for instance, Otto Weber, *Grundlagen der Dogmatik* (Neukirchen Kreis Moers, 1955–62), 2 (1962), pp. 106f., who appeals for support to Reinhard Wittram, *Das Interesse an der Geschichte* (Göttingen, 1958), p. 16, passim. In any case, even Weber has to admit in view of the contemporaneous character of the historical quest itself "that history is not 'dead' in every sense" (p. 108).

hermeneutical work of Hans-Georg Gadamer.[3] In order to evaluate the step Gadamer's work has taken, and which also prompts certain counterquestions to him, we must first of all have before us the history of our theme within the discipline of hermeneutic.

It has already been mentioned that the modern historical method has developed out of the hermeneutical task of interpreting texts. The relationship between the two was subsequently reversed. Philology became an auxiliary science to that of history.[4] This development is to a certain extent the result of consistency of procedure, since textual interpretation had taught itself to view the texts as merely historical documents. Therefore, it is very questionable whether one can share Bultmann's judgment: "But the result was simply that philology lost its real subject matter, the interpretation of texts for the sake of understanding them."[5] This judgment is questionable because it is just this interpretation of the text for the sake of understanding it that led to the historical step of going behind the texts because of the methodological requirement of understanding every author on the basis of the situation of his time. This requirement led, as we saw, to the discernment of the fundamental "tendency" inherent in every text in relation to its essential content, so that henceforth the essential content dealt with by a text had to be distinguished from the way in which this found expression in language. This was to be accomplished precisely through reflection upon the "tendency" of the text. Since in the "process" of the development of "tendency criticism" textual interpretation itself succeeded in inquiring behind the text, it could very well be the case that hermeneutic here has sublimated itself [*sich aufhebt*]

---

[3] Hans-Georg Gadamer, *Wahrheit und Methode; Grundzüge einer philosophischen Hermeneutik* (Tübingen, 1960; ²1965). Supplementing his book is Gadamer's article "Hermeneutik und Historismus," *Philosophische Rundschau* 9 (1962); pp. 241–76 (reissued as an appendix to the second ed. of *Wahrheit und Methode*, pp. 477–512).

[4] Gadamer, *Wahrheit und Methode*, p. 320.

[5] Bultmann, "The Problem of Hermeneutics," in *Essays on Old Testament Hermeneutics*, ed. Claus Westermann (London: SCM Press and Richmond: John Knox Press, 1963), p. 237.

into history and continues to exist only as an auxiliary science to history.

Such a sublimation [*Aufhebung*], however else it might be regarded, is nevertheless incomplete so long as the historical outlook has not been broadened into universal history. If history uses the texts at its disposal only as documents of the period of their origination, then the text retains a dimension that has not entered into historical understanding. This is particularly clear in the case of works of art, but also with respect to religious texts. If one describes the Greek tragedies of the fifth century only as expressions of the classical period of Greek history, then he has obviously not touched the artistic truth of the works of Aeschylus or Sophocles, which speak to man regardless of his place in time. These works are more than simply expressions of the Greek spirit of the fifth century, for they created an image of human behavior which has proved its formative power in our cultural tradition. Just as little are the Pauline letters exhausted in being taken as merely expressions of the situation of primitive Christianity. As long as there is a Christian church, someone will find in these texts, despite all changes of time, something that still brings to consciousness the true situation of man before God. The same thing could be exemplified with legal, mathematical, or philosophical works. To all appearances such texts have a dimension which is not accessible to historical inquiry, at least so long as those "generally human" contents are not themselves recognized as historical structures (law, religion, art, philosophy), and as long as, on the other hand, the historical interrogation of such texts limits itself to the period of their origin. As opposed to such a restricted formulation of the historical question, however, the transmitted texts contain a surplus because their truth continues to be effective beyond the situation of their origin. Just for this reason they are able to make a "direct appeal." To evaluate them as mere documents of a long bygone age constitutes an abridgment. This is true even of historiographical works. Herodotus' historical treatise, as he states in the introduction, intended to set up a monument to the deeds of the heroes of his time, and he obviously believed that these deeds contained in an exemplary way something of what it means to be human universally. Historiography itself never wants to portray a completed epoch of the past merely as past. That would not be worth the effort. Quite the contrary, historiography is guided by an interest in the present.

The fact that transmitted texts of the widest variety are not exhausted when they are used as nothing more than sources for the period of their origination is the basis of a relative independence of hermeneutic over against historical research. So long as historical science treats universal history as a marginal problem and remains content with more narrowly defined tasks, it has no right to view hermeneutic as a mere auxiliary discipline, but will rather itself remain only a branch of hermeneutic. To be sure, this final conclusion had not yet been drawn by even the most significant theoreticians of hermeneutic in the nineteenth century, Schleiermacher and Dilthey. History and hermeneutic remained juxtaposed.

Schleiermacher's hermeneutic arose out of a theological interest in connection with the task of interpreting Scripture, and not with reference to the historical task.[6] This does not mean that Schleiermacher laid claim to special principles of interpretation for the biblical writings. On the contrary, the biblical texts were to be interpreted in accordance with such rules as had general validity. Here, as elsewhere, Schleiermacher explained, the general takes precedence over the particular.[7] His point of departure is to be found, however, in the understanding, not in the first instance of texts, but of oral speech and the thought expressed in it.[8] In this way, Schleiermacher became the first to view hermeneutic as a science of understanding as such, something reaching beyond the task of interpreting given texts. Reciprocal understanding is grounded in man's "consciousness of kind" [*Gattungsbewusstsein*, lit. "species consciousness"], which

---

[6] Gadamer, *Wahrheit und Methode*, p. 185.

[7] Friedrich D. E. Schleiermacher, *Hermeneutik*, newly edited from the manuscripts and introduced by Heinz Kimmerle, Abhandlungen der Heidelberger Akademie der Wissenschaften, Philosophisch-historische Klasse 2 (Heidelberg, 1959), p. 55 (= first draft of 1810).

[8] Kompendium of 1819, secs. 3–5 (Schleiermacher, *Hermeneutik*, pp. 8of.).

links single individuals to each other insofar as it involves each of them in the generally human and in what is meaningful for man as such.[9] As Niebuhr has shown, Schleiermacher's conception of hermeneutic is grounded in his idea of the common consciousness of kind. Only by means of the common consciousness of kind is it possible to understand not only the words but also the gestures, inflections, mimicry, and total behavior of another person. It enables us to grasp in our own self-consciousness, in the mode of feeling, the meaning of the words and gestures of the other person. Thus, intuition, empathy with the other on the basis of common participation in humanity, is the foundation of all understanding.

Nevertheless, Schleiermacher did not develop a universal hermeneutic of human interrelatedness, corresponding to such general considerations as have just been mentioned. Rather, he immediately turned back to the traditional task of the interpretation of texts. This task obviously did not appear to him to be essentially different from the task of understanding oral conversation. The fact that Schleiermacher did not find any additional problem in this transition from the dialogical understanding of oral exchange to the interpretation of transmitted texts shows that he was not aware of the true depth of the problem of historical understanding.[10] Comprehending the particularity of an author – beyond the general character of the grammatical structure of his language – was simply a psychological, not a historical, task for Schleiermacher. This has had its effects, through Dilthey, down to the present time, even if today we no longer speak of a psychological but of an existentialist interpreta-

---

[9] Richard R. Niebuhr, "Schleiermacher on Language and Feeling," *Theology Today* 17 (1960), 150–67, esp. 153ff. [The translation of *Gattungsbewusstsein* as "consciousness of kind" is taken from Richard R. Niebuhr, *ibid.*, p. 153. He also gives "fellow feeling" in his *Schleiermacher on Christ and Religion* (New York: Charles Scribner's Sons, 1964), p. 127.—Tr.]

[10] Kimmerle writes in his introduction to Schleiermacher's *Hermeneutik* (p. 16) that Schleiermacher did not see "that knowledge of historical relationships [*Zusammenhänge*] . . . belongs to the process of understanding itself" and does not constitute merely its presupposition. Cf. also Gadamer, *Wahrheit und Methode*, p. 179.

tion. Schleiermacher's theory of psychological interpretation was at first intended simply to lead to the determination of the individual style of an author's linguistic usage, but later it was also to lead to the reconstruction of the origin of a text from the mental processes of the author.[11] The object of understanding is now no longer a specific, essential content [*Sache*] expressed in the text, but rather "the process of emergence from the inwardness of thought into language."[12] In order to accomplish that kind of psychological reconstruction of a text as formed by the thought of its author, one must put himself into the place of the author, entering into the particular conditions of his peculiar characteristics and situation. For only by means of such empathetic understanding is it possible, as Schleiermacher stressed in 1829, "*correctly to reproduce that creative act*, [to show] how the necessities of the moment could have influenced the living fund of language, hovering before the author, in precisely the way it did and not otherwise."[13]

The psychological intention of Schleiermacher's hermeneutic was retained by Dilthey. Understanding appeared to him, too, as a "psychological imitation," which had as its task the reconstruction of the "creative process" by which some work originated. In order to characterize the relationship of a text to its author, Dilthey used the concept of "expression" [*Ausdruck*], which at the same time constituted the point of departure for overcoming the psychological conception of the hermeneutical task. The concept of "expression" had already been employed in Droysen's historiographical works, and may go back to

[11] Since the Academy courses, "Über den Begriff der Hermeneutik," etc., 1829.

[12] Schleiermacher, *Hermeneutik*, Introduction, p. 23. Kimmerle sees a loss of substance in this development (*ibid.*). This development was already posed as a problem, however, in the earlier distinction between the general meaning of words and the individual nuance (cf. *Aphorismen* from 1805 and 1809, p. 34). The question of how the one passes over to the other was to be solved later by means of psychological construction. Nevertheless, it was Schleiermacher's opinion already at an early stage that the concrete assertion is to be taken as "an empirical modification of an ideal quantity" (Schleiermacher, *Hermeneutik*, 23), as is clear from the passage indicated.

[13] Schleiermacher, *Hermeneutik*, p. 138.

Hegel.[14] Dilthey not only saw texts as "expression[s]" of the intentions and thoughts of their authors, but understood all events in general as expressions of the acting persons. The sphere of hermeneutic was in this way widened to an amazing degree. It now included not only oral discourse, as in Schleiermacher, but even the wordless event or the remaining traces of it. Dilthey could comprehend all the events of history as expressions of human behavior because he held – calling upon Vico for support – that all historical events are to be understood as workings of the human spirit in which the historian also shares, so that he can always imagine the possibility that he himself could produce similar effects. Dilthey writes: "The first condition for the possibility of historical science lies in the fact that I myself am a historical being: that he who investigates history is the same (!) as he who makes history."[15] Doubts cannot be suppressed at this point. It is really extremely questionable that any average historian, *by virtue of his having the same psychic nature*, can "empathize" with any activity of men of earlier time he pleases whether they be criminals, founders of religion, or rulers. Besides this, history does not have to deal with unique occurrence only with respect to how men acted, but also with respect of what happened to them.[16] It is simply not the case that the historian may concern himself only with man's mental activity and leave the rest to physics.

The reference of the past to the interpreter's present can no more be called into question for Dilthey than for Schleier-

[14] Georg W. F. Hegel, *The Phenomenology of Mind*, tr. George Lichtheim (New York: Harper Torchbooks, 1960), pp. 179ff. ("Force and Understanding, etc."). Cf. also Gadamer, *Wahrheit und Methode*, p. 193. On J. G. Droysen's *Outline of the Principles of History*, tr. E. Benjamin Andrews (Boston: Ginn and Co., 1893), sec. 9, pp. 12f. and the corresponding section in Droysen's *Historik; Vorlesungen über Enzyklopädie und Methodologie der Geschichte*, ed. R. Hübner (Munich, [3]1958), pp. 21ff., cf. Gadamer, *Wahrheit und Methode*, p. 204. But see already Schleiermacher, *Grundriss der philosophischen Ethik*, ed. D. A. Twesten (Berlin, 1841), sec. 61, p. 64.

[15] Wilhelm Dilthey, *Gesammelte Schriften* (Leipzig and Stuttgart, 1927; [2]1948), 7, p. 278; on which see Gadamer, *Wahrheit und Methode*, p. 209.

[16] Cf. Bultmann's argument against Collingwood in *The Presence of Eternity: History and Eschatology* (New York: Harper and Brothers, 1957), pp. 136ff.

macher. Both of them seem rather to have presupposed this reference: the identity of life and the possibilities of experience on the part of the interpreter and on the part of the men of the past is the common element that from the outset connects the interpreted past and the present. The interpreter can therefore find in the past only what is also accessible to present experience, at least as a possibility. The pre-understanding of life and the possibilities of experience thus determines and limits the interpretation from the *start*.

However, Dilthey's idea that the possibilities of life are really first revealed to us by history stands in tension with what has just been stated. This idea, for its part, is closely related to the psychology of expression. Just as the individual, according to Dilthey, is unable to know himself through introspection, but know himself only from the forms he produces, so the possibilities of the human soul generally are to be understood only from the forms in which it has expressed itself at some time or another. To that extent, contemporary life is directed for its own possibilities to that to which earlier generations have given form as human possibilities, and thus made accessible to the comprehending recollection [*der verstehenden Besinnung*].

Bultmann fastened on to this side of Dilthey's thought. To be sure, he also sought a structure of man's being – now no longer a psychological kind, but an existential one – on the basis of which the possibilities of human activities and experience were to be understood. But the existential structure of man's being, according to Bultmann, is at once marked by the fact that the one who understands deals with his text as a questioner because questionableness [*Fraglichkeit*] determines the very structure of human existence. In this sense, Bultmann says that interpretation always requires "the interpreter's relationship in his life to the essential content which is directly or indirectly expressed in the text."[17] Which content this is depends upon the interest of the interpretation.[18] This interest can be directed toward the

[17] Rudolf Bultmann, "The Problem of Hermeneutics," in Westermann, *Essays*, p. 241 [tr. slightly altered].

[18] *Ibid.*, pp. 243f.

historical reconstruction of a course of events; it can be psychologically or aesthetically oriented. Lastly, it "can be established by an interest in history as the sphere of life in which human existence moves, in which it attains its possibilities and develops them."[19] It is with such considerations in mind that Bultmann turns to the interpretation of New Testament texts. Since he thinks of God, of whose actions the New Testament witnesses speak, only in connection with man, only as the one who is asked about in the questionableness of human existence, the pre-understanding of an exegesis of the New Testament must consist in "the inquiry into the understanding of human existence which finds expression in the Scriptures."[20] Thus, for Bultmann, the necessity of an existentialist interpretation follows as a consequence of the fact that we know God as the one about whom man asks in the questionableness of his own existence. This is the conclusion of the essay he wrote in 1925, "What Does it Mean to Speak of God?,"[21] and it forms the basis of the program of an existentialist interpretation of the New Testament writings.

Although Bultmann's emphasis on the questionability of human existence as the presupposition of interrogating a transmitted text about the possibilities of human existence and self-understanding does tie in with Dilthey's recognition that man attains knowledge of his own possibilities only by means of a comprehending perception [*verstehende Wahrnehmung*] of the forms produced by men in history,[22] it nevertheless surpasses Dilthey's psychological interpretation in a fundamental way. This is particularly evident in the fact that Bultmann replaces the questionable requirement of an empathetic interpretation with "the simple fact that the presupposition for understanding is the interpreter's relationship in his life to the essential content which is directly or indirectly expressed in the text."[23] Thus, the

[19] *Ibid.*, p. 253.   [20] *Ibid.*, p. 258.
[21] Rudolf Bultmann, *Faith and Understanding* I, tr. by Louise Pettibone Smith (London: SCM Press and New York: Harper and Row, 1969), pp. 53–65.
[22] Bultmann, in Westermann, *Essays*, pp. 250f.
[23] *Ibid.*, p. 241 [tr. slighty altered].

questioning without which the text could not be understood as an answer is the only presupposition of understanding. Accordingly, the "pre-understanding" of Bultmann's existentialist interpretation is also to be conceived in terms of the questioning character [*Fraglichkeit*] of human existence. With respect to the New Testament, it consists in "the *inquiry* into the understanding of human existence that finds expression in the Scriptures."[24] Thus, the pre-understanding involved does not, as has been repeatedly misunderstood, prescribe answers of an already determinate content in the sense of a prejudgment. At least, that is not the hermeneutical intention of Bultmann's concept of pre-understanding. Rather, the questioning character of the pre-understanding makes room for a revision of any given preconception about the essential content of a text by means of the confrontation with the text itself. In spite of this, the considerations against Dilthey's attempt to undergird all historical forms with a general psychological typology must be raised, in part at least, against Bultmann, too.

Existentialist interpretation, like the psychological interpretation of Schleiermacher and Dilthey, also restricts the question about the contemporary significance of the past to that which a transmitted text expresses concerning the question of human existence. Although the intention is not to tone down the particular thing the text has to say, but, on the contrary, to bring it into view for the sake of contemporary understanding, nevertheless that content is constricted from the outset: anything other than possibilities of human existence cannot become relevant for existentialist interpretation. Or better: absolutely everything becomes relevant, but only *as* the possibility of an understanding of human existence. Now, it is very much a question whether such a treatment allows the texts being interpreted still to say what they themselves have to say: for example, the New Testament texts deal (at least at the explicit level) with many other matters than possibilities of understanding human existence, although everything that they do deal with will *also* be an element of a New Testament author's understanding of

[24] *Ibid.*, p. 258 (italics mine).

existence. Yet this latter element is not always intended. The New Testament writings deal also, indeed primarily, with God and his works in the events of the world and its history. Whatever they say about man is conditioned by this perspective. Bultmann's way of formulating his question forces him to proceed the other way round. He must regard the statements about God, the world, and history as merely the *expression* of an underlying understanding of human existence. In a certain sense this procedure is doubtless appropriate, since the statements involved unquestionably always *also* have such an expressive value. But this value only comes into view when one takes the statements about God, world, and history, not in their direct intention (*intentio recta*) but rather according to an indirect intention (*intentio obliqua*), that is, by understanding them through reflection upon their character as expressions of this or that author. Such a hermeneutical obscuring of the *intentio recta* of the statements about God, the world, and history in favor of the meaning of the text as an expression of an understanding of human existence evidences an anthropological constriction in the formulation of the question, in the pre-understanding. Is it not true that the question concerning the possibilities of human existence is after all always referred for its clarification to the questions about the world, about society, and beyond both of these, about God? Is it not the case that man cannot expect an answer to the question about himself without knowledge of the world, of society, of history, and of God? If this is the case, however, then self-understanding cannot become thematic irrespective of previous understanding of the world and also, in a certain sense, of God.[25] The understanding of the world and of

[25] I certainly agree with Bultmann that God can be thought of today only as the one who is asked about in the questionableness of human existence. But even if, since the beginning of the modern era, God can only be thought of by beginning with man, he must nevertheless be conceived of as the indispensable *presupposition* of human self-understanding, and not merely as the *expression* of man's questionableness. To that extent, however, the understanding of God logically (not psychologically) precedes the understanding of the self. Incidentally, the inappropriateness of a proof for the existence of God which proceeds from an understanding of the self also stems from this

God are not merely the *expression* of man's question concerning himself, but, on the contrary, the relationship to the world, to society, and to God is what first *mediates* man to himself. Only by means of the mediation of these relationships does he gain his self-understanding.

The existentialist constriction of the hermeneutical theme raises the further question of whether the historical distance between the texts to be understood and the interpreter's own time is retained in all its profundity if one subjects the texts to an anthropocentric understanding of existence, as do Dilthey and Bultmann.[26] How could that be possible if the texts, quite the other way around, express precisely the priority of the understanding of God and of the world over the self-understanding of man? It is just at this point that the historical distance between the New Testament texts and Bultmann's intellectual situation stands out quite clearly, and perhaps it is here that a question is put to our contemporary modes of thought. If this distance is obscured beforehand by an existentialist mode of inquiry, then the attempt to build a hermeneutical bridge, which is supposed to set the text in all its antiquity in relationship to the present, cannot succeed.

Texts coming from a past epoch demand, nevertheless, an interpretation that links the historically past *as such* with the time of the interpreter. What happened then [*das Damalige*] cannot be stripped of its "then-ness" [*Damaligkeit*] and in such a way construed as a contemporary possibility; for in that case its "then-ness" would be missing. On the contrary, it must be

---

point. The objective priority of the understanding of God over the understanding of the self manifests itself in the fact that God is experienced in the world as the ground of a total view of the world and of man in it, in relation to the whole current experience of reality. The questionableness of human existence is essentially involved in the relationship to the world insofar as the wholeness of human existence is to be attained only in relation to the wholeness of the world. Therefore man cannot acquiesce in any answer to the questionableness of his existence which does not include his relationship to the world, and which does not render his experience of the world (even that of physics!) intelligible as a whole.

[26] See Bultmann's statements about man as the "subject of history" in *Presence*, pp. 138ff.

related to the present precisely in its character as having happened then. This undertaking is meaningful, to be sure, only so long as the present age does not regard itself as self-sufficient, but asks about its historical heritage for the sake of giving shape to human existence in the present. That contemporary man can become aware of and comprehend his own possibilities of existence only by means of such questioning, is the pioneering idea which Bultmann's hermeneutic shares with Dilthey and Heidegger.[27] In the fact that the interrogation of transmitted texts is indispensable for the understanding of contemporary possibilities of human existence, Bultmann sees, conversely, that man is questioned by the tradition – and that is his own further step. "True understanding would therefore be to listen to the *question* which is imposed in the writing to be interpreted, to the claim which is met in the writing. . . ."[28] Bultmann himself found the difference between his way and that of Dilthey in the fact that the interpreter not only observes the variations of human life aesthetically[29] – a method of observation which leads to relativism[30] – but rather experiences from history a "claim," a question concerning his own self-understanding, and in that way is summoned to responsible "decision."

This basic idea of Bultmann's points beyond the existentialist limitation of his formulation of the question. If a transmitted text, precisely in its character of having happened then, can make a claim upon the interpreter, then one obviously cannot set boundaries around this claim (for instance, by means of reflection upon the intellectual situation of the present), but

[27] On Bultmann, in Westermann, *Essays*, pp. 251ff., cf. Heidegger, *Being and Time*, tr. John Macquarrie and Edward Robinson (London: SCM Press and New York: Harper and Row, 1962), pp. 434f.

[28] Bultmann, in Westermann, *Essays*, p. 226.

[29] Bultmann specifically abjures the "aesthetic standpoint" of Dilthey's historical understanding in *Presence*, pp. 125ff. He can nevertheless also emphasize (in Westermann, *Essays*, pp. 250f., in the context of the passage mentioned in n. 27, above) that Dilthey, through his idea that only history shows man what he is, because only the abundance of historical forms reveals the possibilities of human existence, actually points beyond the aesthetic standpoint.

[30] Bultmann, *Presence*, p. 148.

the interpreter must instead expose himself utterly to the particularity of what happened then. He must apprehend the past situation to which the text refers in its disparity from his own present, and may relate that situation to the present only in its disparateness. The pre-understanding or the interpreter's formulation of the question would thereby be set in motion by the text in a way which is no longer reflected in Bultmann's thought. If the historical distance of what happened in the past is retained, then the link connecting the events and forms of the past to the present can scarcely be found anywhere else than in the continuity of history itself which joins today with yesterday. The hermeneutical formulation of the question would thus expand into the question of universal history.

Bultmann, of course, did not take this step. He did not even relativize the pre-understanding of the existentialist analytic in relation to the historical context within which it arose. Accordingly, the "claim" of the historical heritage is not discussed in its substantive diversity, but is referred to the formal "either-or" of the authenticity or inauthenticity of human existence, to the true or false understanding of existence, to being at one's own disposal or the renunciation of this in faith.[31] The fruitful start toward apprehension of the conditioning of man by history, precisely in recognition of the fact that the past confronts the understanding of existence on the part of those who come after with a claim, a question, was not carried through in its full consequences. It is true that this fundamental idea of Bultmann's is tied up with his view of the "Word" or the "proclamation." The proclamation allows the claim that appeared in Jesus, through which the possibility of a believing understanding of existence is disclosed, to be heard by contemporary men. But it is just this idea that is neutralized by the reference to the formal either-or of the understanding of existence. Gadamer could remark about this that in Bultmann the summons of the Christian proclamation releases "almost a

---

[31] *Ibid.*, 140ff., 148; on the second alternative, cf. pp. 150ff., and especially the discussion in the essay, "New Testament and Mythology," in H. W. Bartsch (ed.), *Kerygma and Myth* I (London: S.P.C.K., 1963), pp. 1–44.

privative experience of human self-disposal."[32] It is a fact that the substantive bearing of the claim of Jesus and of the proclamation of him is misplaced by referring it to the formal structure of human existence. It is characteristic that what is decisive for Bultmann is simply the "that" of the claim, and not any specific content. This seems to confirm the contention that the claim of the Christian proclamation does not disclose any new content, but only releases that "privative experience of human self-disposal."[33]

Ernst Fuchs and Gerhard Ebeling have taken up Bultmann's suggestive but incompletely developed idea of the "claim" with which a transmitted text confronts the interpreter.[34] For Fuchs, the "claim" or "Word" of the New Testament texts to us includes the "support" which faith needs and on which it can ground itself. "Jesus anticipates us in that he meets us in the *Word*."[35] The character of the text as address becomes for Fuchs the center of the hermeneutical theme. In this connection, Fuchs can appeal to the later writings of Heidegger where the "dimension of language" is opened up,[36] but he clearly finds the decisive idea already indicated in the analysis of the call of conscience in *Being and Time*.[37] According to Fuchs, man

[32] Gadamer, "Hermeneutik und Historismus," p. 261 (=*Wahrheit und Methode* [²1965], p. 497).

[33] Compare, on this point, the discussion concerning the knowledge which the self that has taken over responsibility for itself (here = being at one's own disposal?) has of the "other possibility" of faith that it has thus rejected, in "The Problem of Natural Theology," *Faith and Understanding* I (London: SCM Press and New York: Harper and Row, 1969), pp. 313ff. On the whole problem of the bare "that" in Bultmann's thought with respect to the event of salvation itself as well as to the proclamation, cf. Gerhard Ebeling, *Theology and Proclamation* (London: Collins and Philadelphia: Fortress Press, 1966), pp. 36ff., 48, 67ff., 118f.

[34] Fuchs emphasized this relationship himself in the supplement to his *Hermeneutik* (Bad Cannstatt, ²1958), p. 6: "Bultmann's term 'address' [*Anrede*] provides sufficient reason for regarding faith as a 'speech-event.'"

[35] *Ibid.*, p. 75.

[36] *Ibid.*, pp. 70f.

[37] *Ibid.*, p. 64. To that extent, Fuchs rightly defends himself against the conjecture, most recently repeated by Gadamer (*Wahrheit und Methode* [²1965], p. 498), that he has been particularly influenced by the "later" Heidegger (*ibid.*, *Ergänzungsheft*, p. 5).

exists as man "linguistically between call and answer."[38] Man is already constituted as such in understanding the call: ". . . the I that speaks within the realm of mankind is always an I that has already been called."[39] Fuchs' discussion of language and address is often related, in a dubiously direct way, to ethics. In that way one leaps on occasion from the breadth of the problem of language into the area of the traditional theme of Law and Gospel.[40] This is reminiscent of the abrupt relationship in which the "question" and "claim" a text directs at the interpreter stands to the either-or of authentic versus inauthentic existence in Bultmann's writings. Yet Fuchs sees that man hears the "call" upon which his existence is oriented from out of the historical context in which he stands. Thus he can say: "History is . . . essentially 'saga,' and thus the history of language. The language which is carried to us from history is fundamentally that *essential* language in which we from time to time answer 'with ourselves.' "[41] In this way, however, history places "our given self-understanding linguistically in question."[42]

III

The comprehensive critique of the hermeneutical tradition and the analysis of the process of understanding in Hans-Georg Gadamer's work *Wahrheit und Methode* (1960) largely corresponds to the hermeneutic of the language event which was opened up by Fuchs and likewise by Ebeling. Here, too, it is a matter of keeping in view, without prior restrictions, the claim laid upon the bearer, reader, observer, or interpreter, as the actual center of the hermeneutical theme. For precisely this reason, Gadamer struggles to maintain without effacement the difference between the historical situation of the text to be interpreted and the interpreter's present era. For it is just this

[38] Fuchs, *Hermeneutik* [²1958], p. 133.
[39] *Ibid.*
[40] Cf. Ernst Fuchs, *Zum Hermeneutischen Problem in der Theologie* (Tübingen, 1959), pp. 282f., 190f., 193; as well as *Hermeneutik*, pp. 133, 147.
[41] Fuchs, *Hermeneutik*, p. 137.
[42] *Ibid.*, p. 138.

difference that articulates the claim the text makes upon contemporary understanding. Thus, hermeneutical and historical motifs, in the narrower sense, interpenetrate in Gadamer's thought. In this case, historical difference acquires decisive significance for the structure of the process of understanding itself. With Schleiermacher, this difference remained outside the hermeneutical considerations as a merely external presupposition of understanding. In Dilthey and even more clearly in Bultmann we found starting points for taking up the historical difference between text and interpreter into hermeneutical thought. In Dilthey, there was the idea that man can gain knowledge of what is human only from history. And in Bultmann this idea was sharpened to the extent that the historically formed factor, for instance, something transmitted by a text, confronts those who live in the present with a specific claim upon their self-understanding. Nevertheless, such starting points for appropriating the historical difference between text and interpreter into hermeneutical thought are consistently developed for the first time in Gadamer's work.

Gadamer, too, developed a theory of the linguisticality [*Sprachlichkeit*] of understanding. He achieved this by way of a critical discussion of Dilthey's hermeneutic. He spotted the difficulty of that position in the fact that Dilthey did not conceive deeply enough as a hermeneutical structure the historical character of understanding something handed down from the past.[43] But it is precisely the temporal distance of the interpreter from the situation in which the text originated that immediately opens up for the first time the possibility of conceiving the process of understanding as one of interpretation.[44] In any case, this temporal distance is fundamentally taken into account by Gadamer with respect to the hermeneutical relation, so that he can say: "the hermeneutically schooled consciousness will . . . include historical consciousness."[45] Of course, it will also have to "think of its *own* historicness at the same time," so that "the

[43] Gadamer, *Wahrheit und Methode*, p. 228.
[44] *Ibid.*, pp. 280f.
[45] *Ibid.*, p. 282.

reality of history is exhibited in the process of understanding itself."[46]

Gadamer excellently describes the way in which the past and the present are brought into relation to each other in the process of understanding as a "fusion of horizons" [*Horizontverschmelzung*].[47] The horizons of the interpreter and of the text to be interpreted are different at first, but that is only their initial position, so to speak, in the process of interpretation. The interpreter's own horizon is not fixed, but capable of movement and expansion. In the process of understanding, the interpreter's horizon is widened in such a way that the initially strange matter along with its own horizon can be appropriated into the expanded horizon he attains as he understands. In the interpreter's encounter with his text, a new horizon is formed, "a single horizon which includes everything which the historical consciousness contains within itself."[48] To place oneself into the strange situation that is to be understood always means, therefore, "the elevation to a higher universality, which overcomes not only one's own particularity, but also that of the other."[49] That corresponds to a successful conversation insofar as the agreement reached in conversation represents "a transformation into mutual possession, in which one does not remain what he was."[50] What occurs in conversation is precisely the fusion of horizons by means of an elevation of the partners to a new, comprehensive horizon that comprises the two originally separate horizons. Despite the analogy to a conversation, however, interpretation in the proper sense can hardly be designated a "conversation with the text," as it is by Gadamer.[51] While in a conversation the partner takes care to avoid premature absorption into the other's horizon, in the case of the interpretation of a text the interpreter himself must see that the peculiar form, the alien horizon of the text, is allowed to assert itself in contrast to the horizon he brings with him. Gadamer himself calls attention to the fact that

every encounter with the tradition that is effected by the historical con-

---

[46] *Ibid.*, p. 283.   [47] *Ibid.*, pp. 286–90.   [48] *Ibid.*, p. 288.
[49] *Ibid.*   [50] *Ibid.*, p. 360.   [51] *Ibid.*, p. 350.

sciousness experiences in itself the tension between the text and the present. The hermeneutical task consists not in concealing this tension by a naïve assimilation, but rather in deliberately developing it.

For this reason, the projection of a historical horizon that is distinct from the horizon of the present era necessarily belongs to the hermeneutical procedure. The historical consciousness is aware of its own otherness and therefore contrasts the horizon of the tradition with its own. On the other hand, however, it reunites itself with the contrasting horizon in order to mediate itself to itself in the unity of the historical horizon produced in this way. The projection of the historical horizon is therefore only one *phase* in the achievement of understanding, and . . . is overtaken by the present's own horizon of understanding.[52]

In this masterly description of understanding as a fusion of horizons, historical thinking is in fact incorporated into the hermeneutical achievement. Whether the hermeneutical formulation of the question, in the narrower sense, is not thereby burst through and displaced by universal-historical thinking is something we must take up shortly. Before we do this, however, the advances that this conception of hermeneutic makes over the hermeneutic of Dilthey and Bultmann should be highlighted.

(1) Gadamer does not begin by relating the text to be understood to a presupposed understanding of the structure of human existence by way of the formulation of the question (pre-understanding), but rather is concerned first to grasp the strange object that is to be understood precisely in its *distance* from the total horizon the interpreter brings with him. "The hermeneutical task consists not in concealing this tension by a naïve assimilation, but rather in deliberately developing it."[53] In this way, there is some prospect of overcoming any constriction of viewpoint which might be lodged in the very formulation of the question a person brings with him.

(2) The agreement that is striven for in the accomplishment of understanding takes shape through the formation of a comprehensive horizon which comprises the two, at first alien, contrasting horizons of the interpreter and his text. This comprehensive horizon is formed in every case only in the course of the process of understanding itself. It is precisely what under-

[52] *Ibid.*, p. 290.   [53] *Ibid.*

standing consists in. The comprehensive horizon is not already presupposed (as a pre-understanding) in the formulation of the question.

(3) The distinction between (questioning) pre-understanding and (projecting) preconception is superseded in Gadamer by the idea of the horizon that the interpreter brings with him. By this means, not only the given preconception but also the formulation of the question are set in motion, because the horizon which the interpreter brings with him is not a rigid presupposition. "The horizon is rather something into which we move, and which moves with us. Horizons change for the one who moves."[54] Thus, after the interpreter becomes aware of the temporal distance between the text and the horizon he has brought with him (1), he builds up a new, comprehensive horizon (2), and thereby succeeds in moving beyond the limits of his original preconception and formulation of the question (3).

In applying these insights to the interpretation of New Testament texts, the interpreter must first of all attain clarity about the difference between his own intellectual situation, the situation of "modern man" in which he shares, and the horizon of the New Testament authors with whom he has become occupied. He will then attempt – but that is always a creative act! – to achieve a synthesis, to formulate a comprehensive horizon of understanding within which both the intellectual world of the biblical texts as well as the differing intellectual world of modern man will each have their place and can thus be related to each other. Everything depends here on the newly projected horizon being wide enough to comprehend not only "something" of the texts, but all of their complex riches.

Such an application already presupposes that the comprehensive horizon formed in the process of understanding will also be explicitly formulated as such. This would be a way of distinguishing between an interpretation which is to be carried out methodically and an unreflective mode of understanding such as occurs in a conversation. In a successful conversation, the partners understand one another without being obliged to

[54] *Ibid.*, p. 288.

articulate explicitly the comprehensive horizon within which their understanding takes place. Rather, one is assured of complete mutual agreement by reaching agreement on this or that particular subordinate theme. Such agreement on a particular point constitutes the test, so to speak, of an anticipatory certainty of mutual understanding of the whole. Only rarely will that totality, within which one reaches agreement, become itself the subject of conversation. This will happen especially when the presupposed agreement is endangered.

An unreflective interpretation of a tradition may proceed in a similar way. In a methodical execution of an interpretation, however, the process of understanding must be reflected upon because only in that way can the correctness of the interpretation be tested. The comprehensive horizon of understanding must be formulated so that one can test whether or not it is capable of including both the horizon of the text and the contemporary horizon of the interpreter. To be sure, the effort to formulate that most comprehensive horizon within which a person lives his own life has still other roots than the technical requirements of a methodical interpretation of a transmitted text. Man can become sure of the wholeness of his own life only through being linked with the whole of reality generally. And he can become sure of the whole of reality only by trying to become conscious of it. Even the agreement reached in a conversation is propelled by a quest for the one all-embracing truth, although this is not always articulated as a theme. This same quest for the unity of truth provides the impulse for projecting comprehensive horizons. That the particular requirements of methodical interpretation provoke such projections only makes plain the fact that the methodical interpretation of what has been transmitted shares in the basic human task of understanding reality as a whole.

The projection of a total understanding of reality which, in view of the distance between the interpreter and the tradition he is interpreting, can only be a historically differentiated one, and, thus, a mediation of the present by the totality of history, is not the consequence Gadamer draws from his description of understanding as a fusion of horizons. With the form of Hegel's philosophy of spirit in mind,[55] he regards such an undertaking as claiming "to perform a total mediation of history and the present."[56] Against this, Gadamer insists on the "openness . . . in which experience is acquired."[57] He points to the negative character of the process of experience, in the course of which "false generalizations are continually refuted by experience,"[58] and thus arrives at the thesis that experience stands in irreducible contrast to knowledge.[59] One can object to this thesis that experience nevertheless tends toward knowledge insofar as it opens itself to new knowledge. Still, it remains true for the one who wishes to have experiences as well as for the one who is experienced and who knows about being overtaken by continually new experiences, that they can never regard as complete the knowledge they possess or that they may somehow attain. To that extent, Gadamer is right when he observes that genuine experience is "that experience in which man becomes aware of his finitude."[60] With this, Gadamer has formulated the state of affairs that does in fact separate all possible con-

---

[55] The whole work of Gadamer's is engaged in a partly open, partly tacit debate with Hegel. As early as the transition to the second section, which deals with the hermeneutic of the cultural sciences, Gadamer remarks that Hegel points beyond "the whole dimension" within which Schleiermacher posed the problem of understanding. Hegel recognized, according to Gadamer, that "the essence of the historical spirit is not in the restoration of the past, but in a mediation of it by thought to contemporary life" (*ibid.*, p. 161). He sees it as his "task . . . to follow Hegel more than Schleiermacher" (*ibid.*, p. 162), and in fact the theory of understanding as a fusion of horizons has its home on the ground of the Hegelian dialectic (cf. *ibid.*, p. 290). Nevertheless, Gadamer shuns the "speculative claims of a philosophy of world history" (*ibid.*, p. 343), because he sees – with good reason – in Hegel's attempt to sublimate history into "the absolute self-consciousness of philosophy" (*ibid.*, p. 338) a contradiction to the finitude of human experience (*ibid.*, pp. 339f.). For that reason, he is at pains to prove that it is linguisticality, instead of universal history, that provides "mediation of past and present" (*ibid.*, p. 451), with the explicit allusion that in this way a misguided ideal of objectivity in the cultural sciences as well as "the idealistic spiritualism of a metaphysics of the infinite in the style of Hegel" should be avoided (*ibid.*).

[56] *Ibid.*, p. 328. [57] *Ibid.*, p. 335. [58] *Ibid.*

[59] *Ibid.*, p. 338. [60] *Ibid.*, p. 340.

temporary thought from Hegel, and which makes any simple repetition of Hegel's system impossible: finitude as the vantage point of thought, and the openness of the future. But how can the mediation, in thought, of history to contemporary life still succeed? Gadamer attempts to do justice to this hermeneutical task by reflecting on the linguisticality of the hermeneutical experience, instead of attempting a total mediation of the present by means of history.

Gadamer finds the model of the hermeneutical process in conversation.[61] His demand that the interpreter ascertain the question to which the text was an answer is not to be disputed. But Gadamer combines with this the statement that the text (i.e., the answer to that question which is to be reconstructed) "itself" poses "a question, and thereby brings our supposition into the open."[62] "The reconstruction of the question to which the text is supposed to be the answer stands itself within a question through which we seek the answer to the question posed to us by the tradition." The reconstructed question, to which the text is supposed to be the answer, passes over into the question "which the tradition is for us."[63] Manifestly, the latter has to do with the question whether the text can still be an answer for us. The stylistic device of speaking about a "question" which the text poses to the reader and interpreter has, to be sure, no more value than that of an image which expresses the peculiar inescapability of the context of tradition within which one stands, whether he relates himself to it positively or negatively.[64] Gadamer himself concedes that the text does *not* speak to us "as a thou," since "we, the ones who comprehend, must on our part first enable it to speak."[65] What this last insight means, however, is precisely that talk about the "question" the text poses to us can only be metaphorical: the text becomes

---

[61] *Ibid.*, pp. 344ff.   [62] *Ibid.*, p. 356.   [63] *Ibid.*

[64] To be more exact, this should say: "to specific traditional contents." For one cannot take a position with reference to the whole context of tradition within which he stands, because he can find no standpoint that would be situated completely outside this totality.

[65] Gadamer, *Wahrheit und Methode*, p. 359.

a question only for the one who asks questions; it does not have this character in and of itself.

Before we follow up these considerations, which press in the direction of the distinction between interpretation and conversation, it must be expressly emphasized that Gadamer is right in understanding the hermeneutical process as a linguistic process. The fusion of horizons that occurs in understanding is inconceivable without linguistic expression, even if this fusion is perhaps not to be flatly designated, with Gadamer, as "the proper effect" of language.[66] The process of understanding indeed has to do with "the coming-into-language [*zur-Sprache-kommen*] of the essential content itself," insofar as the "understanding of the essential content . . . necessarily (attains) linguistic form."[67] Language is truly "the universal medium in which understanding itself is accomplished," insofar as in understanding the essential content that is to be understood enters language.[68] Thus, it is also the essence of tradition "to exist in the medium of language."[69]

Yet, even if one gladly agrees with these vigorous remarks about the linguisticality of understanding, the concealment of the difference between the interpretation of a text and a conversation renders Gadamer's argument suspect. The interpretation of a transmitted content does not become a language event [*Sprachgeschehen*] by the fact that someone speaks to me, as is the case in conversation. Rather, it becomes such only when *the interpreter* finds the language that unites him with the text. To that extent, the fusion of horizons, too, is not in the first instance something produced by language, but, on the contrary, the formation of a new manner of speaking is the expression of the fusion of horizons accomplished by understanding. The hermeneutical process is certainly articulated in language. But this is much more a matter of the creative formation of language by the interpreter than of being called by a "thou." The text does not "speak," but rather the interpreter finds a linguistic expression which combines the essential con-

---

[66] *Ibid.*, p. 359. On this matter, see the text that follows.
[67] *Ibid.*, p. 360.   [68] *Ibid.*, p. 366.   [69] *Ibid.*, p. 367.

tent of the text with his own contemporary horizon. It is always a matter of formulating the essential content of a text, in other words, of formulating an assertion [*Aussage*]. And here we reach the point at which we can no longer follow Gadamer.

Gadamer would like to separate the language event of understanding from the predicative function [*Aussagefunktion*] of language.[70] The concept of "assertion" stands, in his opinion, "in an extreme contrast to the essence of hermeneutical experience and the linguisticality of human experience of the world generally." Plato, as well as Hegel, is reproached for having rested his dialectic "in essence on the subordination of language to the 'assertion.' "[71]

How does Gadamer establish such a negative assessment of the assertion? He maintains that the furnishing of assertions is not an appropriate way of "saying [*Sagen*] what one means," because the language event of an understanding holds together "what is said [*das Gesagte*] with an infinity of what is unsaid [*das Ungesagte*] in the unity of one meaning," and in this way gives it to be understood.[72] Precisely in this way "what is unsaid and what is to be said" are brought into language.[73] The words will thereby "express a relationship to the totality of being, and allow it to enter into language." In contrast to that, anyone who only "repeats what has been said" [*Gesagtes weitersagt*] will unavoidably and without exception "change the sense of what has been said," because precisely in the repetition the unspoken context of the meaning of the original utterance disappears.[74] For Gadamer, this point is demonstrated with particular clarity in the process of a judicial hearing. The "statements" which are recorded are already reduced, severed from their unsaid but accompanying horizon of meaning, with the result that their meaning is from the outset a "distorted meaning" in comparison with the original speech.[75] Thus, Gadamer concludes: "In the assertion, the horizon of meaning of what actually wants to be said is concealed with methodical exactitude,"[76] – precisely by its abstraction from the background of what is unsaid.

[70] *Ibid.*, p. 444.   [71] *Ibid.*   [72] *Ibid.*   [73] *Ibid.*, p. 445.
[74] *Ibid.*   [75] *Ibid.*, p. 444.   [76] *Ibid.*

For a closer understanding of the devaluation of the predicative character of language as this is established by Gadamer, attention may be called to the different basis Gerhard Ebeling gives for countering an understanding of language from the standpoint of the assertion. Ebeling distinguishes between the predicative function of language and its communicative function in relations between persons.[77] Although one fully acknowledges the concern to free the essence of language from the narrowness of an abstract view of the word as a mere instance of assertion, one must nevertheless ask, in view of Ebeling's "not this . . . but rather that," whether the rubric "communication" is meant to include within itself the element of assertion, too, or whether – as appears to be the case in his discussion – it is to be set in opposition to the assertion. In the latter case, one would have to object that reference to content and relation to persons always belong together: that personal association arises within the horizon of common substantive interests, just as, conversely, all relationships to substantive matters are already socially conditioned. Accordingly, the personal dimension of language (as communication) is only accessible in its concrete substantiveness (with which, at any rate, its predicative character is connected). Gadamer seems to have seen this connection

---

[77] Gerhard Ebeling, "Word of God and Hermeneutic," in *Word and Faith* (London: SCM Press and Philadelphia: Fortress Press, 1963), pp. 305–32, esp. pp. 326f. Ebeling emphasizes the mutual relatedness of the content and power of a word in an event "to which at least two belong," and continues: "The basic structure of word is therefore *not assertion* – that is an abstract variety of the word-event – *but apprisal*, certainly not in the colorless sense of information, but in the pregnant sense of participation and communion" (*ibid.*, p. 326, italic mine). Furthermore, communication is defined as promise. As such, it occurs in its purest form when "in word the speaker pledges and imparts himself to the other and opens a future to him by awakening faith within him" (*ibid.*, p. 327). Friedrich Gogarten (*Der Mensch zwischen Gott und Welt* [Stuttgart, 1956], pp. 234ff.), in discussing the concept "Word of God," had already emphasized, in a way analogous to Ebeling's distinction, the personal character of the word as gift and demand (*ibid.*, p. 241), with stress on the power (*ibid.*) of this word and its character as a divine "promise of himself to us" (*ibid.*, p. 246), as opposed to an understanding of the word as "a means of communication and understanding" (*ibid.*, p. 244).

quite clearly. He does not place the character of language as personal communication in opposition to the understanding of language based on assertion, but rather opposes the latter to "the finity of what is unsaid,"[78] which forms the horizon of meaning and of situational understanding of the spoken word, whereas the assertion allows this horizon to disappear.

Gadamer's reference to the unspoken horizon of meaning of every spoken word is, at first glance, convincing. The primary hermeneutical task consists precisely in restoring the word of a transmitted text to its original, if also unspoken, context of meaning, in order to understand it from within its original situation, the situation of its author in which he composed the text we now have. Nevertheless, *in the first place*, such a procedure can only begin from an exact grasp of what is stated. The implicit, unspoken horizon of meaning is accessible to the understanding only on the basis of the assertion and not without it. And, *in the second place*, the interpreter can only become clearly conscious of the unity of that background of meaning made accessible by assertions, if this unity, for its part, also becomes the content of assertions. Gadamer's correct insight, that every spoken word has an infinite, unspoken background of meaning, does not therefore demolish the significance of the assertion for the spoken word and for an understanding of it, because that background of meaning can only be grasped on the basis of the assertion, and it will then – in the course of the interpretation – be itself turned into something that is asserted. Gadamer's arguments only affect an abstract handling of assertions which does not pay attention to their unspoken horizon of meaning (including the personal relationships within which the word in question was originally spoken or written). If one follows Gadamer's argument, as indeed one must, then one will not somehow go beyond or behind the assertion form of language, but will instead, as an interpreter, also convert into the form of assertion the unspoken horizon which accompanied the original assertion. Precisely by means of interpretation, to the extent that interpretation really intends to understand

78 Gadamer, *Wahrheit und Methode*, p. 444.

the author, *everything* must be turned into assertion; everything that was involved in the formulation of a text – nuances, or frames of reference, of which the author himself was partly unaware – must be made explicit. The interpreted text is precisely the text which has been *objectified* with respect to the previously unanticipated proportions of its horizon of meaning.[79]

Gadamer himself cannot really get away from the predicative sense of language. Following the anthropological suggestions of Scheler, Plessner, and Gehlen, he understands language as an expression of the freedom in relation to its environment [*Umweltfreiheit*] that characterizes all human behavior.[80]

> The peculiar objectivity [*Sachlichkeit*] of language is a consequence of its relationship to the world. What enters into language are states of affairs [*Sachverhalte*], i.e., an objective content [*Sache*] that is related in such and such ways [*sich so und so verhält*]. Therein is acknowledged the independent existence of the other, which presupposes that it has its own measure of the distance between the objective content and what is being said about it. That something can be lifted out as a state of affairs in itself and be made into the content of an *assertion* which others also understand, depends upon this distance.[81]

These sentences provide an excellent description of the significance of the predicative structure of language. For one thing,

[79] This sentence deliberately links the by now infamous word "objectify" with a quantitative viewpoint. The question of the given "proportions" of the objectification and objectifiability could perhaps (as I suggested already in *Theologische Literaturzeitung* 83 [1958], cols. 327ff.) avoid the false alternative between, on the one hand, the scientific ideal of absolute objectivity (as a complete disregard of everything subjective), which has not once proven attainable in the natural sciences or in mathematics, and, on the other hand, the illusion of a totally non-objectifying discourse, which is probably equally unattainable. In opposition to the faddish, sloganeering demand for "overcoming" objectifying thinking, Martin Landmann has rightly pointed out that the ability to *objectify*, to grasp the encountered reality in its (of course, only relative, greater or lesser) independence over against the experiencing subjectivity, characterizes the distinctively human relationship to the world, namely, man's specific objectivity, which is based on his extensive freedom from instinctual drives (*Philosophische Anthropologie* [Berlin, 1955], pp. 215f., 219f.). Cf. also Jürgen Moltmann, *EvTh* 22 (1962), pp. 45ff., as well as the way Gadamer links up with the relational anthropology [*Verhaltensanthropologie*] referred to in the text above.

[80] Gadamer, *Wahrheit und Methode*, pp. 420ff.

[81] *Ibid.*, p. 421 (italics mine).

they express the very objectivity that is the specific character-istic of the human, open-to-the-world [*weltoffen*] mode of relationship. In addition to that, however, Gadamer also says that the possibility of men reaching an understanding among each other depends upon the predicative structure, upon the separability of the intended objective content from the one making the assertion. "That something can be lifted out as a state of affairs in itself and made into the content of an assertion which others also understand, depends upon this distance." Thus, without assertion, without the objectification that always occurs in the assertion, men cannot come to an understanding among themselves about something. Without assertions, there is no language. To be sure, the assertion itself is not understood as long as its unspoken horizon of meaning is disregarded. For that reason, the *interpretation* of the assertion must take into account the situation in which it arose, and to that extent the interpretation goes *behind the assertion* to its original conditions in order to be able to understand the assertion.

The priority of the assertion for hermeneutic is further con-firmed by Gadamer's finding that understanding always means "coming to an understanding with reference to an objective content [*Sache*]."[82] "Carrying on a conversation means to place oneself under the guidance of the objective content to-ward which the conversants are directed."[83] The objectivity of language which is expressed in the form of the assertion thus constitutes the meaning of the conversation, too. A conversation has to do with bringing the objective content into language, i.e., putting it into the form of an assertion. When people come to an understanding on the objective content, they also under-stand each other. This matter of having reference to the objec-tive content applies to the interpreter's craft, too. Although, as we saw, interpretation has a different structure from a con-versation, it also has to do with bringing out of the assertions of the text themselves the essential content (including the unspoken horizon of meaning which accompanies it) that they intended, and putting this into the form of assertion.

[82] *Ibid.*, p. 361.   [83] *Ibid.*, p. 349.

IV

It is a peculiar spectacle to see how an incisive and penetrating author has his hands full trying to keep his thoughts from going in the direction they inherently want to go. Gadamer's book offers this kind of spectacle when he strives to avoid the Hegelian total mediation of the truth of the present by means of history. As was noted, the point about the finitude of human experience which can never be sublimated into absolute knowledge provides a very good reason for this concern. But strangely enough, the phenomena which Gadamer describes move time and again in the direction of a universal conception of history, something which he would like to avoid in view of the Hegelian system. This applies first of all to Gadamer's new formulation of the hermeneutical event as a "fusion of horizons." If interpretation has to do with the relationship between the then and the now in such a way that the difference between them is preserved when the hermeneutical bridge is built; and if, further, one must inquire behind the text into its unspoken horizon of meaning, into its historical situation, so that the first task of the interpreter is to project the historical horizon to which the text is native; then the only way that the historical situation of the text can be adequately linked to the interpreter's present is by investigating the historical continuity between the present and the past situation from which the text stems. This means that the text can only be understood in connection with the totality of history which links the past to the present, and indeed not only to what currently exists today, but also to the horizon of the future based on what is presently possible, because the meaning of the present becomes clear only in the light of the future. Only a conception of the actual course of history linking the past with the present situation and its horizon of the future can form the comprehensive horizon within which the interpreter's limited horizon of the present and the historical horizon of the text fuse together. For only in that way are the past and the present preserved in their historical uniqueness and difference in contrast to one another within the comprehensive horizon. Nevertheless, they are preserved in such a way that they are as moments which enter into the unity of a comprehensive continuity of history that embraces them both.

Gadamer himself has seen that the description of understanding as a fusion of horizons moves in the direction just indicated.[84] He is of the opinion, however, that he can escape this tendency by being able to avoid the "speculative claim of a philosophy of world history,"[85] through reflection upon the experience of the linguisticality of transmitted tradition. We have reviewed this attempt and have seen that this route does not bring us to the desired goal without doing violence to the phenomenon of language itself. The objectivity of the human experience of the world, which constitutes such a thing as language as a specifically human mode of behavior in the first place, and which is expressed in a particular way within language itself in its predicative character, excludes an unmediated relationship of the present to the "claim" of a transmitted text. Understanding is always mediated by the essential content expressed by the text. But always this content is brought into language in the text only within the totality of a horizon that remains unspoken, which is not the interpreter's horizon of the present, but is rather connected with the particular historical situation within which the text originated. So reflection upon the relationship between the interpreter and the text leads back to the historical difference between their horizons which is to be bridged over by means of a fusion of horizons. *Consideration of the linguisticality of this relationship by itself is, thus, unable to accomplish this bridging.* The bridging must occur within the realm of the stated content itself as this becomes visible in its historicness, so that art, religion, law, and even such an apparently nonhistorical matter as mathematics, are to be understood as contents that have undergone historical development and have been historically structured both in essence and in concept: art as creative projection; law as positive deposition; religion as having become historic and mediated by its forms; mathematics as the instrument of mastering the world by means

----

[84] *Ibid.*, p. 324.   [85] *Ibid.*, p. 343.

of abstraction. The concept of truth itself is essentially to be conceived as history.[86] This by no means signifies its relativistic dissolution, but certainly does mean that it is impossible to conceive of the unity of truth as a timeless identity of a given essential content. It can be conceived only as the whole of a historical career. Always it is the merely abstract concepts of man, nature, architecture, law, etc., that are thought of as timelessly identical. Their timeless generality consists precisely in their abstractness, however, and therewith also their merely *provisional* truth. They all attain their authentic truth only by their sublimation in the history of the essential content intended by them. This does not call into question the fact that all knowledge begins with abstract, general representations of its object, but such preliminary, unavoidable and abstract representations must allow themselves to be sublimated into a differentiated understanding of this object in its historical movement.

Only by devaluing the predicative structure of language[87] – which he is himself nevertheless elsewhere compelled to acknowledge as a primary phenomenon[88] – can Gadamer get around the fact that the understanding of the essential content of a text requires a projection of the history of this content (at least an intellectual history of man's understanding of it), because only within the horizon of such a projection can the historically conditioned perspective of the text on this content and the interpreter's contemporary perspective on it be properly brought into relation to each other. Since, also, the various subject matters [*Sachbereiche*] are in turn connected to each other, the hermeneutical task requires not only projections of the history of this or that particular subject matter, but also universal-historical projections which encompass the changing associations of all the various subject matters. Only within the

---

[86] On this, see my article, "What is Truth?", forthcoming in vol. 2.

[87] Gadamer calls the assertion a "de-naturing" of the occurrence of understanding (*Wahrheit und Methode*, p. 445), with the exception of the poetic assertion, which, however, is assertion [*Aussage*] in another sense, viz., as expression [*Ausdruck*].

[88] *Ibid.*, p. 421.

context of universal history can the "then" of the text be bound to the "today" of the interpreter in such a way that the temporal, historical difference between them is not eliminated but rather preserved and bridged over in the nexus of events linking them both. For even the delimitation of the subject matter about which a transmitted text is to be interrogated can mean that the formulation of the question would be constricted by the presupposition of a modern division of subject matters which would do violence to the perspective of the text itself.

It is true that the motivation of an actual interest in associating with transmitted texts is the fact that the contemporary perspective on a given matter [*Sache*] has become questionable. This perspective is not a fixed datum which the interpreter has to take over *en bloc* simply in order to distance himself from the alien perspective of his text as a still inadequate standpoint. On the contrary, the transmitted texts – in highly varying degrees, to be sure – cause the interpreter himself to be concerned about his current understanding of the matter he is interested in. Since the truth about such a matter is not given with final and absolutely universal validity even in a contemporary perspective on it, but rather remains in question and open to further experience, even transmitted texts can therefore become the occasion for noting new aspects of this matter which have not been given adequate recognition in the current perspective. Even if the transmitted text in its historical sense can never simplistically provide the model solution to the substantive issue in its contemporary form, it may nevertheless provide the impetus for a better, creative mastery of it. That is the significance of the hermeneutical requirement that the transmitted text be related not merely to a currently *available* horizon on some matter, but to the present age's horizon of the future, in order that it might be related to the questionableness of the current understanding of this matter and thus, perhaps, discover new possibilities for a contemporary understanding of this matter itself. Herein lies the justification of the idea of turning toward the present on the basis of the "claim" made by a transmitted text, which, since Bultmann, had played so great a role in theological hermeneutic – and surely it was not by accident that this development happened precisely here.[89] It is true that such a claim is itself always questionable. It must prove itself anew in every period by the power the transmitted material exhibits in relation to the contemporary state of the problem. But the fact that such a power of disclosure can proceed from a transmitted text at all is linked to the fact that the current understanding of the matter in question is not yet absolute but is itself bound to a finite perspective and is thus submitted to questionableness. In its questionability, and in view of the openness of the future, the current understanding of a matter is referred to tradition. This means that the matter about which one is presently concerned cannot be understood without looking back to what was written and spoken about it in the past.

Here we hit upon the significance of the *application* of what has been transmitted, on which Gadamer has laid special emphasis. It forms a phase of the hermeneutical task which is forced upon legal and theological hermeneutic especially, but which is nevertheless essential for hermeneutic of all the cultural sciences.[90] Insofar as it is precisely the application that has the "task of mediating the then to the now,"[91] since it goes beyond the historically ascertained self-understanding of the text to the contemporary possibilities, it flows once again into the problem of universal history. For the "fabric composed of custom and tradition," on which the philologist, as well as the lawyers and theologians, weaves,[92] is for its part the hermeneutical object of the historian.[93] His act of application consists in projecting the "unity of the totality of tradition" by going beyond the text of his widely varying "sources,"[94] but he thereby projects the horizon within which the jurist and the philologist already move. Only the unity of the totality of tradition provides the horizon – this is what is to be concluded, beyond the points

[89] The tradition with which theology has to do claims for itself in a special way that it reveals the true situation of man and the truth of reality generally.

[90] Gadamer, *Wahrheit und Methode*, pp. 290–323.   [91] *Ibid.*, p. 316.

[92] *Ibid.*, p. 321.   [93] *Ibid.*, pp. 322f.   [94] *Ibid.*, p. 322.

Gadamer has made – for an assessment of the results of applications made in working with the transmitted texts, even though philological or legal interpretation of texts, on the other hand, can burst through a specific, overly narrow projection of the totality of tradition and thus, likewise, have a critical function to observe over against it. The latter point does not cancel the fact that the appropriateness of the application of a transmitted text to a current substantive problem cannot be scrutinized without reflecting upon the historical difference between the present and the past situations, and on that which nevertheless links the two together. Indeed, just such historical reflection on the totality of tradition may, under certain conditions, free one for the first time for the present's particular possibilities of action and thus, also, for the particularity of a present application of what has been transmitted.[95] It cannot be disputed that a projection of universal history, by means of its speculative claim, can also obscure such possibilities instead of opening them up. But that simply demonstrates the finitude which, just as it qualifies all human thought, naturally also inheres in projections of universal history. What it means in concrete cases is that we are summoned to produce ever better projections of universal history.

Here, in closing, we must return once more to Hegel. Gadamer correctly points out that Hegel's system of the absolute idea had overleaped the irreducible finitude of experience. Closely related to that is the further fact that the future could no longer be thought of as an open one, from Hegel's standpoint, insofar as its openness would consist in its continuously bringing forth surprising experiences. Also related to the failure to recognize the irreducible finitude of experience is the further failure to recognize the impossibility of taking account of the contingent and the individual by means of the universal. All these points indicate the limits of Hegel's philosophy and, thus, of his philosophy of history, too. But the task

[95] Of course that does not mean leaping clear of the context of tradition as such, as though historical research freed one in principle from the power of tradition!

of a philosophy or a theology of world history dare not be sacrificed on account of the failure of the Hegelian solution, as it is by Gadamer for the sake of a hermeneutical ontology within the horizon of language.[96] This conception remains exposed to the criticism that it understands the nexuses of events abstractly, namely in abstraction from the predicative function of language by means of which the word points beyond itself as a "mere" word. It was shown that by virtue of its predicative character, language leads back to the problem of universal history. Instead of avoiding this problem, we must instead ask how it is possible today to develop a conception of universal history which, in contrast to Hegel's, would preserve the finitude of human experience and thereby the openness of the future as well as the intrinsic claim of the individual. The task thus formulated might seem like that of squaring the circle, since the totality of history could only come into view from the perspective of its end, so that there would then be just as little need to speak of a further future as there would be to speak of the finitude of human experience. But the Hegelian conception of history is not in fact the only possible one, because the end of history can also be understood as something which is itself only *provisionally* known, and in reflecting upon this provisional character of our knowledge of the end of history, the horizon of the future could be held open and the finitude of human experience preserved. It is precisely this understanding of history as something whose totality is given by the fact that its end has become accessible in a provisional and anticipatory way that is to be gathered today from the history of Jesus in its relationship to the Israelite–Jewish tradition. Hegel was unable to see this because the eschatological character of the message of Jesus remained hidden to him, as was the case with the New Testament exegesis of his time. To this extent, we have here a paradigm of the way philology, on the basis of transmitted texts (though not on the basis of just any text one pleases!), can not only call into question a given conception of universal history, but can also point the way for its replacement by means of a better projection.

[96] *Wahrheit und Methode*, pp. 415ff.

That is certainly related in this instance to the fact that the biblical tradition constitutes the origin of universal historical thought as such. For this reason, a deeper understanding of this tradition can provide the impetus for projections of universal history that do more justice to reality.

The possibility of taking a new look at the problem of universal history, on the basis of the original eschatological meaning of the history of Jesus as an anticipation of the end, is relevant in the context of our considerations, because the hermeneutical theme itself leads back to the problem of universal history. This is so because it appears that an understanding of transmitted texts in their historical differentiation from the present cannot be adequately and methodically carried out apart from universal historical thought which, to be sure, must include the horizon of an open future and with this the possibilities of action in the present. The significance of Gadamer's book lies in its having forcefully demonstrated that this whole problem is inescapable for hermeneutical thought, partly by his explicit reference to the task of mediating to the present the past to which the text belongs; and partly, also, by his own futile attempt to avoid the universal-historical consequences of his own description of understanding. It is precisely the impasse which a hermeneutical ontology runs into when it tries to establish its independence from the philosophy (or theology) of history that points all the more emphatically to the task of elevating the hermeneutical theme, whose own logic moves it toward the universal-historical perspective, into a projection of a universal history which goes beyond the inadequacies of the Hegelian conception.

5

ON HISTORICAL AND
THEOLOGICAL HERMENEUTIC

This previously unpublished lecture was delivered at a meeting of the smaller circle of the *Allgemeine Gesellschaft für Philosophie in Deutschland* on May 1 and 2, 1964, in Heidelberg. The overall theme of the meeting was "Analytical and Hermeneutical Method in the Cultural Sciences." This lecture has been revised for publication, especially sections I and III.

I

IN RECOGNIZING the hermeneutical character of its task and of the procedure which it had always tacitly followed, contemporary Christian theology finds itself in the vicinity of the cultural sciences which likewise work with hermeneutical methods. Of course, certain features that are peculiar to the theological hermeneutic become apparent even upon merely cursory inspection. Reflection upon the hermeneutical task of theology typically speaks of texts with respect to their "normative character," their "authority" as witnesses to the "revelation of God" and the "apprisal" [*Mitteilung*] involved in that, and of the "translation" of these texts into our own contemporary situation.[1] Someone hearing such expressions through untheological ears could easily gain the impression that theological hermeneutic is something completely different from the hermeneutics of the other cultural sciences. Nevertheless, if one looks into the matter more closely, it appears that the peculiarities just mentioned are determined less by a special theological

[1] These catchwords were taken from Ernst Fuchs' *Hermeneutik* (Bad Canstatt, 1954).

hermeneutic than, on the one hand, by the distinctiveness or the essential content with which theology deals, and, on the other, by the unique correlative accentuation theology gives to specific phases of the general structure of the hermeneutic process. The latter aspect, which will be taken up first, can be summarized by saying that the phase of *application* attains a central and highly distinctive function in theological hermeneutic.[2]

The hermeneutical reflection of theologians is not focused primarily on the fact that, in opposition to all positivistic urges toward unambiguous determinability, one and the same matter, the same text, and the same historical personality, are susceptible of a plurality of interpretations which remain irreducible.[3] Although theology might find it very rewarding to consider whether such a multiplicity might be rooted in the nature of the content which has been and has to be continually reinterpreted in a fresh way in the advance of the process of its transmission, this consideration does not occupy the foreground of its hermeneutical interest.[4] Of course, the multiplicity of possible and actual interpretations of the same content also plays an important role in theological discussions, viz., with reference to the history of interpretation and to the historicness

[2] Hans-Georg Gadamer, *Wahrheit und Methode: Grundzüge einer philoso-phischen Hermeneutik* (Tübingen, 1960; [2]1965), pp. 290ff., 313ff., has rightly established a close relationship between theological and legal hermeneutic in this respect.

In the *Hermeneutik* of Ernst Fuchs, concentration on the phase of applica-tion is especially evident in the category of "apprisal," which is of central importance for him (*ibid.*, pp. 98ff., 140ff.).

[3] This plurality of meaning was especially emphasized by Georg Simmel in *Die Probleme der Geschichtsphilosophie* (Leipzig, [4]1922), p. 71, in opposition to a "naïve realism" which took historical knowledge to be a simple mirror image of a given reality. I am indebted to D. Heinrich for this reference to Simmel.

[4] The point of view just mentioned can be of help in understanding the multiplicity of interpretations of the Christ-event in the history of the Christian tradition as having arisen from the unique character of the history of Jesus itself, having been released by it from time to time. Only such a point of view would allow the historicness of every new phase in the history of Christianity to be understood as having been obtruded by the history of Jesus itself in its novel and peculiar particularity.

of the interpretation to be achieved in the present age.[5] Nevertheless, such a multiplicity is in many respects more an embarrassment than a cause for satisfaction. For the most part, the theologian finds himself able to come to terms with it only in a somewhat laborious manner by means of the insight that one and the same message has to be delivered to different men and ages in different and therefore new ways. The difficulty in this insight is that in such circumstances the unity and identity of the message can scarcely be made evident any longer. But the actual interest of theology hinges precisely on that. Testing the multiplicity of interpretations that have appeared is exactly what theology is all about. The theologian can no more remain satisfied with an abundance of possible constructions than can the jurist. The reason for this is not to be sought merely in the theologian's responsibility to the church, but primarily in the ultimate validity of the truth theology is concerned about. For this reason, theology, faced with the fact of a multiplicity of interpretations of the Christian message, inquires after criteria that allow such interpretations to be measured against the source of the Christian tradition, whether this be the already differentiated primitive Christian proclamation of Christ, or the historical Jesus himself.

The requirement that interpretation be controlled by the essential content to be interpreted touches on a matter that is fundamental for historical hermeneutic, viz., that "the meaning we call the historical one be inherent in the object itself."[6] It follows from this that the facticity of the content must somehow remain the measure of the multiplicity of its interpretations, although interpretation of it must go beyond bare facticity and therefore can appear in a manifold form. These two opposing viewpoints in relation to content and interpretation can be

[5] In this connection, one should not, as so often happens, think only of the changes in the historical situations to which the new interpretations correspond that arise from time to time. One must also take into account the diversity in anticipations of meaning that are possible in one and the same situation, and which result in a corresponding diversity of possible perspectives on the content to be interpreted.

[6] G. Simmel, *Probleme der Geschichtsphilosophie*, p. 193.

unified only on the presupposition that the facticity of the content to be interpreted always contains more than is immediately present in it: that it implies an anticipation of meaning, of consequence,[7] and does so in such a way that this anticipation of meaning cannot be expressed exhaustively and definitively within any limited horizon of meaning or in any particular interpretation. This means, however, that the criteria that should govern the interpretation of some content are not themselves formulable in a final way, but must for their part, too, come up for fresh discussion in the course of the interpretation.

The parallels between theological and historical hermeneutic in binding interpretation to the facticity of the content to be interpreted should not, however, permit us to overlook the peculiar character that this backward linkage attains in theology. In theology, the historical phenomenon – be it Jesus of Nazareth, Pauline theology, or Johannine theology – does not come up for inquiry merely as such, but rather as the origin and norm of a tradition that is still continuing today, as the norm of contemporary proclamation. This circumstance has, in fact, repeatedly been taken as an occasion to contest the constitutive significance of the historically factual within theology, precisely because historical facticity as such appeared to be unable to provide normative content for contemporary preaching. At any rate, the phase of application or "communication" was characteristically thrust into the foreground in the way in which the essential content transmitted by means of Christian proclamation was conceived in theology as the norm of its interpretation. Although historical portrayals and even historical research are also always guided by a present interest,

---

[7] Accordingly, Simmel sees historical manifestation as given through *individuality*. Individuality is not to be confused with the exceptional, something that in every case stands outside the general. Rather, individuality consists in the fact that in a particular and unique manifestation, another, otherwise inaccessible aspect of the universally human comes into view (*Probleme der Geschichtsphilosophie*, p. 89). The multiplicity of possibilities of interpretation a historical manifestation opens up is supposed to be grounded in this state of affairs, since the universally human always comes in for fresh discussion thereby.

the distinctiveness of theological hermeneutic in contrast to historical hermeneutic can be suggested at just this point. In order to determine whether this distinctiveness involves a difference in principle, i.e., whether it indicates a fundamental difference between theological and historical hermeneutic, or whether it signifies only a variation a more comprehensive mutuality, we will first investigate the peculiar significance of application in theological hermeneutic.

It has already been shown that the motive for application is grounded in the peculiar authority ascribed by the Christian tradition to the New Testament texts, or to the figure of Jesus, this tradition's source of vitality. The tendency toward application which stems from this source is especially evident in the way in which an increasing number of theologians today affirm, at least in principle, the necessity of controlling theological assertions by means of the current experience of reality belonging to the hearer to whom the Christian message is addressed. Strictly speaking, this does not entail introducing any second criterion for theological statements alongside their subjection to the norm constituted by the source of the Christian tradition. For the factual source of the Christian tradition, the appearance and destiny of Jesus, already claims for itself universally decisive meaning. This anticipation of universal meaning inherently presses for confirmation by the totality of man's experience of reality at any time whatever. This impulse has been the moving force behind the history of the transmission of the Christian tradition as the gradual alteration of the self-explication of the Christian message, and has to be understood as intimately related to the character of Christian history as a history of mission. Only the universal significance of Jesus justifies speaking of "God" in connection with his history and person, just as, conversely, Jesus' speech about God has become constitutive for the universal significance of his message and history. For this reason, theological assertions must be tested against the whole wealth of experience of reality accessible at any given time. Such testing may not be confined to some isolated experience of ethical existence, as happens all too easily in pietistic circles. The universal significance of the history of Jesus as the revelation of the all-determining reality of God cannot be adequately tested solely in relation to the individual's experience of conscience.

Application of the contents of the Christian tradition is made particularly difficult for our modern historicized consciousness because it involves the continuing necessity of bridging the historical distance between primitive Christianity and the present age ever anew. This problem was expressed in an earlier form as the question of how to overcome the "nasty ditch" [*garstige Graben*] between accidental truths of history and necessary truths of reason. The real core of the problem, viz., the historical difference and its surmounting, did not yet attain full, conscious clarity in this conception. The eighteenth century did not recognize that the accidental historical truths of Christianity were experienced in relation to the contexts of meaning taken as more or less evident in their own time. Nor did it notice that the convictions of its own age which were regarded as necessary truths of reason were themselves also historically conditioned, and were bound to lose their self-evidence and appearance of *a priori* validity in a later age. Thus, the dualism between accidental truths of history and necessary truths of reason which was characteristic of eighteenth century criticism of tradition constitutes an imperfect, preliminary stage of the question regarding the possibility of bridging the historical distance between primitive Christianity and the present age. Since then, the more the spirit of the present age has shucked off the outgrown husks of an authority-bound Christianity, the more has this problem proven to be the central hermeneutical problem of theology. It became increasingly clear that the difference between primitive Christianity and the present age was precisely what had to be overcome by means of a contemporary application of Christian revelation, but also that this difference was the obstacle to this application – and thereby to the extension of the Christian tradition as a whole.[8]

---

[8] It is only a relatively innocuous and superficial form of this difficulty which still describes it as the task of obtaining acknowledgment in the present

The historical thought that has given rise to this problem is by no means something that has been foisted upon theology from outside, by its surrounding world. It was much more the case that Christian theology itself was a decisive factor in the formation of historical thought, since the task of the transmission of the Christian message demanded such a development. In what way could the essential content to be transmitted, God's revelation in Christ, remain the norm of the chain of interpretations arising from it? It was for the sake of providing such a norm that the New Testament canon arose in the early church alongside the office of bishop which had been traced back to the apostles.[9] This was done on the basis of the assumption, justified then, although uselessly revived today, that the oldest witnesses to the history of Jesus put one in immediate contact with the "norm of truth" itself. Nevertheless, for a long time it was taken for granted that the authentic interpretation of the divinely inspired Scriptures was that of the ecclesiastical teaching office, which was specially equipped with the same Spirit that inspired the Scriptures. It was Scholasticism's elevation of the historical sense [*sensus historicus*] of the biblical texts, which had been consolidated in the course of the Middle Ages, that for the first time made it not only possible, but a conscientious duty, for Luther, as a doctor of Holy Scripture, to confront the interpretation of the teaching office of the church with an appeal to the self-evidence of the biblical texts.[10] Scripture, interpreting itself, allowed Christ, the origin and content of the Christian tradition, to become effective as the norm of all interpretation with a new clarity.

The requirement that the Scriptures be interpreted by means

---

age for the (supposedly) already known essential content of Christianity. The more profound difficulty consists in the fact that the historical difference makes an open question just what really constitutes the essential content of Christianity.

[9] For a more detailed discussion of this point, see Hans Freiherr von Campenhausen, "Ursprung und Bedeutung der christliche Tradition," in *Im Lichte der Reformation,* Jahrbuch des Evangelischen Bundes 8 (Göttingen, 1965), pp. 22–45.

[10] For a fuller discussion of this matter, see above, "The Crisis of the Scripture Principle," pp. 1–14.

of themselves led inevitably, however, to the further principle that the interpretation must adhere to the intention of the apostolic authors at the time of the composition of their writings, bearing in mind the author's contemporaneous surrounding world as well as the original readers. The present interests of the later interpreter were to be kept in the background. This procedure allowed the difference between the world of primitive Christianity and the present age of the interpreter to emerge ever more clearly, even if the interpreter still continued naïvely to identify himself with his text and allowed the historical difference to assert itself only in the form of opposition between the text and the manifestations of contemporary church life of which he was critical. Even here the preponderance of application within theological hermeneutic had its effect. It was indeed the case that in one respect, namely, with respect to the controlling function of the biblical texts in relation to contemporary preaching that was to be grounded on them, the exhibiting of the historical difference made things easier. For this purpose the biblical content had to be clearly distinguishable from later interpretations, just as much as from all forms of contemporary thought available to the interpreter *beforehand*. The historical difference thus gave sharp expression to the placing of the essential content to be transmitted above the chain of interpretations of it. To this extent, J. S. Semler was completely justified in his conviction that historical-critical interpretation of Scripture was the inescapable consequence of the Reformation Scripture principle.[11]

But the full sharpness of the historical difference is first felt only when the interpreter can no longer naïvely identify himself with the content of his text. Such a development does not necessarily mean that the advance of the Christian tradition's process of transmission has been crippled, although the feeling of strangeness with regard to the spiritual world of primitive Christianity which was experienced in connection with the

---

[11] That Semler was a protagonist of this conviction has been shown by G. Hörnig, *Die Anfänge der historisch-kritischen Theologie. Johann Salomo Semlers Schriftverständnis und sein Verhältnis zu Luther* (Göttingen, 1961), pp. 176ff.

discovery of the apocalyptic conditioning of even the message of Jesus himself, together with all the attempts to repress
this knowledge which abound in the history of recent theology
right down to this very day, easily lend themselves to such an
interpretation. Nevertheless, the insight that the interpreter
himself can no longer unqualifiedly identify himself at any
point with the message of Jesus or with any New Testament
text at all, may also have a liberating effect. It can encourage
conscious adoption of the in one way or another inevitable
particularity of its own questioning and thought (as present-
day types) in contrast to primitive Christianity, and consider
from the standpoint of this presupposition the question of what
possibility of continuity might still be open in relation to the
Christianity transmitted by tradition and thereby also to
primitive Christianity. The insight that it is no longer possible
for a present-day interpreter naïvely to identify himself with the
primitive Christian texts – unless by means of a self-deception –
makes it possible for the first time to seek the continuity of the
Christian tradition in the *way* in which, from its inception, ever
new forms of its interpretation were released.

The event of transmitting a tradition always has the form of
constructing a bridge – to previously distant men, or a new
generation, or an altered situation. Until the Enlightenment,
this bridging could be accomplished in the medium of a nonhistorical, general consciousness of truth, e.g., by the application of general truths to the particular situation of the individual
recipient of the message (by means of moral or tropological
exegesis of Scripture), and by theological certification of the
general truth of Christian revelation through combination and
comparison of scriptural passages and statements of the tradition with each other and with other truths (in the scholastic
dialectic, which combined these truths in an essentially nonhistorical metaphysics, despite the presence of many historical
components in it). Even in the early days of historical-critical
exegesis of Scripture within Protestantism, the depth of the
problem that had emerged with respect to application remained
hidden because the exhibiting of the historical difference was

used chiefly for the purpose of becoming unburdened of the tradition – from the Catholic "human traditions" [*traditiones humanae*] at first, but later from its own orthodox dogmatics, too. During this period, Protestantism still continued immediately to discover or rediscover its own tendencies in primitive Christianity, or at least in the figure of Jesus. It was the knowledge of the apocalyptic conditioning of primitive Christianity and of the message of Jesus himself that first brought about full realization of the depth of the historical gap between the twentieth century and primitive Christianity, and with this, also, an awareness of the difficulty of the problems burdening the enterprise of advancing the Christian tradition in the present age.

The most currently used label for the process of application is termed "Word of God." This catch-word is no longer understood in the classical Protestant sense as the divinely inspired – insofar as spoken by God himself – word of the Bible, but instead as either the whole process of Christian tradition (understood in a Protestant light) from Jesus Christ to Scripture and proclamation, or else, preferably, as the last of these alone, following Luther's idea of the "living voice of the Gospel" [*viva vox Evangelii*] which goes forth through the preaching and whose form has not been fixed once and for all since it proclaims "the same thing" in an ever new form.

The symbolic and tradition-weighted term "Word of God" at least designated (although in a very enigmatic way) the exceedingly complex process of application that is involved in carrying out the transmission of the Christian tradition. But, in any event, it only *designated* the process: it by no means made it possible to carry out that process – except perhaps in an epoch which in by-passing the foundations of its secular form of life had become unsure of itself, and could once again be confronted with the authoritarian claim of being able to proclaim divine revelation directly. Instead of using the formula "Word of God" (whatever one understands by that) as evidence of its own orthodoxy and as something to be mouthed at any time in order to shatter opponents, theology should perhaps rather devote itself more to the less pretentious task of clarifying the problem of application designated by this term, and taking as its theme the problem of the possibility of transmitting the Christian tradition in the present age. In any case, the task of theology is not accomplished in the long run by mythologizing talk about the Word of God (which was originally a mythological expression, anyway), nor by confronting the hearer, threatened by the *asserted* authority of this divine Word, with a naked demand for obedience.

Theology must free itself today from a pseudo-orthodox terminology which is a symptom of a flight from the full scope of the hermeneutical task posed by the present situation of Christianity. The same applies to the ever present temptation, arising out of the Lutheran and pietistic tradition, of limiting hermeneutical reflection to, or at least focusing it upon, the problem of application to the individual. Such a procedure, which obscures the universal meaning of God-talk and the problems related to this, readily allies itself with a view of revelation – that belonging to a theology of the Word of God, for instance – which it simply assumes to be authoritative and does not adhere to because it has been demonstrated by critical reflection right down to its foundations. In that way, it circumvents the genuine and more comprehensive problem of application.

Another form of abridgment of the contemporary hermeneutical task grows out of concentrating upon application itself. Theology certainly does give exceptional importance to the application of the content of its tradition to contemporary man. Nevertheless, an isolated interest in the phase of application in theological hermeneutic easily results in interpretations that obscure the historical difference between primitive Christianity and the present age. This is already indicated by the naïvete, so difficult to overcome, with which an interpreter will identify himself with the interpreted text – or at any rate, with its "authentic" core – and will use the historical difference only to jettison a tradition felt to be oppressive or else to turn back toward the dominant consciousness of the present age from another quarter.

The consequences of such a way of requisitioning New Testament texts can be observed even in Bultmann, whose program of demythologization made clear to many people for the first time the full depth of the contrast between the present age and the primitive Christian picture of the world. Since Bultmann's interest as a theologian is concentrated entirely upon the application of the Christian message, that is, upon the reception and understanding of its claim on the part of a contemporary hearer or reader, he can regard the historical attempt to go behind the New Testament texts as theologically unimportant, or even characterize theological extrapolation from such a basis as illegitimate (because this would mean calling into question the divine authority of the kerygma), even though such inquiry is an inevitable feature of historical-critical interpretation of texts. Furthermore, it is consistent with Bultmann's interest in the application of the primitive Christian message that he finds in the New Testament such an extensive uniformity in self-understanding, despite contradictory objectivizing forms of expression, that he can, in addition, relegate the historical difference between primitive Christianity and the present age wholly to the side of the forms of expression and the world-picture determining them, while regarding the self-understanding of primitive Christianity as a possibility one may still avail himself of today. The violence of this attempt to dissolve the correlation between self-understanding and world-picture (together with all its related objectifications) and by historical analysis relativize the latter but not the former,[12] is

[12] Rudolf Bultmann, "New Testament and Mythology," in H. W. Bartsch (ed.), *Kerygma and Myth* I (London: S.P.C.K., 1963), pp. 1–44. The specific character of this undertaking appears even more clearly in Bultmann's pupil, Herbert Braun, who designates the *anthropology* of the primitive Christian writings as the constant (and also still appropriable by us), taking the *Christology* of these writings as the variable ("Der Sinn der neutestamentlichen Christologie," *ZThK* 54 [1957], pp. 368, 370f., 376; reprinted in H. Braun, *Gesammelte Studien zum Neuen Testament und seiner Umwelt* [Tübingen, ²1967], pp. 272, 274f., 280f.). He won Bultmann's approval in so doing (Rudolf Bultmann, "The Primitive Christian Kerygma and the Historical Jesus," in Carl E. Braaten and Roy A. Harrisville [eds.],

worthy of note and becomes fully intelligible only from the standpoint of passionate concern for contemporary application of the Christian tradition. But even if it could be shown that the New Testament contains as extensive a uniformity in self-understanding as Bultmann contends, this could hardly be declared to be the central content of the Christian tradition without tracing it back to the historical Jesus. If it really were a matter of indifference for the content of the Christian message whether or not Jesus was a historical person, or what the manner of his historical existence was, then it would be impossible to see why the transmission of this understanding of human existence would have to appeal to Jesus any longer. The appeal to Jesus encountered in the New Testament could then be relegated to the accidental historical conditions out of which this understanding of human existence which entered the world as Christianity happened to arise. Since, on the contrary, appeal to Jesus, indeed, confession of faith in him, constitutes the fundamental feature of all Christian tradition, its content cannot consist simply in a particular understanding of human existence which is common to the New Testament writings but would itself be independent of the historical Jesus. This is, surely, the most important application to theology of the general maxim that in the realm of history meaning must remain bound to facticity, so that all meaning has its criterion in the fact in which it inheres, even though as meaning it may transcend this fact. As long as the Christian message remains a message about Jesus Christ, it must have a "foothold" in Jesus himself, as Gerhard Ebeling has put it. Even if the Christian message were only a matter of a self-understanding (in contradistinction to a world-picture), it would still require legitimation by means of a proof of its agreement – even on this point! – with Jesus. Inquiry behind the kerygma, behind the New Testament texts to the historical Jesus himself, is theologically unavoidable. Once this is admitted, however, it will be difficult in the long run to limit such inquiry to the question of the self-understanding

---

The Historical Jesus and the Kerygmatic Christ [New York and Nashville: Abingdon Press, 1964], p. 36).

of Jesus and its correspondence with the self-understanding of the primitive Christian proclamation. Rather, by exposing the total historical phenomenon of the figure of Jesus in all its strangeness, it will tend to call into question the limitation of the interpretation of Scripture to the sphere of the understanding of human existence.

The line of thought we have been following thereby returns to our starting point, to the proximity we observed between historical and theological hermeneutic in view of the fact that theological as well as historical meaning inheres in something historically factual, so that historical individuality in its facticity, which is inexhaustible as a source for general structural statements or of appreciative interpretation [*deutende Auslegung*], remains the norm of all interpretation. Meanwhile, it has been shown that this principle holds even for the application of the revelatory significance of Jesus with which theology is concerned. The reopening of the quest for the historical Jesus in recent theological discussion means that theology has decided that it cannot resolve its hermeneutical task purely by means of the interpretation of texts in the sense of a direct application of the "Word" of the text, the kergyma, to the present situation. Rather, the interpretation of texts intrinsically demands that a detour be taken which is routed around the essential content articulated by the Christian writings. For they express this content in language as something previously given which must therefore be sought out by inquiring behind the texts. Only in that way will the interpreter follow their real intention. In this sense, theological hermeneutic requires a detour around the question of the historical Jesus in order to be able to bring the primitive Christian message of Christ, transmitted by the New Testament writings, closer to the present age. All interpretations of the historical Jesus – past as well as present – must allow themselves to be tested with regard to whether or not they explicate the meaning warranted by this history itself. It is possible to do this only on the presupposition that the significance of this history transcends its location at a point in the historical past. But, as was shown above, this presupposition is valid for all historical individuality and thereby for all historical events.

From this standpoint, every dualism between theological and historical hermeneutic is excluded. If interpretation has to do with the unique meaning warranted by the very content which is to be interpreted, then differences between the various perspectives and formulations of the problem employed by the interpreters cannot be taken as fixed boundaries which would justify different hermeneutical principles.[13] Certainly interpretation always presupposes a relationship in life to the "essential content" of the text and, thus, a pre-understanding of the same – in the sense of an open question about it. Such pre-understandings, as well as those that grow out of them which guide the formulation of the question involved in the interpretation,[14] can be of the most varied kinds. A distinction should be made here, however, between formulations of the question whose intention is from the outset only a particular aspect of the content in question, and those which are open to the content itself. In the latter case, the content comes into play as the norm of its interpretation and decides the appropriate way of inquiring into it, since it imposes the necessity of integrating its various aspects in a total comprehension of its content. Insofar as the unity of the content functions as the norm of its interpretation and requires a unified understanding of this content, the multiplicity of hermeneutical principles which have hardened in opposition to each other will be overcome precisely in the process of understanding the unity of the content being inquired into. In this sense, even the distinction between *historical* investigation of New Testament texts as "sources" for the history of Jesus, and *theological* investigation of the same texts regarding the possibilities of human existence (inasmuch as it is motivated by the question of God) expressed in them, does not justify any ultimate difference in their hermeneutical principles. Rather,

---

[13] A different view is expressed by Rudolf Bultmann, "The Problem of Hermeneutics," in Claus Westermann, *Essays on Old Testament Hermeneutics* (London: SCM Press and Richmond: John Knox Press, 1963), p. 252.

[14] *Ibid.*, pp. 239f., 243f.

this distinction indicates only a difference in the aspects whose unity will have to be perceived in the light of the essential content animating the texts in question, viz., in the light of the history and person of Jesus. This point is all the more urgent since the historical as well as the theological quests for Jesus intend to uncover not merely a partial aspect but the totality of his figure. Thus, if the historical and the theological aspects are not to exclude each other, their unity must be given in and made intelligible through the unity of the history of Jesus.

Initially, of course, that is only a postulate – albeit one grounded in the content itself. It still contrasts, at first, with the phenomenon that the New Testament texts are interrogated by theologians in a way that seems to deviate fundamentally from the usual procedure of the historian, even if these texts are interpreted as testimonies to Jesus of Nazareth. The theologian claims them not only as sources or as evidence for historical hypotheses, but uses them also as guidance for the interpretation of the significance warranted by the history and person of Jesus, which permits of being characterized even to the extent of the modern slogan that Jesus has to be understood as the revelation of God. Disregarding, for the time being, the substantive problem involved, and concentrating on the form of such a way of using a text, a fundamental difference between historical and theological hermeneutic already suggests itself. The former appears not to assess its sources as providing both access to an event and guidance for the interpretation of the event thus made accessible. In contrast to this, it has to be pointed out that even within historical work the given sources can acquire very different relevance and function. This may depend decisively upon the relation in which the source being treated stands to the events it attests. But it may also depend upon whether and to what extent the source had become determinative for the history of the interpretation of a specific historical figure right down to the time of the present interpreter. An example may be found in the importance of Plato, especially his earlier dialogues, for the mediation of our *information* [*Kenntnis*] about Socrates as well as for our *knowledge* [*Erkenntnis*] of his significance as a philosopher. The point of comparison here is to be found as much in Plato's relationship to Socrates as a student as in the fact that Plato originated a traditional view of Socrates which is still influential today. Here, too, of course, it has to be demonstrated that the source of our knowledge of a historical figure is at the same time an indispensable guide for the understanding of his significance. Naturally, the profound difference between Plato's relationship to Socrates and that of the New Testament writers to Jesus cannot be overlooked. Let us disregard all of the peripheral and more external differences, such as, for example, the fact that the New Testament writers – as far as we can tell today – were not disciples of the earthly Jesus. Regarding the hermeneutical relation of the interpreter to the content to be interpreted, however, the most important difference consists in the fact that in the Christian tradition it is above all a matter of finding application for the history and person of Jesus, and not only his teachings. This is in turn connected with the nature and mode of the relationship – an indirect one, to be sure, but also indissoluble – of the person of Jesus to the particularity of his message. In addition to this, there is the further circumstance that the significance of Jesus was handed down in the form of confessions of faith in him. Despite such differences, however, the example of the relationship of Plato to Socrates nevertheless shows that historical sources can at the same time provide guidelines for interpreting the significance of of the historical figure they attest.

A consideration of fundamental importance explains this state of affairs. While it is necessary to distinguish between the individuality of a historical figure and the "history of influences" [*Wirkgungsgeschichte*] stemming from him,[15] they nevertheless

---

[15] This point has to be made against Martin Kähler, who expounded the togetherness mentioned in the text in a one-sided way with his conception of the unity of the historical and suprahistorical elements in the "historic Christ of the Bible" (*The So-called Historical Jesus and the Historic, Biblical Christ*, ed. and tr. Carl E. Braaten [Philadelphia: Fortress Press, 1964], p. 65. On the concept of the suprahistorical, see *ibid.*, p. 6, as well as *Die Wissenschaft der christlichen Lehre* [second revised ed., Leipzig, 1893], pp. 12ff.). According to this conception, a "historic figure" is to be discerned in "a man who has been

belong together. They do so in such a way that not only must
the "history of (his) influences" be understood from the side of
the historical figure that constitutes its point of origin,[16] but
also, conversely, in such a way that this figure cannot be comprehended in his individuality unless it is understood as the
starting point of this history of influences. The latter idea is
highly illuminating if one starts out from the viewpoint stated
earlier that historical individuality constantly includes, beyond

---

influential in molding posterity" through his "permanent influence" (*So-
called Historical Jesus*, p. 63), which in the case of Jesus consists in "the faith
of his disciples" (*ibid.*). Thus, Kähler could say of "the historic Christ of the
Bible" that he alone is the real Christ (*ibid.*, pp. 65f.). In his *Wissenschaft*, the
concept of the historic is, by comparison, more limited. There, it is stated
that "the reports of the historical facts" must "still have added to them" the
"testimony to their supernatural value" (sec. 22, p. 21). Kähler could now
also write that faith has the "means of verifying its objectivity" in "the simple,
rational comprehension of historical information" (sec. 16, p. 16). Nevertheless, this means of verification has nothing to do with a verification, which
is reserved for faith, of the "attestation of revelatory value" (*ibid.*) warranted
by this history. For Kähler, the historical can never be a criterion for judging
this value, since it is just this which has to be "added" to the historical (*ibid.*,
p. 21; cf. sec. 14a, p. 14, as well as sec. 18, p. 18). In spite of this, Kähler
based his concept of the suprahistorical on the observation that there is "in
the contents of this history . . . a permanent, universally valid content"
(sec. 13b, p. 13) – a formulation reminiscent of Simmel's emphasis on historical individuality (see above, p. 140, note 7). If, however, the universally valid element of "this historical fact" is supposed to "belong to it"
(*Wissenschaft*, sec. 13b, p. 13), then it must also be capable of being adduced
from this fact and of being used as a criterion for its interpretation. Otherwise there is no defence against the thought, rejected by Kähler, that the
universal validity asserted has been appended in a purely external way to
the historical fact to which Christianity appeals, so that "that about him
which is historical would be viewed as a matter of indifference" (sec. 12,
p. 12).
    [16] The term "history of influences" [*Wirkungsgeschichte*], which has become
current through the work of H.-G. Gadamer (*Wahrheit und Methode*, pp.
284ff., passim.), is open to misunderstanding insofar as it suggests a conception of historical processes analogous to physical connections of cause and
effect. Gadamer himself found fault with historicism's use of the categories
of natural philosophy (as, for example, the concept of force, *ibid.*, pp. 192ff.),
because they obscure the specific problems connected with historical events
and their interrelations. The same applies, however, to the expression
"history of influences." At best, it is useful as an abbreviation for a complex
process in which tradition and reception interpenetrate in many ways.

its abstract facticity, an anticipation of meaning (see above, pp. 140f.).

A fundamental difference between theological and historical hermeneutic would arise at this point only if the New Testament writings were understood as *authoritative* guides for the interpretation of the historical Jesus in such a way that their function was not simply that of pointing to the significance of Jesus which his history itself seeks to disclose, but was instead that of a supplementary interpretative principle [*Deutungsprinzip*], alien to the history of Jesus, which claimed to be binding upon its interpretation because its validity could not be questioned. Although in this case the fundamental, theological presupposition that Jesus himself must be the norm of all proclamation of the Christ would be lost sight of, it cannot be denied that theological interpretation of Scripture has been and still is widely understood in this sense. But such an understanding of itself is by no means a necessary and absolutely constitutive element of a theological hermeneutic of the New Testament texts as witnesses to Jesus. On the contrary, as explication of the meaning warranted[17] by the history of Jesus itself, these texts allow themselves to be questioned and, if occasion arises, judged critically insofar as the interpretation they offer falls short of or in some other way deviates from the anticipation of meaning that the history of Jesus allows to be advanced for itself. Viewed in this way, no fundamental difference between historical and theological hermeneutic needs to be assumed. The peculiarity of the interpretation of the New Testament texts as witnesses to Jesus can be traced back to the particularities of the history and person of Jesus himself, so that such interpretation constitutes only a special case of historical hermeneutic, not a completely different type of hermeneutic. Even the extraordinary peculiarity

[17] One could also say that the meaning belongs to or inheres in the event. In that case, the emphasis is on the claim that the significance is not arbitrarily ascribed to the event. However, that way of putting it does not express the fact that the meaning transcends the individual fact and has to do with its place in a wider context. This becomes clearer if one says that this or that meaning is warranted by a specific event, whereby, likewise, willful and arbitrary ways of construing it remain excluded.

of theological interpretation, viz., the urgent significance of application, can meaningfully be shown to arise out of the particularity of the history and person of Jesus without thereby having to postulate a special theological hermeneutic.

If no fundamental difference between theological and historical hermeneutic is to be deduced with regard to the form of the hermeneutical process, it nevertheless seems to be only too clear that such a difference is indicated by the significance ascribed to the content of the history of Jesus. "Revelation of God" seems to be a category that has no place within the realm of historical hermeneutic. This is the most difficult of the problems to be considered, yet while it has beclouded attempts to understand the relationship between historical and theological hermeneutic, it is not insoluble. Everything depends upon giving a precise meaning to the expression "revelation of God." It can be shown that it is closely related to the concept of history as such, so that it cannot be ignored by historical hermeneutic, either. This connection will be demonstrated, in the first instance, by examining the theological problem of the idea of a revelation of God.

If it is justifiable to speak about God at all – something that cannot be further investigated at this point – then, in any case, such talk implies a reference to the whole of reality, provided that God can be meaningfully conceived only as the all-determining power. Speaking about God and speaking about the whole of reality are not two entirely different matters, but mutually condition each other. Presumably it is not even possible to speak of the whole of reality without in some way thinking of God. In any case, the converse is true: it is utter thoughtlessness to leave undecided or even to repudiate the idea of the whole of reality while at the same time speaking about God as the all-determining reality. That the idea of "God" implies a whole of finite reality (even if in such a way that God is thought of as free in relation to it) remains valid even when the whole of reality is not present since it must be conceived as still unfinished and incomplete. This only states that the whole of reality is not something presently available, but must rather be thought of as a process of history moving toward a still open future. The all-determining reality is then – if it be personal – to be thought of as the God of this history. The open future of man and the world then appear as an expression of the freedom of God.

The idea of the freedom of God is not to be thought of as some sort of subsequent interpretative key appended to the openness of man and the world to the future, such as is approximated by those arguments about the secularized understanding of man and the world (which come about as the result of a historical process). It is much more the case that the experience of the freedom of God has been historically and materially fundamental for the experience of the openness to the future on the part of man and the world. The God of Israel and of the Christians manifested himself in this way as the God of history – a history which is still, in individual matters as well as a whole, very much unfinished. Also grounded in that is the fact that the deity of God – as the all-determining reality – has itself not yet been definitively demonstrated and made evident. Insofar as the history of Jesus was marked by the nearness of the ultimate future of this God and thus is the unsurpassable anticipation of the ultimate revelation of God, it generates an impulse toward the confirmation of this ultimacy that took place in Jesus, a mission to all peoples, and toward the integration of all realms of life under the divine truth which appeared in Jesus but which still needs confirmation of its divinity through the fulfillment of this integration. Thus, the history of Jesus releases a new history through the impulse toward integration emanating from it. Inasmuch as such integration and the reciprocity arising from it alter the reality of man and his world (together with the anticipations of their fulfilling wholeness which free the present from its nullity), they also alter the understanding of God as the constitutive power of the whole of this reality and of its revelation in Jesus. Thus, although God's revelation occurred in Jesus with final validity, it nevertheless did not appear as something already on hand in finished form. Rather, because the history of Jesus is not finished in this sense, the revelation of the God of history, whose reign is always still coming, must always be understood anew. Thus, the whole of history will constantly be constituted anew in the process of the transmission of the revelation of God in Jesus of Nazareth. The God who constitutes history has himself fully entered the process of history in his revelation. But he has done so in such a way that precisely as he is here transmitted in a process of tradition, he is at the same time the future of this history, the coming God who remains distinct from, or, better, who is always distinguishing himself in a new way from, what happens in this history.

God is immanent in history in the process of the transmission of his eschatological revelation, determining it in its totality from within, from the intra-historical event of the history of Jesus. It is thus that he proves himself to be the God who determines all reality. The totality of reality is constantly coming to light in ever new ways through the influence of Jesus on the hermeneutical process of the transmission of the Christian tradition. The hermeneutical process is thereby kept from being arrested and is driven instead, by the struggle for confirmation and realization of this totality and by the concomitant experience of the narrowness of the determinate content thus far attained, toward an ever new stage of the process characterized by a new understanding of reality as a whole. Since every such understanding of the whole rests on an anticipation, however, it bears an internal contradiction which will drive it beyond itself again, insofar as it reaches out to the whole and yet presents itself as a *mere* anticipation, thus showing that it is not the whole. Even though this holds for every individual stage, however, the process that leads from stage to stage is itself comprehensible in its unity as the explication of the anticipation of the ultimate end (i.e., the future of God himself) in the history of Jesus. Only within the horizon of the totality of history in general, as disclosed at some given time, is it possible to understand the particular present age in relation to Jesus, the origin of the history of the transmission of the Christian tradition, in such a way as to preserve the historical difference and thereby the particularity of Jesus in contrast to that present age. From this, however, there must proceed the impulses for changing the present which keep the hermeneutical process of the history of Christianity in motion.

It has been shown that the peculiarity of the historical figure of Jesus which has been described as "revelation of God" is the basis of the specific historicness of the process of tradition which has emanated from him. The biblical idea of God, with that peculiar reference to history which constitutes its totality, no longer stands in a merely external relationship to the deeds of men. Rather, it allows the totality of history already to take shape in the present through the process of the transmission of a specific event, the history of Jesus. On the other hand, the totality of history to which theological talk about God and his revelation in Jesus are related now constitutes an unavoidable theme of historical hermeneutic, for the reason that all historical study remains oriented to the problem of universal history. If this latter assertion is correct, then one may conjecture that the theme of the totality of history is a strictly common frame of reference for both historical and theological work. The historian as such may not usually speak explicitly of God, but his work nevertheless remains oriented toward that theme which on its part, justifies speaking about God, viz., the problem of universal history. Conversely, theological speech about an "act of God" in specific historical events would have to be defended with regard to the current actuality of the *whole* of the reality which is determined as history and of the power constituting it for this or that particular event.[18]

Thus, with regard to the fact that theology deals with the historical person of Jesus in such a way that it speaks of the revelation of God in him, it appears that it is unnecessary to assert without qualification that there is a *fundamental* difference between historical and theological hermeneutic. The obvious dissimilarity between a theological interpretation of the meaning of Jesus and the usual form of historical work can be adequately accounted for by the dissimilarity of the particular

---

[18] Cf. the concluding remarks of my essay "Kerygma and History," above, pp. 94f.

historical objects with which the Christian tradition and theological hermeneutic have to deal – objects with which historical
hermeneutic has still to concern itself. If historical research
really inquires into the individuality of a historical person in a
comprehensive manner, then what theology has found in Jesus
of Nazareth cannot in principle transgress the boundaries of
historical inquiry – or else theology is not rendering a true
account in its explication of the inherent meaning of the historical figure of Jesus.

But is the presupposition that all historical work, whether it
wants to or not, is oriented toward the problem of universal
history a tenable one? There is much today that seems to favor
bracketing out such questions as a sign of scientific sobriety.[19]

---

[19] The Göttingen historian, Reinhard Wittram, has greeted the theme of
universal history with marked reserve, and wants to view every "total construction" [*Totaldeutung*] – whether Christian or of some other lineage –
"with unmitigated skepticism" ("Möglichkeiten und Grenzen der Geschi-
chtswissenschaft," *ZThK* 62 [1965], 430–57; citation from p. 455). He
gives a theological reason for just this attitude, viz., the Christian conviction
"that God makes history" confers a "confidence of meaning" [*Sinnvertrauen*]
that "renders every total construction superfluous" (*ibid.*). The only question
is how one can attain this conviction that God makes history. Does not this
sentence already imply a total construction of history, and is not just this the
reason why any other is unnecessary? It is not necessary, at any rate, for this
"total construction" to coincide with any one specific form in which a presentation of universal history has been carried out. One might even rule out
the ability of any portrayal of universal history to claim final validity on the
grounds that human knowledge always has a provisional character. To this
extent, I can agree with Wittram. But this "confidence of meaning," the
conviction that God makes history, nevertheless has to satisfy itself – for all
the provisionality this involves, which is the reason why it must always be
done again – that it is not an empty, subjective meaning, which is powerless
in relation to reality and which must even be judged to be arbitrary and
unconvincing. The attainment of such confirmation involves, however, in
addition to concrete historical experience, attempts at universal-historical
understanding and portrayal, fragmentary though their results may remain.
Wittram himself, a few years ago, in connection with my theses on the
theology of history, declared: "Perhaps we have made it too easy for ourselves in that we have lost consciousness of the continuity of world history
and relinquished this to secular projections" ("Die Verantwortung des
evangelischen Historikers in der Gegenwart," in *Im Lichte der Reformation*,
Jahrbuch des Evangelischen Bundes, 5 [Göttingen, 1962], p. 40).

On the other hand, this theme was thought through in a penetrating manner in the hermeneutic of the historical school of the nineteenth century. Does it not still remain at least an open question today?[20] Justified as the repudiation of all premature and short-sighted constructions of universal history may appear, especially when they pretend to convey ultimate knowledge, the unavoidability of this theme and, therefore, concern for its clarification should continue all the more to be acknowledged. The last theoretician of the hermeneutic of historicism, Wilhelm Dilthey, was still fully aware of the impossibility of circumventing this theme. At the same time, Dilthey's reflections make clear why the theme of the totality of history has since lapsed into the background not only in the practice of historians but also in the further development of Dilthey's hermeneutical thought in Heidegger. Since reluctance with regard to this theme burdens every attempt to renew the problem of universal history today with the necessity of justifying its motives, it is advisable to examine more carefully the thought of Dilthey and its transformation by Heidegger.

[20] In this sense, Wilhelm Mommsen judged that as a "guiding idea" [*Leitidee*] "the principle of universal history is more actual today than ever before," even if every "attempt at concrete realization of a universal history . . . must remain, today more than ever, a mere patchwork" (article on "Universalgeschichte" in: Waldemar Besson [ed.], *Geschichte* [Fischer-Lexicon 24 [Frankfurt am Main, 1961], p. 328). A series of newer portrayals and philosophical interpretations of world history are discussed by Joseph Vogt, *Wege zum historischen Universums: Von Ranke bis Toynbee*, Urban-Bücher 51 (Stuttgart, 1961). In the concluding section "Menschheitsgeschichte als Aufgabe" (The history of mankind as a task), Vogt, following O. F. Anderle, speaks in favor of a "procedure of historical integration" which moves from particular wholes ("closed structures, genuine unities as complexes that are essentially more than the sum of their parts") to "a more comprehensive, higher unity," which could "help disclose the meaning of history" by "the demonstration of a step-wise order – culture, cultural sphere, cultural synthesis" (*ibid.*, p. 134). Dilthey had already, in a similar fashion, taken this way out of the impasses of historical relativism (see the text that follows). It remains unsatisfactory, however, because the successively larger wholes never grow out of their parts alone, but also, conversely, knowledge of the parts as such always already presupposes an understanding of the whole.

II

In the hermeneutic of the historical school and in Dilthey the theme of universal history is intimately related to the old hermeneutical principle that in the process of interpreting a text, the whole and its parts reciprocally illumine each other. The result of the application of this principle to historical knowledge was, for Dilthey as well as for the historical school, that "basically, there can be no other history than universal history because the meaning of the individual itself is determined only from the standpoint of the whole."[21] The fundamental point here is that Dilthey defines the key hermeneutical concept of meaning [*Bedeutung*] by means of the relationship between part and whole: "The category of meaning designates the relation rooted in life itself, of parts to the whole."[22] This applies first of all to individual life. The individual life-moments, the experiences undergone by an individual, have their meaning in the context of the course of his life.[23] But the individual is himself, in turn, a part of life-forms and nexuses of meaning that transcend individualized human existence. These, in turn, are coordinated within still more encompassing totalities of historical life – such as peoples and states – and refer beyond all of them to the totality of mankind and universal history. Thus, "the relationship between whole and parts"[24] exists everywhere in society and in history. And it is only this conclusion, as Dilthey explicitly pointed out, that justifies "the application of the concept of meaning to the whole breadth of reality."[25]

If we look past Dilthey to Heidegger's analysis of the historicness of human existence, which indeed purports to want to

[21] Gadamer, *Wahrheit und Methode*, p. 187.

[22] *Meaning in History: W. Dilthey's Thoughts on History and Society*, ed. and intro. H. P. Rickman (London: Allen and Unwin, 1961), p. 106 [= Dilthey, *Gesammelte Schriften* [Leipzig and Stuttgart, 1926; ²1948], 7 p. 5), p. 233].

[23] *Meaning in History*, pp. 99f. [= Dilthey, *Gesammelte Schriften*, 7, p. 73].

[24] W. Dilthey, *Gesammelte Schriften* (Stuttgart and Göttingen, 1958), 7, p. 257 [not in Rickman, *Meaning in History*].

[25] *Ibid.*, p. 255 [The sentence quoted by Pannenberg is omitted in *Meaning in History*, p. 162, which nevertheless does present the context from which this sentence is taken – Tr.].

demand the "appropriation" [*Aneignung*] of Dilthey's thought, it comes as a surprise that here the concept of the "whole" – and, correspondingly, that of the category of "meaning," too – is limited to the description of the individual human being. At first sight, this is strange, in view of Dilthey's references to the encompassing supra-individual nexuses of meaning which, together with the individual human beings themselves, constitute the latter as meaningful wholes. However, one can find reflections in Dilthey himself in the light of which Heidegger's restriction of talk about totality and meaning to the existence of the individual appears understandable.

Dilthey once remarked that "wherein resides the meaning of the life an individual – I, or another, or a nation – has lived through," is "not unambiguously determined by the fact that such a meaning exists." The latter point is certain, to be sure, viz., *that* generally in the course of a life meaning "happens" [*stattfindet*]. But wherein it consists is not clear at every stage of the course of a life. It withdraws itself not only from present experience, but frequently even from a retrospective view, although such a view already sees the individual event or experience in larger contexts. This certainly does not mean that immediate experience or retrospective memory perceive no meaning whatever in what has been experienced, but rather that the true, ultimately valid meaning of what was experienced has not yet come to light. "Only in the last moment of a life can the balance of its meaning be struck, and so it can be done only for a moment, or by another who retraces that life."[26] In another place, Dilthey expanded the idea about the life of the individual.

One would have to wait for the end of a life and, in the hour of death, survey the whole and ascertain the relation between the whole and its parts. One would have to wait for the end of history to have all the material necessary to determine its meaning.[27]

Naturally, Dilthey was aware of the difficulty that for the time

---

[26] *Meaning in History*, pp. 74f. [= Dilthey, *Gesammelte Schriften*, 7, p. 237; translation slightly altered – Tr.].

[27] *Ibid.*, p. 106 [= Dilthey, *Gesammelte Schriften*, 7, p. 233].

being no historian stands at the end of history in such a way as to be able to view its continuities of meaning as they would finally appear. But does it not follow from this that there is no prospect of success for any inquiry into the meaning of even the individual within the given whole to which it belongs, as long as universal history is not completed? Is not the definitive meaning of even the smaller unities – nations and cultural wholes, and individual men, too – rendered precarious by the incompleteness of universal history, since this may be decided with final validity only from the standpoint of the encompassing whole of universal history?

Dilthey sought a way out of this difficulty by reflecting that the whole might be "only there for us when it becomes comprehensible through the parts."[28] But does not this approach to the problem leave the nexuses of meaning suspended from merely partial truths, since the parts can disclose no more than partial aspects of the whole? The main reason why the parts themselves cannot attain any firm footing without knowledge of the whole is that only knowledge of the whole can make clear what significance the parts really deserve. Thus, insight into the inaccessibility of the whole of history leads to the impasse of relativism.

From this standpoint, it is easier to understand the fact that Heidegger, in his analysis of historicness, no longer began by posing the question of a totality of history transcending the individual human being. To be sure, even his own talk about a possibility of wholeness for the individual human being must also appear problematical as long as the whole of universal history encompassing the individual remains beyond our grasp. For the individual human being receives the meaning that constitutes his wholeness only in relation to an encompassing whole.

Nevertheless, Heidegger has discovered a new mode of access to the question of the wholeness of human existence which apparently makes it possible for him to conceive this wholeness independently of a preliminary experience of encompassing totalities or even of universal history. It is character-

[28] *Meaning in History*, p. 106 [= Dilthey, *Gesammelte Schriften*, 7, p. 233].

istic of Heidegger to speak not only of wholeness absolutely, but also of the existing human being's *possibility* of wholeness. The transformation of Dilthey's conception entailed in this nuance can be defined more precisely. Let us recall once more one of Dilthey's thoughts which was cited earlier: "Only in the last moment of life can the balance of its meaning be struck, (and) so it can be done only for a moment, or by another who retraces that life."[29] Heidegger follows Dilthey in accepting the idea that the death of the individual life rounds it into a whole. But Heidegger does not have to "await"[30] the hour of death, as Dilthey does, but instead knows of the specifically human possibility of anticipating [*vorzulaufen*][31] one's future death and thereby attaining the wholeness of human existence. As the only being that knows of its coming death, man is always at the possibility of being whole as a human being "in advance."[32]

This step of Heidegger's beyond Dilthey is coupled with the insight, heard only occasionally in this connection and first elaborated in a fundamental way by Heidegger, that the nexuses of meaning of what Dilthey called courses of life are constituted from the side of the future. In the case of Dilthey, this insight was obscured by the representation of history as a "connection of forces" [*Kräftekonnexes*] or "web of influences" [*Wirkungszusammenhang*] which he shared with the historical school. This picture of history allowed its continuity to appear as a linear process from the past through the present into the future, despite the fact that Dilthey, in his description of the historical consciousness itself, had noticed that the nexuses of meaning were accessible only from the standpoint of the end. Heidegger drew this consequence from this description – as did Count Yorck before him – since he had turned against the conception of history as a "connection of forces,"[33] which Dilthey had still accepted, and described temporality as well as the historicness

[29] See above, p. 161, n. 26.
[30] *Meaning in History*, p. 106 (see above, p. 161, n. 27).
[31] Martin Heidegger, *Being and Time*, tr. John Macquarrie and Edward Robinson (London: SCM Press and New York: Harper and Row, 1962), pp. 306f.
[32] *Ibid.*, p. 303.　　　[33] *Ibid.*, p. 451.

Basic Questions in Theology

of human existence on the basis of their relation to the future. The sharpest expression of this turn is found in the sentence: "The character of 'having been' arises, in a certain way, from the future."[34] Heidegger's concentration on the future has in fact liberated the authentic outcome of Dilthey's analysis of historicness from the husks of the historicist conception of history as a chain of effects stemming from forces. In addition, "the belongingness of the interpreter to his object" thus attained "concrete, demonstrable meaning" for the first time.[35]

Heidegger's new answer to the problem of the wholeness of human existence clearly has made it possible to recognize the priority of the future for the historicness of human existence. In other words, death need not merely be awaited in order for man to participate in his wholeness, but in knowledge of his own future death he is already present to this his most extreme possibility.

Since anticipation of the possibility which is not to be outstripped discloses also all the possibilities which lie ahead of that possibility, this anticipation includes the possibility of taking the *whole* of human being [*Dasein*] in advance in an existential [*existentiell*] manner, that is to say, it includes the possibility of existing as a *whole potentiality-for-Being*.[36]

Does such anticipation of one's future death really make it possible to acquire the wholeness of human being in advance? Various difficulties stand in the way of this. In the first place, the material abundance of possibilities of life preceding death are by no means provided by knowledge of the inescapability of one's own death. To this extent, the anticipatory knowledge a man has of his own death remains abstract. The events which mark and determine the direction of our lives right up to our deaths are characterized by contingency, and it is by no

[34] *Ibid.*, p. 373.

[35] Gadamer, *Wahrheit und Methode*, p. 249.

[36] M. Heidegger, *Being and Time*, p. 309. [While Macquarrie and Johnson prefer to leave *Dasein* untranslated because of the lack of a precise English equivalent for the peculiar sense Heidegger gives it, Pannenberg uses this term in an anthropological sense, as if it designated the fundamental structure of specifically human existence. Hence, it has been translated here, as often in this essay and throughout the book, "human being," or sometimes "human existence." – Tr.]

means from the direction of death that they rush upon us. The uncertainty of the events that are determinative for our lives was once finely intimated by Dilthey: "The wonderful and dreadful (things) that become significant for our lives always seem to enter through the door of chance."[37] For this reason we cannot adequately anticipate the real course of our own existence. It becomes accessible to us only in retrospect, when its end has really appeared.

The second and decisive objection to Heidegger's idea of anticipating death is aimed at the presupposition, held by both Heidegger and Dilthey, that death rounds out man's existence into a whole. Is it not rather the case that death breaks off our life, so that even in the best instances the successful life remains a fragment? That is to say, putting it the other way round, does not human being's intention toward wholeness, toward well-being [*Heil*], necessarily reach beyond death? If this is the case, the wholeness of the individual's existence would not come into view from the standpoint of his death, but only from the standpoint of a determination transcending the finitude of individual human being. The first thing to be considered at this point is the web of social life. However, the destination of the individual human being hardly coincides with his exhausting himself in the service of some kind of group, be it the family, the nation or the society. On the contrary, the criterion of social progress is to be found just as much in the extent to which the forms of social life require the freedom of the individual, so that the purpose of mankind must be the individual as well as the society, both reciprocally conditioning each other. Thus, the question about the wholeness of human being can find a satisfactory answer only when it is directed beyond death toward the participation of the individual in the destination of mankind as such.

The doubts that have just been raised leave untouched, however, Heidegger's idea that the wholeness of human being is to be attained only by means of an *anticipation* [*Vorwegnahme*], corresponding to the primacy of the future for temporality. This

---

[37] *Meaning in History*, p. 101 [= Dilthey, *Gesammelte Schriften*, 7, p. 74].

idea must be severed from the attempt to attain the wholeness of human being from the standpoint of death. Knowledge of the inescapability of his own death can make a man conscious of the seriousness of the question of his own destination, but cannot itself be that knowledge of man's final destination from which the wholeness of his being is constituted. This point makes all the more convincing the insight that the wholeness of human being can be spoken of only in an anticipatory manner. And the impossibility of such an anticipation is clarified by Heidegger's critical comment against Dilthey that all talk about "life" remains short-sighted as long as this life is not thought of in anticipation of its future wholeness.[38]

This sentence may perhaps be generalized by saying that statements expressing essences [*Wesensaussagen*] and, indeed, all designations of essential contents [*Sachbenennungen*] whatever, depend upon anticipations of a future that has not yet appeared. Far from designating only what is on hand at present, language names the essence of what appears by an anticipation of its future. It can be shown that in precisely this way man is able through his language adequately to reflect the incompleteness, the openness to the future, of the being of appearances. The idea in *Being and Time* that the wholeness of human being – i.e., of that which it is – can only be conceived by anticipating its future (and, indeed, its final future) might form a bridge to many of Heidegger's later utterances about language. If language names the essences of things, then it obviously says more than what is already present in them. In the later writings of Heidegger the inseparability of being and future returns. This probably has to do with the fact that in *Being and Time* there was no future beyond death and therefore no eschatology either. If the restriction of the phenomenon that occurred there in Heidegger's existentialist analytic is set aside, then it is possible to conceive of a reference of all beings to the future through the incompleteness of their nature, in line with the originally intended general ontological scope of the descriptions in *Being and Time*. Only man, as the being that in a special way

[38] Heidegger, *Being and Time*, pp. 363f.

has its being in anticipating its future by means of language, has the ability to do justice to this reference to the future in which all beings participate. If reference to the future characterizes not only man but all beings, then only in anticipation of their future can one adequately state what something is. And then what is present in its appearance is essentially a fore-conception [*Vorgriff*] of its future.[39] If this is correct, then the anticipatory character of naming essences implies a peculiar form of agreement between thought and being which again emerges in concrete substantiveness only in the form of anticipations whose final truth remains a theme of eschatology.

Now let us turn from this extrapolation back to the discussion of the wholeness of human being which is accessible only by anticipation. It has become clear that human being – with regard to both the individual and to "man" universally – can be spoken of only by means of such an anticipation. It is just as evident that the provisionality of being a mere anticipation always clings even to the surpassing anticipation of the wholeness of one's human existence from the standpoint of its future destination. The anticipated goal of life, in the light of which one's own human existence discloses itself as a whole from time to time, must confirm itself by the extent to which it is able to provide an actual integration of the moments of human existence. In so doing it will be shown that it is always only a more or less happy anticipation, which receives its luster from the anticipated future; it succeeds, but as a mere anticipation it can and must be superseded.

The positive element in the anticipation reveals itself by confirming in contemporary life that it is genuinely an anticipation of the future-constituted wholeness of a man's own human being. Since it is a matter of the wholeness of human being, confirmation or the lack thereof are decided only by the fulfillment of human being. Since, however, the anticipation of the

---

[39] This idea is developed in my lecture, "Appearance as the Arrival of the Future," in the *Journal of the American Academy of Religion* 35 (1967), pp. 107–118. [On the concept of *Vorgriff*, see the translators' note in Heidegger, *Being and Time*, p. 191, n. 2. – Tr.]

wholeness of human being includes the necessity of its confirmation, it thereby also includes the possibility of the opposite so that where the limits of its integrative power become evident, a new anticipation, superseding the first, is required. The new anticipation will be related to the first, as a reflection upon it. Therefore, rightly understood, this process does not lead to an infinite progression of anticipations which indifferently dissolve each other.

Because of the social involvements within which the individual stands, but also because of the commonality of the human destination of all individuals, the individual cannot anticipate the wholeness of his own human being without simultaneously including in this the more encompassing whole of the society which he serves and by means of which he lives his life. But the individual society in turn stands in an over-arching historical context. The anticipation of the wholeness of one's own current society, in the form of political or social utopias, for instance, always implies an anticipation of the whole of mankind in its whole history. In order to overthrow, but also to confirm and develop, an existing form of social life, it is necessary to appeal to *the* human. What was intended by this was never the form of life among all men at some present time, but always the still unrealized destination of men to true humanity. And even here, once again, it is the degree of actual integration provided that decides the measure of the anticipation, the degree of participation in the anticipated destination of mankind.

The category of fore-conception [*Vorgriff*] makes it possible to conceive the history of mankind as ordered toward a final destination without skipping over the unfinished character of the factual course of events. Just as the anticipation of the whole of one's own human being made possible by its futurity is always presupposed in one way or another in all talk about "life" or about the existence of this or that individual, so also is the whole of universal history already anticipated and presupposed in all talk about this or that particular event and its meaning. It is impossible to see why this implicit anticipation should not be reflected upon and thematized.

The category of fore-conception, the ontological determination introduced by Heidegger into the analytic of historicness, leads beyond the impasses of relativism if one drops the restriction imposed by the idea, stemming from Dilthey, that death is the uttermost possibility of human being. With that idea out of the way, it would then be possible to conceive of the presence of the whole – of individual existence as well as of the history of mankind – in the midst of unlimited historical relativity. The whole of universal history is not finished, although it is indeed capable of being anticipated, just as the life of the individual man is for his comprehending attitude toward himself. The two questions are not merely parallel. Since the individual man relates himself to the still outstanding wholeness of his own existence, he relates himself to the whole of the world and its history.[40] In this way he also always relates himself to God as the mysterious power that constitutes this – absent – wholeness. Every such anticipation is conditioned by its standpoint, bound to its location in history. To this extent, it is a *mere* anticipation, and not the whole itself. Nevertheless, to the extent that it is an anticipation, it is the presence of the whole constituted by the future.

In themselves, every projection of universal history, every existential (and existentialist) projection of the whole of human being, and even such plain statements concerning essence that attempt to say what this or that matter is, have the character of a fore-conception. Nevertheless, only an anticipation that is reflected upon, that is conscious of itself as a mere anticipation, includes historical relativity as an intrinsic element. Only in the mode of intrinsically reflected anticipation can the whole of history be conceived without doing violence to the openness of the future, and thus without basically failing to recognize the relativity of one's own position. The relativity and finitude in which reason is involved make it possible to conceive the whole

[40] This formulation also includes, beyond the history of mankind, the relationship of man to extra-human nature, without which mankind and its history are inconceivable. The wider sphere is not otherwise taken into account here, but see my "Erwägungen zu einer Theologie der Natur," which will be published in the near future.

at each of its stages – from the simple designating of essential contents, to universal history as the history of mankind and of the cosmos – only in fore-conception, and not definitively in concepts. The concept itself may be set forth as a mere fore-conception in the light of reflection upon that which actually takes place in the process of forming concepts. In that case, the intrinsically reflected anticipation would have to be regarded as the true concept of conception, although it would no longer be put forth as having been concluded as a necessary consequence.[41] With the establishment of the point that all concepts of wholeness as well as all statements expressive of essence depend upon thought's fore-conception of a not-yet-present wholeness and truth, post-Hegelian philosophy, with its insistence on the finitude of human thought, would receive its due without thereby surrendering the theme of wholeness or even that of absolute being. However, in distinction from the Hegelian philosophy of the concept [*Begriff*], a type of thought that understands itself as anticipation, and thus as an intrinsically reflected anticipation, would not be able to be self-constituting. Rather, as anticipation, it would always refer to something preliminary, in relation to which all thought and knowledge prove also to be once again *mere* anticipation, which can never be overtaken or superseded by means of a type of thought that itself has anticipatory structure.

That applies not only to any anticipatory concepts one pleases, but also to the very form of anticipation itself. A form of thought that understands itself as a mere fore-conception of the truth does not have the truth in itself but is rather the process that strives beyond itself toward it. This process can be maintained only on the presupposition that existing being itself is not what it is, i.e., has not yet attained its own essence.

Now such a self-understanding is obviously apt to revert to the dualism of the unhappy consciousness. Even when the anticipations are partially – but always only partially – con-

---

[41] That all thinking is determined by anticipation would have to be elaborated in relation to the function of the productive imagination for thought, as was already seen in Kant's critique of reason.

firmed, experience and anticipated reality (in its totality at that time) can still fall apart. The fore-conception easily falls under the suspicion of being empty yearning. And the yearning threatens to unmask it as an expression of a self-alienated subjectivity.

The dualism of the unhappy consciousness, which believes itself separated by its finitude from the truly real, falls into untruth because the agreement of consciousness and reality and thus the presence of truth are presupposed even in the consciousness of its lack. The insight about the thorough-going anticipatory structure of all thought can be maintained only on the condition that consciousness can nevertheless be certain of the presence of the truth. If it is correct, however, that we have access to the truth only in anticipation, then the truth's presence can be conceived, from its side, only as an anticipation in the sense of a pre-appearance [*Vorschein*] of that which has ultimate validity and of the whole constituted by the end of all history. Nevertheless, it would not necessarily call into question the presence of the truth if there should be given an experience of a pre-appearance of the ultimate which so far has not been superseded and which is at least not involved in any inherent necessity of being superseded. There would prove to be a pre-appearance of this sort if there were one which would not be superseded, but would rather, as the entrance of the ultimate into history, constitute its wholeness from that point. But this statement is again an anticipation whose validity can only be proven in the future. Until then, the difference between a pre-appearance and the ultimate, which is inherent in the fact that the former is the appearance of the latter, will be mirrored by the anticipation of that which appears in a pre-appearance, in such a way that such anticipations will anticipate the ultimate truth of events as the definitive *arrival*-in-pre-appearance [*Zum-Vorscheingekommensein*] of the ultimate.[42]

Thus, on the basis of the experience of something that has

---

[42] A more precise discussion of the concept of appearance which is only sketched here can be found in "Appearance as the Arrival of the Future" (see above, n. 39).

not yet been surpassed and is not inherently subject to being surpassed, and is even an inherently exclusive pre-appearance of the ultimate, there can be a consciousness that understands itself as anticipatory through and through without thereby losing the presence of truth and being stricken with the impasses of the uneasy consciousness. It would then know itself to be supported in the process of its anticipatory movement by the presence of the ultimate – and only in that way. Thus, it has its essence and its truth by and in itself only in going beyond itself, since it is anticipatorily referred to the ultimate that transcends it.

III

In line with what has just been said, the reflections of the preceding section may be understood as an attempt to ponder the implications for ontology, epistemology and the philosophy of history of the peculiar anticipatory structure of the ministry and destiny of Jesus of Nazareth, occasioned by a philosophical situation whose own problems seem to converge upon such a solution. I hope that the admission of the dependence of my philosophical reflections upon Christian presuppositions will not prejudice the possibility of their being discussed philosophically, since these presuppositions have not been introduced directly as arguments but belong only to – as Ernst Topitsch puts it – the psychology of the process of investigation. It is not only the logic of anticipation articulated here that leads to the conclusion that philosophical reflection constantly presupposes a religious basis. This conclusion has also been established again and again by philosophers, with particular emphasis on Hegel in relation to the Christian tradition. To be sure, Hegel coupled this conclusion with the conviction that philosophical thought, as a self-positing concept, must go beyond the religious representations from which it arises. If, however, thinking is accomplished essentially by means of anticipations; if every concept is in truth a fore-conception and only the fore-conception reflected in it is the true "concept"; then it is possible to see through the misguided opinion that pure thought is constituted by itself and must therefore in every case transcend its religious presuppositions. Rather, it belongs to the nature of fore-conception that the thing it pre-conceives allows itself to be pre-given, not indeed as something which is merely future, but rather in the way in which the future-ultimate [*das Zukünftig-Endgültige*] is the truth of everything present and past, and is thus already present itself. Mythical thought, it is true, distorts the coming ultimate into a primordially perfect archetype. Critical thought rightly departs from these mythical archetypes since in forming a fore-conception of something not presently on hand it distances itself reflectively from everything given. On the other hand, reflectively liberated critical thought will not succeed in surpassing its own religiously grounded tradition, to which it is related critically, at the point in the process of criticism at which the absent truth to which thought reaches out in fore-conception is shown to be the genuine truth of the tradition itself. In this case, the critical process surpasses only the previous *interpretation* of the content of the tradition, and does so precisely by releasing its deeper truth. This will be even more the case where motives of self-criticism continually grow out of the religious tradition itself which is in question. This was shown above to be true of the hermeneutical process of the history of Christianity with regard to the fact that the ultimate and universal that was anticipated in the ministry of Jesus and in his history supplied the motive for requisitioning every new experience to test itself, and thus it for ever after forced the transformation of the forms of the Christian tradition which had until then been considered valid.

But to what extent have ultimate reality and truth so appeared in the public ministry [*Auftreten*] and destiny of Jesus that as yet no new experiences have surpassed it and every new experience of the meaning of what appeared in Jesus has, rather, been immediately claimed for the sake of revising earlier, time-bound interpretations of the Christ-event? The answer to this question is to be sought in the peculiar, eschato-logical character of the history of Jesus. It is necessary, first of all, to reflect upon the content of the eschatological expectations that formed the horizon of the ministry of Jesus, the modification of which resulted in an understanding of his history which determined the original form of the message about Christ. The expectation of the coming reign of God must be mentioned here, above all, since it includes the other eschatological motifs – such as, the hope of the resurrection of the dead and the renewal of the creation, as well as the prospect of final judgment. Conviction about the nearness of the coming reign of God constituted the basis of Jesus' own message. It was directed toward the coming God as the ultimate future of the world through which the totality of the world and its history would become manifest. In this connection, the relief it was hoped God's reign would bring from the consequences of the final judgment meant at the same time the realization of justice and righteousness among men. The latter was in fact the content of the will of God that was revealed to Israel, and this will finds its fulfillment where God reigns. Thus, through the reign of God, the ordering of human society is brought to its true, human destination for the first time. This is why the Book of Daniel characterized the kingdom of God by the symbol of a man, in contrast to the animal symbols which symbolize the essence of different world kingdoms. The idea that the reign of God realizes the humanity of man accounts for the fact that the hope of the kingdom of God was bound to that of the resurrection of the dead. This metaphor indicates that the destination of individuals is not exhausted in the service of a social order that has become autonomous in relation to them. Indeed, it is much more the case that the height of the development of a civilization is to be seen in the degree of freedom and of human fulfillment it guarantees to individuals. Therefore, a perfected society of the future in which the individuals of previous generations had no share would not be a comprehensive fulfillment of human destination, nor a perfect society, either. On the other hand, the resurrection of the dead, which is supposed to bring to men who open themselves to God's future and to his reign both full possession of the undying life of God and the fulfillment of their human destination, the wholeness in which salvation consists, is expected as an event at the end of history in which all recipients of this salvation will share. Individuals can attain salvation [*Heil*], the fulfillment of their human destination, only in a social mode.

The anticipations of the eschaton which are bound up with the expectation of the coming reign of God, among which are to be reckoned chiefly the transformation and renewal of the creation as well as the idea of judgment, anticipate the end of history that accompanies the kingdom of God (which is what first made possible the idea of a universal history). Taken together, these two anticipations express the realization of the corporate destination of mankind in union with the destination of the individual and in connection with nature, which it was hoped God's reign would bring. Eschatological expectation had to do not with any sort of tangential and dispensable extravagances, but with the humanity of man himself, and that can receive its perfection only through God and his reign because it has its origin in him.

In the light of such anticipations of the eschaton, it becomes possible to make projections of preliminary fulfillments of human existence in individual as well as social life. These must not be confused with the eschatological consummation, but should be striven for as preliminary realizations of a form of human existence worthy of man. It is disgraceful and shocking that often – and especially in recent history – it has been just such confusion, that is to say, by a secularization of the eschatological hope, that released energies for the realization of the human progress that was possible at a given time. However, the confusion of preliminary projections with the eschatological consummation led without fail to disillusionment and violence. Thus, secular utopias, championed as political programs, become blind to their own provisionality and onesidedness, as for example, the history of Marxism shows. Its alleged finality reacted upon individuals as spiritual coercion until ecstasy vanished and disillusionment took its place. It is a different story where the difference between all human projection and the eschatological destination of man beyond death to a life under the rule of God is not forgotten. Here, all projecting of inner-worldly integration is sobered by the consciousness of its provisionality. Thus, tolerance is retained toward those who think otherwise. Yet, rightly understood, Christian faith in the presence of the coming reign of God in and through Jesus Christ constantly releases impulses toward transforming any given present which suppress the tendency toward flight from the world that always lies close to such sobriety. Thus, eschatological consciousness has a twofold political relevance: with regard to the difference between the eschatological destination and the present world, it drives toward altering present circumstances; and it nevertheless guards against identification of the consummation with the particular change being striven for.

The last sentences already imply the specifically Christian brand of eschatological consciousness which is most intimately related to the finality of Jesus. It is characteristic of Jesus' message about the nearness of the reign of God that the eschatological future of this reign does not remain a distant beyond,[43] but rather becomes a power determining the present without thereby losing its futurity. For this reason, Jesus himself stepped forward claiming the authority of the reign of God which he nevertheless preached as future. In this way, the present became eschatologically qualified without thereby becoming closed to the future. Its eschatological quality consisted much more in its being determined by the future of God, and therefore being involved in the movement of ever renewed transformation. This is the evidence that what appeared in the public ministry and history of Jesus is unsurpassable.

It is true that the unsurpassability of the history of Jesus as the revelation of God was not yet decided by his earthly ministry, but by the event his disciples proclaimed as his resurrection. The earthly ministry of Jesus was burdened with an

---

[43] A future which is only set in opposition to the present in a dualistic way cannot be the basis of the wholeness or salvation of the present world and the men of the present. Rather, it can at most signify the negativity and – with the entrance of that future – the negation of everything, past and present.

ambiguity that was dispelled for the first time by his death and resurrection. Since his message that the present age was already wholly determined by the nearness of the reign of God already brought about this nearness of God with it, the one who proclaimed this message inevitably had to claim for himself the authority of God. This claim stood in sharp contrast to the authority of the Jewish law, which could be discharged only by the dawning of the reign of God itself. Jesus' fore-conception of this future, which he announced as an imminently arriving final event, would have been surpassed by its delay if it had not been – according to the testimony of his disciples – that the resurrection of the dead, which Jewish apocalyptic expected as an event of the last days, likewise appeared – in him, at any rate. It is true that so far this event has happened only in the case of Jesus, contrary to the Jewish expectation, shared by Jesus, which was oriented toward the resurrection of all men to face the judgment, or of all the righteous to participation in the life of God. To this extent, the event of the resurrection of Jesus is itself only an anticipation of the end, not the end itself. Its difference from the eschatological future of the general resurrection is nevertheless only a quantitative, not a qualitative one. For in the resurrection of Jesus, the eschatological reality itself became an event that occurred in him in advance. For this reason, the anticipation of the end in the way it occurred in the resurrection of Jesus is no longer surpassable by any inner-worldly event. Rather, the question of its truth is decided only by the occurrence – or non-arrival – of the general resurrection, which is now no longer bound to any fixed day of an imminent expectation.[44]

It is by means of such unsurpassability that the anticipatory meaning of Jesus' resurrection is distinguished from the prophetic anticipations of a future to be ushered in by God, of which

[44] Consciousness of the nearness of God, to whose coming reign faith is oriented, no longer has to be bound to a chronological form of imminent expectation just because now the nearness of God in Jesus has been definitively confirmed and has become accessible even to distant and later generations through the transmission of the tradition of what happened through and to Jesus.

Israel lived in hope, and which was also the context in which Jesus' ministry itself was accomplished. The prophetic announcements of historical events were always surpassed again by their "fulfillment," because the events declared to be the fulfillment only approximately, and hardly ever exactly, coincided with their corresponding prophetic announcements. And such "fulfillments" as the return of the exiles from Babylon to Jerusalem were also surpassed again because the flow of history brought with it new needs and new tasks. The difference between the prophetic promises of an ultimate, future salvation and the reality of final fulfillment which they intended can be recognized already by the fact that they employ metaphorical language. This applies to the eschatological language of the preaching of Jesus, too. But that which was declared in the language of metaphor already became a living presence in the preaching of Jesus and was completely so in his resurrection. To be sure, in speaking of the reality present in and through Jesus, one can again employ only eschatological metaphors or fore-conceptions which still lack complete definiteness. We do not yet have definitive knowledge of what really happened in the ministry and destiny of Jesus. But this reservation itself belongs to the ultimacy of that event. It was the only way possible, in the midst of the historical relativity of ongoing time and of the knowledge which is bound to it, for knowledge of the meaning warranted by the destiny of Jesus to remain non-definitive.

Within the horizon of primitive Christian thought, the resurrection of Jesus signified that the end of history had already taken place in him, so that his pre-Easter claim that the final destiny of each man is decided by their relationship to him and his message, has now been confirmed – in an unforseen form, to be sure. But because the end of history that was to have been ushered in by the coming reign of God has already become a present reality in the ministry and destiny of Jesus so that the wholeness, the essence of all events and of every human life is decided in relation to him, the Christian tradition can speak of the ultimate revelation of God in Jesus.

It is not quite decisive for this claim that in general Jesus' ministry and history cry out to be understood, in the light of the final destination of man, as the anticipation of the future salvation of mankind in the light of the coming reign of God. It may indeed be the case that living in fore-conception of the future is a basic and universal feature of human existence, and may, in one way or another, perhaps even be constitutive for all beings whatever. But in the destiny of Jesus the end of history occurred in advance in a way which is no longer qualitatively different from its proper reality. It was on account of this specific form of anticipation that primitive Christianity could proclaim that Jesus was the eschatological revealer of God. It is true that primitive Christianity, under the pressure of the imminent eschatological expectation that still prevailed within it, had hardly reflected upon the merely anticipatory character of the event that took place in Jesus. One rather understood the resurrection as the onset of the end event itself. However, the eschatological horizon of the public ministry of Jesus and the significance of his destiny were lost in the following generations. Their rediscovery by means of historical exegesis about eighty years ago at first made the figure of Jesus appear so strange to the present age that this knowledge was widely felt to be unbearable. The attempts of theology to circumvent this knowledge in order to be able to rescue the relevance of Jesus for the present time extend right down to Bultmann's new existentialist construction of the temporally intended primitive Christian eschatology. Nevertheless, it is just this, at first sight so seemingly alien, basically apocalyptic characteristic of the ministry and destiny of Jesus that, by means of its anticipatory structure, can become the key to solving a fundamental question facing philosophical reflection in the problematic post-Hegelian situation in which we still seem to be involved. It is possible to find in the history of Jesus an answer to the question of how "the whole" of reality and its meaning can be conceived without compromising the provisionality and historical relativity of all thought, as well as openness to the future on the part of the thinker who knows himself to be only on the way and not yet at the goal.

6

WHAT IS A DOGMATIC STATEMENT?

This essay was originally a lecture delivered at a joint conference of a Protestant and a Roman Catholic ecumenical work group on March 22, 1961, in Paderborn. It was first published in *KuD* 8 (1962), pp. 81–99.

I. DOGMATICS AND DOGMA

To ask about the peculiar character of dogmatic statements from a Protestant point of view already presupposes that Protestant theology really permits of being understood as dogmatics. This presupposition was variously disputed by Neo-Protestantism. It was said that dogma, as ecclesiastically sanctioned doctrinal law, was something specifically Catholic, and that therefore a science of dogma was impossible in Protestant theology, except in a merely historical sense and not as dogmatics. This was the view of Adolf von Harnack, Wilhelm Herrmann, and Ernst Troeltsch, among others. Today, such misgivings seem for the most part to have subsided.[1] Explicit reference to dogmatics in the full sense of that term, as an enterprise related to dogma, is widespread. In this connection, the words "dogma" and "confession" are usually used synonymously.[2] Thus, dogma is understood as essentially church dogma,

---

[1] The late Paul Tillich rejected the concept of dogma on somewhat different grounds. According to Tillich, this expression has been discredited by the "demonic activities of states and churches, Catholic as well as Protestant, against theological honesty and scientific autonomy" (*Systematic Theology* [Chicago: University of Chicago Press and Welwyn: James Nisbet, 1951], I, p. 32).

[2] Werner Elert, *Der christliche Glaube: Grundlinien der lutherischen Dogmatik* (Hamburg, ³1956), p. 39. (As dogma, the confession expresses the "mandatory content [*Sollgehalt*] of church proclamation" [p. 49]); Heinrich Vogel, *Gott in Christo* (Berlin, 1951), pp. 37ff.; Otto Weber, *Grundlagen der Dogmatik*

as the church's "answer"[3] to the revelation of God. It "formulates" the insight given by revelation and mediated by the biblical witnesses (Prenter); it is "the known and confessed truth of the Word of Holy Scripture heard and believed by the church" (Vogel). On the other hand, revelation itself is not designated as dogma but as the norm set over dogma, the criterion of dogma.[4] In a similar way, the Formula of Concord had already said that Holy Scripture is "the sole rule and norm of all doctrine" [*pro unica regula et norma omnium dogmatum*], to which everything must be subjected.[5] Barth can even formulate the definition of dogma as the agreement with revelation demanded of the dogmas of the church as answering to this: "Dogma is the agreement of the church's proclamation with the revelation attested in Scripture."[6] The concept of revelation is hereby conceived more narrowly than in Roman Catholic usage. It is limited to Jesus Christ himself.

It is characteristic of the evangelical understanding of dogma and dogmatics that it sets revelation, as an independent judiciary court of highest appeal, over against the doctrine and preaching of the church. This opposition remains unchanged even when revelation itself is designated as the dogma of God, following ancient church usage.[7] For in this case one distin-

(Neukirchen Kreis Moers, 1955), 1, p. 43; Edmund Schlink, *The Coming Christ and the Coming Church* (Philadelphia: Fortress Press, 1968), p. 34; Regin Prenter, *Creation and Redemption*, tr. Theodor I. Jenson (Philadelphia: Fortress Press, 1967), the proposition of sec. 1, p. 3; Gerhard Gloege, article on "Dogmatik," *RGG*[3] 2, pp. 224f. Paul Althaus, in *Die christliche Wahrheit* (Gütersloh, [3]1952), p. 242, expresses himself more cautiously because he is primarily concerned with the *present* "sum of the faith-knowledge of the church rendered accessible in God's revelation."

[3] Thus, for example, Vogel, *Gott in Christo*, pp. 68ff.; Schlink, *The Coming Christ*, pp. 18, 28f., passim; G. Gloege, *RGG*[3], 2, p. 222.

[4] Vogel, *Gott in Christo*, pp. 62f., 73; Weber, *Grundlagen der Dogmatik*, 1, p. 49.

[5] Solid Declaration, Summary Formulation (*BC*, p. 505).

[6] *CD* 1, p. 304.

[7] Cf. Otto Ritschl, *Dogmengeschichte des Protestantismus* (Leipzig, 1908), 1, pp. 16ff. on Origen *In Mt.* 12, sec. 23 (cf. *Origenes Werke*, vol. 10, ed. E. Klostermann [Leipzig, 1935], p. 122), and Chrysostom, Homily 29 on 1 Cor. 12:1 (see *The Nicene and Post-Nicene Fathers*, ed. Philip Schaff, Second Series [Buffalo: Christian Literature Publishing Co., 1885–90], 12, p. 175 [reprint

guishes, with Origen, between the "doctrines of God" [*dogmata theou*] and the "instructions of the church" [*logoi ekklesiastikoi*]. The task of dogmatics and, thus, of "dogmatic" statements in the broader sense, derives from this distinction. It has to raise the question of the agreement of dogmas with revelation, of the dogmas of the church with the one dogma of God, and make this question the object of methodical investigation. Thus, dogmatics carries out ever new testing of dogma,[8] "critical interpretation of dogma."[9] At the same time, the critical task of dogmatics has a positive side in that it seeks to show the basis in revelation of the statements of dogma. In so doing, its attention is not only directed to the given dogma, but in that it tests the basis of this in revelation, it already includes a "new inquiry after dogma."[10]

2. THE RELATIONSHIP OF THE DOGMATIC TASK TO SCRIPTURE

The evangelical understanding of dogma and dogmatics is characterized by its intimate relationship to Scripture. The confrontation of church dogmas with revelation has the concrete form of their being bound to Scripture. The Formula of Concord already put it in this way in the sentence cited above (p. 141, n. 5).

It is significant that the oldest Protestant dogmatics, Melanchthon's *Loci Communes* of 1521, was conceived as a summary of the testimony of Scripture. Here, no distinction had as yet been made between dogmatics and what we think of

---

of Edinburgh ed.; reissued by Eerdmans Publishing Co., 1959] = J. P. Migne, *Patrologia cursus completus, Series Graeca,* 161 Vols. [Paris, 1857ff.], 61, p. 250).

[8] Elert, *Der christliche Glaube,* p. 39.

[9] Weber, *Grundlagen der Dogmatik,* 1, pp. 54f.; Prenter, *Creation and Redemption,* p. 5.

[10] Althaus, *Die christliche Wahrheit,* p. 245. According to Weber, dogmatics inquires "*today* (into) *what has become* dogma, in order that the church *tomorrow* may be prepared for *new* decision" (*Grundlagen der Dogmatik,* 1, p. 56). See also, Schlink, *The Coming Christ,* p. 34.

today as the task of New Testament theology. For Melanchthon, dogmatics was concerned with the "fundamental truths" [*loci*] from which the whole of revelation and theology was suspended.[11] Paul's epistle to the Romans was regarded by Melanchthon as a model for a "compendium of Christian doctrine" [*doctrinae christianae compendium*].[12] Calvin formulated the purpose of his 1536 *Institutes of the Christian Religion* in a similar way. He wrote in the preface to the French edition of 1541 that it should assist in finding "the sum of what God wished to teach us in his Word."[13]

It may be questioned whether this definition of the task of dogmatics as a synopsis of the contents of Scripture does not really oversimplify the relationship between the exegetical and dogmatic tasks. There are many problems involved in the word "synopsis" which we shall have to deal with later. Above all, we shall have to ask about the unity of the contents of Scripture themselves, which is what makes something like a synopsis possible in the first place and, beyond this, is a condition for the systematic character of dogmatic statements.

The definition of dogmatics as a synopsis of the witness of Scripture functions primarily to bring out once again the relationship between dogma and dogmatics. Even dogma is "the sum [*Inbegriff*] of the faith-knowledge of the church rendered accessible in God's revelation,"[14] as Althaus formulates it. And the Formula of Concord justified its undertaking by saying that the unity of the church required a "summary formulation" [*compendaria forma*] of doctrine. The ancient church devised its symbols for just this purpose [*in talem usum*].[15] This comes close to the conception of dogma in Catholic theology as expounded

---

[11] "On what topics the whole scheme hangs" (*The Loci Communes of Philip Melanchthon*, tr. and intro. Charles Leander Hill [Boston: Meador Publishing Co., 1944], p. 66 (. . . *e quibus locis rerum summa pendeat; Corpus Reformatorum* 21, p. 84).

[12] *Ibid.*, p. 69 (= *Corpus Reformatorum* 21, p. 85).

[13] On this and the similar expression found in the preface to the Latin edition of 1559 see Wilhelm Niesel, *The Theology of Calvin*, tr. Harold Knight (Philadelphia: Westminster Press, 1956), p. 23.

[14] See above, n. 2.

[15] Solid Declaration, Summary Formulation sec. 1 (*BC*, pp. 503ff.).

by Johannes E. Kuhn, according to which dogma – exemplarily in the Apostles' Creed – provides a "brief synopsis" of the whole of Christian doctrine, the "quintessence of the preaching of all the apostles."[16] Since Scripture and tradition coincide in substance, according to Kuhn,[17] fixed tradition contained in confessions of faith does not differ in content from the witness of Scripture, but only in its form as a synopsis of its essential contents.

For Protestant theology, the normative character of Scripture follows from what has just been said. If dogma and dogmatics have the task of summarizing the content of the apostolic preaching expressed in Scripture, then obviously they cannot add some supplementary content to Scripture, but must remain open to critical review and modification in the light of Scripture.

This inference by no means signifies an underrating of tradition. The traditional view of the *sola scriptura* principle as standing in opposition to tradition generally is no longer tenable on evangelical grounds because research has shown that the scriptural witness itself has to be understood as the precipitate of a history of the transmission of tradition and not as something somehow immediately conceived by its authors, even if by the direct dictation of the Holy Spirit. The origin of Scripture is to be conceived as a process of tradition,[18] and, indeed, in connection with the total process of transmitting the Christian tradition, whose responsible bearer is the church. But in this whole process of the transmission of Christian tradition, the rise of the New Testament writings and their consolidation into a canon constitutes a fundamental break which structures the whole process insofar as all subsequent tradition of the Christ-event is mediated by this written witness and is accomplished

---

[16] Documentation may be found in J. R. Geiselmann, *Die Lebendige Überlieferung als Norm des christlichen Glaubens, dargestellt in Geiste der Traditionslehre Joh. Ev. Kuhns* (Freiburg, 1959), p. 117.   [17] *Ibid.*, p. 158.

[18] This has been shown with regard to the dogmatic conception of Scripture by Kristen E. Skydsgaard in his "Schrift und Tradition, Bemerkungen zum Traditionsproblem in der neueren Theologie," *KuD* 1 (1955), pp. 161–179. "Before there was Scripture, there was tradition" (*ibid.*, p. 170).

in confrontation with it. Thus, the confrontation between the church's post-biblical confessions of faith and dogmatic formulations, on the one hand, and Scripture as their common norm, on the other, takes shape within the total process of Christian tradition and determines its structure.[19]

3. THE CONCEPT OF SCRIPTURE PRESUPPOSED BY THE EVANGELICAL UNDERSTANDING OF THE TASK OF DOGMATICS

If all dogmatic statements, as synopses of the contents of Scripture, are to be grounded in Scripture and testable by it, then this presupposes not only the authority of Scripture in a general sense, but also that the revelation of God is completely expressed by it, at least insofar as is necessary for man's salvation. Furthermore, it presupposes that the unity of this content can be grasped clearly and distinctly through the testimony of Scripture.

If Scripture were not complete with respect to content, it could not be the rule of all statements of faith. The fundamental principle of the sufficiency of Scripture for the content of all theological statements stood in the foreground of the theological controversies of the sixteenth and seventeenth centuries. The point in question was whether Holy Scripture contained the Word of God in its entirety or whether its contents were capable of or in need of supplementation by oral tradition. The polemical situation seems to have changed on this point. The substantive sufficiency of Scripture seems no longer to be or to need to be the chief thesis in the evangelical doctrine of Scripture which the Catholic side is compelled to dispute, nor is there any fundamental objection on the Protestant side today to the intertwining of Scripture and tradition. The Tübingen school of Catholic theology, especially Johannes E. Kuhn, developed a concept of tradition which recognized and presupposed the

---

[19] Skydsgaard judges: "Scripture is certainly not (temporally) prior to tradition. But within the tradition it has to exericse the office of a guardian," viz., as "the absolutely primordial witness of the tradition" (*ibid.*, pp. 177f.).

sufficiency of Scripture with regard to content, without denying the fact that the New Testament witnesses have to be viewed as occasional writings for the most part, and do not aim at being complete presentations of the content of revelation. Here, later tradition is viewed not as completing the content of Scripture, but as having a purely hermeneutical function – although, in fact, this was already the predominant conception in Scholasticism. [20]

Thus, the hermeneutical question has become the actual focal point of theological dialogue dealing with controversy about the meaning of the authority of Scripture. The Reformation solution to this problem was stated in the thesis about the clarity of Scripture. Only if the essential content of Scripture follows clearly and distinctly from its words can Scripture really exercise the function of the supreme norm and guideline of all dogmatic statements.

The fact that Scripture is clear in itself with respect to its essential content was the decisive reason why, in the judgment of the Reformers, it did not allow any independent factor confronting it from the outside to decide its interpretation. In the famous words of Luther, in his 1520 *Defense and Explanation of all the Articles etc.*, Scripture is "of itself most certain, easy to understand, and reliable, interpreting itself, (and so) proving, judging and explaining all other (writings) in everything." [21] A few years later, in *The Bondage of the Will* (1525), Luther explained his thesis about the clarity of Scripture in more detail, expressly contradicting Erasmus' assertion that Scripture is obscure and therefore needs an authoritative teaching office for its interpretation. Against this view, Luther emphasized the clarity of Scripture with respect to its principal content. More precisely, he distinguished between two kinds of clarity. On the one hand, there was the inner clarity which was experienced in the heart, made one certain of personal salvation, and was bestowed only by means of the Holy Spirit. The outer clarity, on the other

[20] Josef Finkzeller, *Offenbarung und Theologie nach der Lehre des Johannes Duns Scotus* (Münster in Westfalen, 1960), pp. 6off.

[21] *WA* 7, p. 97 [Tr. mine – Tr.; see above, p. 62, n. 122].

hand, consisted in the unambiguity and uncontrovertibility of the essential content of Scripture whose exposition and defense were charged to the ministry of the word [*ministerium verbi*].[22] With respect to the outer clarity of Scripture, it is true to say that the meaning of Scripture can be presented in such a way that its opponents, using "the judgment of common sense,"[23] will be unable to bring any serious objection against it. On the basis of the outer clarity of Scripture, the public preaching office, to which the office of theologian also belonged, could, for Luther, "judge the spirits and doctrines of all men, also with the greatest certainty, and now not only for ourselves only, but also for the benefit and salvation of others,"[24] i.e., in order to strengthen the weak in faith and to refute its opponents.[25]

The older Lutheran dogmatics upheld Luther's distinction. Johann Gerhard concluded from it that even those hearers of the Word who were not filled with the Holy Spirit could attain a proper, if not also liberating and saving, knowledge of the content of Scripture: "Indeed, those who are not yet illumined by the Holy Spirit are able to hold the dogmas of Scripture as known and to maintain a historical faith through the external ministry of the Word, although fully assured, certain, sound and saving knowledge cannot be obtained without the interior illumination of the mind by the Holy Spirit."[26] One might

[22] *Martin Luther on "The Bondage of the Will,"* tr. J. I. Packer and O. R. Johnston (London: James Clarke and Co., Ltd., 1957), p. 71 (= *WA* 18, 609).

[23] *Ibid.,* p. 130 (= *WA* 18, 656: *communis sensus iudicio*[!]).

[24] *Ibid.,* p. 125 (= *WA* 18, p. 653, ll. 22ff.).

[25] Rudolf Hermann, *Von der Klarheit der Heiligen Schrift: Untersuchungen und Erörterungen über Luthers Lehre von der Schrift in De Servo Arbitrio* (Berlin, 1958), has provided a very comprehensive interpretation of this idea of Luther's. Despite the misgivings expressed by Hermann on pp. 49ff. and 70ff. against certain of Luther's formulations in relation to this theme, the fundamental significance of the outer clarity of Scripture for the Reformation should not be overlooked, in any event. It was not an appeal to the Spirit (whether in the individual or in the congregation) that led Luther to his criticism of Rome, but the authority of Scripture.

[26] [*Possunt quidem nondum a spiritu sancto collustrati cognita habere scripturarum dogmata, fidemque historicam tenere per externum verbi ministerium at plerophorian certam, solidam ac salutarem notitiam habere non possunt sine spiritu sancto interius mentes illuminante,* Loci Theologici, I (Tübingen, 1762), p. 52 (Locus 2)].

question here whether such a formulation of the outer clarity of
Scripture, which concedes to unbelievers an *ability* to know, is
still in accord with Luther's view. It was not without reason,
after all, that Luther coordinated the outer clarity of Scripture
with the ministry of the Word as a weapon to silence unbelievers. And it is one thing to be reduced to silence so that one
can no longer convincingly object, and another also to possess
even a limited ability. Furthermore, the outer clarity of
Scripture must have some connection with the inner – a
tendency toward the inner, toward the illumination of the
heart – if it is the case that the outer Word bears the Spirit in
itself. In any event, Gerhard maintained that the historical
faith [*fides historica*] (or, as it was called elsewhere, the literal
sense of Scripture) becomes compelling for every man through
itself without the additional condition of some higher form of
understanding. So it was also held during the Rahtmann
controversy (Danzig, 1621–1628), from which Lutheran theologians drew strength against the opinions of early Pietism,
according to which an additional illumination by the Spirit
was necessary to enable one to understand the content of
Scripture. The Spirit works only through the Word itself,
namely, where the Word is trustingly received and one is
brought to silence before it (by the ministry of the word
[*ministerium verbi*]), and that not only as an opponent.

Now what is the content (the *res*) of Scripture which is made
manifest by its clarity? Luther speaks of the *res* in the plural:
Incarnation, substitutionary suffering, and heavenly reign of
Christ, all revealed by his resurrection.[27] He further speaks of
the trinitarian and christological dogmas as objects of the outer
clarity of Scripture.[28] All the contents of Scripture are ultimately concentrated in one thing, however, viz. in Christ:
"Take Christ from the Scriptures – and what more will you
find in them?"[29] For this reason, Luther calls it the true touch-

---

[27] *The Bondage of the Will*, p. 71 (= *WA* 18, p. 606).
[28] *Ibid.*, pp. 73f. (= *WA* 18, pp. 608f.).
[29] *Ibid.*, p. 71 (= *WA* 18, p. 606: *Tolle Christum e scripturis, quid amplius in illis invenies?*).

stone "by which to judge all books, when we see whether they deal with Christ or not."[30] Luther asserts that it is only the central context and not every word of the Bible that is transparently intelligible. He even concedes that there are unclear sentences in Scripture. Nevertheless, its essential content is clear, and if the words are sometimes obscure in places, this same central content is all the more clearly expressed in many other places.[31]

According to Gerhard's conception, too, the literal sense [*sensus literalis*] of Scripture, or "historical faith" [*fides historica*], deals throughout with the central dogmatic content of the Bible, i.e., with the "dogmas of Scripture" [*scripturarum dogmata*]. This corresponds to the statement of the Augsburg Confession that the knowledge of the resurrection of Jesus also belongs to the historical faith which even the devil and unbelievers have.[32] Here, as with Luther, no fundamental distinction is drawn between a historical husk and a dogmatic kernel of the scriptural content. The only thing the unbeliever does not see is the "for me" [*pro me*] aspect of the event attested by Scripture, the article concerning the forgiveness of sins.

The dogmatic significance of the results of historical-exegetical study of Scripture follows immediately from Luther's doctrine of the outer clarity of Scripture, the heart of which is his conviction of its self-evident nature. The dogmatic content of Scripture must be demonstrable by means of historical arguments. This is the true "significance of the critical historical method for church and theology in Protestantism."[33]

---

[30] *The Works of Martin Luther*, 6 vols. (Philadelphia: A. J. Holman Co. and Castle Press, 1930), p. 478 (= *WA*, Deutsche Bibel 7, p. 384).

[31] *The Bondage of the Will*, p. 71 (= *WA* 18, p. 606).

[32] Art. 20, sec. 23 (*BC*, p. 44).

[33] Gerhard Ebeling in his essay with this very title (*Word and Faith* [London: SCM Press and Philadelphia: Fortress Press, 1963], pp. 17–61) arrives at a highly paradoxical answer to the problem formulated by the theme when he states that the significance of historical research is to be seen in its "shattering of all historical assurances that supposedly render the decision of faith superfluous" (*ibid.*, p. 56). Nevertheless, the factual connection in cultural history between the Reformation and the rise of historical

4. THE PROBLEM OF THE UNITY OF SCRIPTURE

The clarity of Scripture as a presupposition of the Protestant understanding of dogmatic statements is not to be separated from the unity of Scripture. It is precisely its clarity that opens up a vista of its essential and harmonious content. It is this content which then makes it possible for the first time to raise he question of the sufficiency of Scripture in a meaningful way.

The unity of Scripture was so self-evident for classical Protestant dogmatics that it did not even stress it as a special property of Scripture. In substance, Protestant dogmatics expressed this idea in the principle of the mutual non-contradictoriness of all the passages of Scripture. This principle was put into practice in orthodox Scriptural exegesis by means of the hermeneutical schema of the analogy of faith [*analogia fidei*]. Thus, the unity of Scripture was understood as the doctrinal unity of its statements, whose implicit systematic connections needed only to be made visible by a corresponding systematic arrangement.

There was no polemical problem on this point, but modern historical research certainly did pose one for both Protestant and Catholic theology. Protestant theology had to be particularly sensitive to this problem since in its case exegesis itself, working under the aegis of the literal or historical sense [*sensus literalis seu historicus*] – in other words, the clarity of Scripture! – had led to the dissolution of the unity of Scripture in the traditional sense.

In the Protestant sphere, the dissolution of the unity of Scripture in the sense of a doctrinal unity must be judged as a theologically legitimate turn of events. The procedure of classical Protestant dogmatics, which secured the unity of Scripture by means of a summary of doctrine oriented toward a specific set of scriptural sayings to which the rest were coordinated in keeping with the fundamental maxim of the analogy of faith, must in fact lead to the undermining of the

criticism ought rather to be seen as residing in the task of establishing a positive basis for theology in scriptural exegesis.

normative character of Scripture. Hermann Diem rightly concludes on this matter, "but it became ever more dubious how Scripture was in practice to fulfill this function of arbitration if from the outset it was presupposed that its interpretation must correspond with a specific *summa doctrinae* [sum of doctrine]."[34] As historical investigation of Scripture progressed, the biblicistic harmonizing procedure of interpretation controlled by the analogy of faith became increasingly questionable, and its distance from the literal sense of Scripture, which according to it was supposed to be normative, became ever clearer. Historical research showed that the contradictionless doctrinal unity which had been presupposed was not in fact present in the New Testament writings. The New Testament witnesses not only contradict themselves on details, such as in the accounts of the day of Jesus' death, but in addition they exhibit considerable differences and even contradictions in the theological conceptions that occasionally leave their imprint on an entire book and cannot be removed from its individual formulations. These contradictions cannot be understood as complementary parts of an organic unity. At least this much has become clear since the New Testament research of the Tübingen school of F. C. Baur. More recently, the essays of Philip Vielhauer on the Acts of the Apostles[35] and of Ernst Käsemann on the Second Letter of Peter[36] have brought such contradictions to light and have linked the question of the unity of the canon to this phenomenon. Last year (1960), this question was discussed further by Marxsen and Ratschow in the *Zeitschrift für systematischer Theologie*. The most recent work on the theological outlooks of the individual evangelists reveals the differences among them – not only between the Synoptics on the one side and John on the other, but between, say, Matthew and Luke – ever more

[34] *Dogmatics*, tr. Harold Knight (Edinburgh and London: Oliver and Boyd, 1959), p. 167.

[35] "Zum Paulinismus der Apostelgeschichte," *EvTh* 10 (1950/51), pp. 1ff.

[36] "An Apologia for Primitive Christian Eschatology," in *Essays on New Testament Themes*, tr. W. J. Montague, Studies in Biblical Theology, No. 41 (London: SCM Press and Naperville, Ill.: Alec R. Allenson, Inc., 1964), pp. 169–95.

clearly. Thus, the assertion of a doctrinal unity of the biblical witnesses has been made impossible by the work of critical historical research. But does not Scripture thereby lose its ability to be the norm of theology? It seems as if one must choose between one or another form of New Testament witness. The canon provides the basis – as the now famous word of Käsemann expressed it,[37] – not for the unity of the church but for the multiplicity of the confessions. The unity of the content of Scripture (*res scripturae*) which, for Luther, was intimately related to the clarity of Scripture, is hardly visible any longer among the differentiation of the witnesses.

In this situation, the call is frequently raised for a canon within the canon, a material center which could be used to measure the individual sayings of the different witnesses. Such a material norm was known in classical dogmatics, too, since it began with a rule of faith in setting out to expound Scripture. In this case, however, the material norm was not used critically against deviant scriptural statements, but was instead employed (as still by Barth) to interpret all other statements in harmony with itself, in accord with the analogy of faith. In contrast to this, Käsemann explicitly searches for a "material center," a "canon within the canon," in order to "test the spirits even within Scripture itself."[38] He finds this center in justification, understood not in the sense of a doctrine, but in the sense of the gracious character of the redemptive event. In spite of this, Hermann Diem is quite right in his criticism that there is at least the danger in this view that justification will be turned into a "principle of interpretation" (*Deutungsprinzip*),[39] which permits only specific aspects of the revelatory event to come into view.

Diem himself understands the unity of Scripture as a "proclamatory unity" (*Verkündigungseinheit*) in contrast to a "doc-

---

[37] "The Canon of the New Testament and the Unity of the Church," in *Essays on New Testament Themes*, pp. 95–107; the formulation referred to is found on p. 103.

[38] "Is the Gospel Objective?" in *Essays on New Testament Themes*, pp. 48–62, esp. p. 58.

[39] H. Diem, *Dogmatics*, p. 231.

trinal unity" (*Lehreinheit*). He means by this that "in the proclamation of these witnesses Jesus Christ is to be heard proclaiming himself."[40] The differences between the individual witnesses are to be explained, according to Diem, on the basis of the differences in their various preaching situations. But the question about the truth of what is said by a specific witness concerns something that does not disappear in the shift of situations. Thus, Diem does not overcome the question of a material norm. Even his own formulation about the proclamation of the Christ who proclaims himself demands, if only in a very formal way, such a substantive criterion.

In the last analysis, there are two basic possibilities for understanding the unity of Scripture after the loss of the conception of it as a doctrinal unity free from contradictions. On the one hand, the unity of Scripture may be grounded ultimately in a hermeneutical principle which is supposed to agree with the spirit of the witnesses themselves, as when justifying faith as a mode of existence is made into a canon of exegesis. Even when the unity of Scripture is incorporated into the process of proclamation, as in the case of Diem, it must ultimately be constituted by the spirit of the interpreter. It will no longer be evident as an "objective" self-existent unity. This conception, therefore, veers into a certain proximity to the conception which binds the interpretation of Scripture to the "living tradition" of the ecclesiastical teaching office.

The other possibility would be to discover the unity of Scripture in the Christ-event attested by its different witnesses. This is what Diem wants, too. But in order to accomplish this, the Christ-event must be distinguishable from the process of its – continually differing – proclamation, and from early on the different[41] forms of the primitive Christian witness must

[40] *Ibid.*, p. 234.

[41] The problem presented by the diversity of the forms of proclamation in the New Testament literature is not, in my opinion, soluble by establishing a "canon within the canon" in the form of a "primitive kerygma," a "first witness" (so, ultimately, Willi Marxsen, in his "Kontingenz der Offenbarung oder (und?) Kontingenz des Kanons?", *Neue Zeitschrift für systematische Theologie* 2 (1960), pp. 355–64; esp. 360f. and 363). This is dubious, in

give evidence of and be capable of supporting the judgment that they represent the unfolding of the inherent meaning of the Christ-event itself.[42] Thus, what is needed is precisely the historical quest, moving behind the kerygma in its various forms, into the public ministry, death, and resurrection of Jesus himself in order in that way to obtain in the Christ-event itself a standard by means of which to judge the various witnesses to it, even those actually within the New Testament. If the Christ-event cannot be distinguished from the kerygma of primitive Christianity, then it cannot be made effective as a norm for "testing the spirits within Scripture itself." On the other hand, however, the Christ-event can be the standard for judging the different forms of primitive Christian kerygma as well as all later church proclamation only if this event bears its meaning in itself. Only if the history of Jesus – understood in its original historical context and not as an isolated event by itself – has its

---

the first place, because constructions of an original kerygma have recently become highly problematical on historical grounds (cf. Ulrich Wilckens, *Die Missionsreden der Apostelgeschichte: Form- und traditionsgeschichtliche Untersuchungen*, Wissenschaftliche Monographien zum Alten und Neuen Testament, [Neukirchen, 1961; ²1962], pp. 1–31 and 187ff.). One has to reckon with a very early development of a multiplicity of forms of proclamation. On the other hand, it will not do to think of Paul as primarily the interpreter of a primitive tradition, as a glance at Galatians 1:12 should already indicate. No matter how much he referred to a body of pre-formed materials, he nevertheless wanted primarily to interpret the event itself, and not a previously developed primitive kerygma about it. Finally, a normative, primitive kerygma of such a kind would inevitably blunt and relativize the diversity of the kerygmatic expositions of the redemptive event in primitive Christianity, if indeed it did not devalue them in comparison with the primitive kerygma itself, while at the same time making all the more plain the inescapability of the task of ever new exposition of the event itself.

[42] The same problem that crops up in Diem appears also in Otto Weber. He says, on the one hand: "The unity of Scripture is not historical. Its coherence can consist only in the relationship of the scriptural witnesses to the redemptive event." Then, however, he goes on to assert in the same line of thought: "This 'center' comes into view *through* the witnesses, and not as a separable quantity of itself" (*Grundlagen der Dogmatik*, 1, p. 293). Here, the question of the theological significance of the historical search behind the kerygma for the event itself, as well as investigation into the process of tradition in the primitive Christian community, drop out. Weber explicitly agrees with the position of Diem.

meaning in itself will one be able to show, positively, how and to what extent the inherent meaning of the event itself has been unfolded in the various forms of the kerygma and in the language of each new situation in this history of the transmission of tradition in primitive Christianity or, negatively, to what extent a specific form of witness must be judged to be a diminished statement of the Christ-event in this or that respect.

This seems to me to be the only way possible to allow the essential content [*res*] of Scripture to become visible as a unity superior to the kerygma of the church and, at the same time, its norm. We hereby find ourselves in the train of the statements of Luther and classical Lutheran dogmatics about the outer clarity of Scripture. Jesus Christ is the one *res*, the proper content of Scripture, and this content comes to light through the outer clarity of Scripture, i.e., through historical study of the Bible. Of course, this content does not appear to us as it did to the historical consciousness of the sixteenth century. We have learned to understand the writings of the New Testament as the results of a process of tradition which had its point of departure in the Christ-event. For us, Scripture no longer appears on the plane of its finished results, so to speak, but has acquired a dimension of depth in the historical process of the transmission of tradition which preceded the collection of its writings into a canon. In this dimension of depth, we also see the Christ-event as distinguished from the different New Testament witnesses. For us, the historical sense [*sensus historicus*] and the literal sense [*sensus literalis*], which were considered identical in the Middle Ages and even in the Reformation, have moved apart as belonging to two different dimensions of the interrogation of a text. Therefore, the dogmatician has not only to deal with exegetical statements that bring out the original meaning of the different writings, but also, beyond this and above all, with historical statements (in the broadest sense of the term) about the history of Jesus himself and the process of its transmission in tradition and interpretation in primitive Christianity. It is precisely this historical understanding of the history of the primitive Christian process of tradition that places dogmatics in the position – both more differentiated and also methodologically clearer than was possible for Luther and the sixteenth and seventeenth centuries – of being able to proceed from Jesus Christ as the touchstone of the New Testament writings. This presupposes, of course, to say it again, that the Christ-event is not value-neutral in itself; it does not have first to be clothed with this or that meaning by a kerygma different from itself. Rather, the Christ-event has its meaning in itself. Like any other event, however, it can only have this if it is understood within the nexus of events to which it originally belongs, and is not artificially removed from this context as "isolated fact," in accord with the positivistic view of history. When referred to the nexus of events in which it originally stood – which includes the Jewish eschatological expectations at the time of Jesus, together with their Old Testament background, and above all the ministry and message of Jesus himself – the event of Jesus' resurrection and, in retrospect, crucifixion bears its meaning in itself. It thus makes it possible to understand and even to verify the explication of the inherent meaning of this event in the history of the transmission of tradition in primitive Christianity. It is in this way that the history of primitive Christianity's transmission of tradition and thereby the New Testament itself receive their unity from the Christ-event.

5. THE RELATIONSHIP OF DOGMATIC TO HISTORICAL STATEMENTS

If, as seems to be the case,[43] the inherent meaning of the history of Jesus is not reserved to the dogmatician, but may also be the content of historical statements, then it will scarcely be possible to distinguish in principle between dogmatic and historical statements about the Christ-event. Therefore, I will

[43] In *Revelation as History*, tr. David Granskou (New York: Macmillan, 1969), pp. 139ff., I have indicated in a preliminary way how the revelatory significance of the history of Jesus is immediately implied in the historical problem of the Easter event, and how the beginnings of the trinitarian and christological dogmas are to be found there.

content myself with a technical distinction, so to speak, between these two sets of statements. This already indicates that what people have become accustomed to separate as historical and dogmatic statements are really two moments in a single cognitive process.

On the whole, dogmatic statements do not refer to historical ones primarily in order to set forth the specific historical individuality of the event with which they are dealing. Rather, they presuppose the historically unique, and seek to formulate its universal meaning for the whole of reality and for man's consciousness of truth. Historical statements, conversely, presuppose a universal horizon of meaning, at least implicitly and in a provisional way. When the historian inquires into the specific individuality of a process, an event, or a figure, he always brings with him a provisional consciousness of reality generally, as well as an approximate idea of the nexus of events in which the occurrence to be clarified belongs. This determines his consciousness of the possibilities with reference to the special object of his investigation. We are talking here about the so-called "pre-understanding." The point of departure for historical work is constituted by a spontaneous pre-projection of nexuses of meaning which then are tested against observation of all the available individual details, and confirmed or modified in accord with each of these. The dogmatician, however, inquires in the opposite direction, asking how a universal context of meaning arises out of a specific event, the history of Jesus Christ. Both aspects, the universal meaning and the specific individuality of Jesus' way, are so intertwined that the process of acquiring knowledge of this always passes from one to the other. The historical individuality of Jesus is rightly understood only in knowing its universal meaning – ultimately, in fact, only through personal trust. Conversely, all dogmatic statements about his universal meaning constantly require grounding in and confirmation by the historical particularity of the message, way, and figure of Jesus.[44]

[44] Thus, exegetical and dogmatic statements are relatively far apart from each other where exegesis deals with a text that has only distant connections

Concretely, to say that the dogmatic statement possesses universality means above all that it takes account of the earthly way of Jesus together with his resurrection from the dead as an act of God. Statements about God refer essentially to the totality of reality and imply an understanding of this whole insofar as we can speak meaningfully about God only by speaking of him as the creator of the universe. The statements about Jesus which speak about God's act and God's revelation in him correspond to a view of the whole of reality as a history effected by God, in other words, to the biblical-Israelite view of reality. For this reason, primitive Christianity sought for the meaning of Jesus in the light of the Old Testament. The universal meaning of the history of Jesus in connection with the prophetic-apocalyptic expectation of the covenant people of the Old Testament is grounded in its eschatological character, that is, in the fact that the ultimate meaning and goal – and, thus, also the origin – of all things is revealed in him. This is especially true of Jesus' resurrection. There, the God of the Old Testament reveals himself as the true God, as the origin and Lord over all men and all things. The assertion of the deity of Jesus is founded on this. In this way, dogmatics explicates the universal meaning of the particular individual event studied by the historian, viewing this in relation to the whole of reality and thus speaking in terms of the act of God that occurred then in the history of Jesus.

The universality of the dogmatic statement is the basis for its systematic character. Viewing things from the standpoint of the distinctiveness of the history of Jesus as the eschatological event, dogmatics sees the whole of reality in such a way that all the particulars in this totality are mutually inter-related. The systematic transparency of these relationships in the statements made by dogmatics expresses the connection of everything in the whole of reality understood as being oriented toward the Christ-event as an eschatological event. This is expressed implicitly in the assertion of the deity of Jesus, in the formulae

---

with the Christ-event, which is especially true in relation to specific Old Testament texts, although not only there.

on predestination and the mediatorial role of Christ in creation, even if only in rather general form.[45]

The inevitability of using philosophical terminology in dogmatics is another implication of the universality of dogmatic statements. Christian preaching and theology are not the first to raise the question about the whole of reality. This question is not first envisaged from the side of Jesus Christ, but is always posed priorly and, indeed, methodically as the question of philosophy. Therefore, Christian theology must avail itself of the language of philosophy, at least entering into critical dialogue with it, if it intends to give expression to the whole of reality. However, while philosophy asks about the whole of reality on the basis of everyday experience of reality, dogmatics asks this question only in such a way that it proceeds from the Christ-event and pursues its universal significance for reality. Thus, dogmatics understands the unity of reality only in the light of the Christ-event. In doing this, dogmatics must use philosophical ideas and concepts which it finds on hand, and those which it employs must be fundamentally transformed because and to the extent that the whole of reality appears in a new light from the standpoint of the Christ-event.

As a universal statement, the dogmatic statement is, in addition, essentially communicative. It belongs to the essence of all truth that it wants to be possessed in common, and this demand applies most strongly to those statements that aim at the most comprehensive truth. This communicative character

---

[45] The statements of proclamation, on the other hand, concretize the universal truth of the Christ-event by relating it to particular situations. The purest form of preaching to which this generalization applies is the catechetical type of sermon. In the case of sermons based on biblical texts, the matter is much more complicated for the majority of pericopes. As a rule, no direct concretization of a deliberately universal formulation of the revelatory truth in relation to a particular situation of the contemporary hearer occurs here. Instead, the universal truth of the decisive revelatory event is more or less tacitly assumed, and the concern is to bring together the particular situation of today's listener with the particular situation of the text in question. For this reason, analogies between the situations and with this the figurative and meditative forms of speech become especially important in such preaching.

of truth forms the foundation of the responsibility of dogmatic statements to the church.

Finally, the time-boundedness of theological statements is also given by their universality. Any understanding of reality as a whole is always approximative and is constantly changing – basically, with the addition of every new piece of knowledge, since this has consequences for the whole. Dogmatics must participate in such change since it may not allow itself to deteriorate into the spirit of a given age but must be "timely" in the sense of confirming the deity of the God of Israel revealed in Jesus in relation to the experience of reality of every successive present age. It is a matter not of establishing a basis [*Begründung*], but of providing subsequent confirmation [*Bewährung*] of the deity of the God revealed in Jesus insofar as he is essentially the God of all men and all times.

6. THE DOXOLOGICAL AND PROLEPTIC STRUCTURAL ELEMENTS OF DOGMATIC STATEMENTS: THE LIMITS OF THE DOGMATIC STATEMENT

The doxological character of dogmatic statements is related to their peculiar universality as statements about the eternal God and his acts. As Edmund Schlink has shown,[46] this characteristic constitutes an essential structural aspect of confession of Christ and, thus, of dogma itself. This doxological character carries over from here to the doctrine of right confession as well, and thus becomes a property of dogmatic statements in the wider sense. The statements used in confession of Christ have a doxological character insofar as they speak, on the basis of the Christ-event, of God himself in his eternal essence [*Wesen*] and of the eternal deity of Jesus Christ. Through confession of Christ, God is praised as being in the eternal essence as he has shown himself to be in the particular events of the history of Jesus. This concept of doxology as a statement about the eternal essence of God based on his action is at once narrower

[46] "The Structure of Dogmatic Statements as an Ecumenical Problem," in *The Coming Christ*, pp. 16–84.

and more general than the form-critical concept of doxology. It is narrower because doxology in the form-critical sense can be found in accounts of the acts of God which contain no explicit mention of his eternal essence. It is more general because the doxological structure set forth here can be found elsewhere than in statements that fit the form-critical classification, namely, in all faith statements about God himself. In any case, this structure appears in an exemplary way in the form of doxology.

Doxology is essentially adoration [*Anbetung*]. In it, as Schlink says, the "I" is sacrificed in the act of praising God.[47] Only in this attitude of adoration can God be spoken of in a theological manner. Therefore, the structure of doxology is characteristic of even the conceptual form of all statements about God's essence. The creaturely content of our concepts is sacrificed when goodness, righteousness, love, wisdom, etc., are ascribed to the eternal essence of God. This means, with regard to the concepts themselves, that they become equivocal in the act of transferring their finite contents to the eternal essence of God. For this reason, doxological formulations are "ultimate (statements) [*letzte Aussagen*], and man cannot go beyond them." "They are a mode of expression in which the worshipper brings himself, his words and the consistency of his thought as a sacrifice of praise to God."[48] They cannot be directly employed as premises for drawing out logical consequences. Otherwise the fallacy of four terms [*quaternio terminorum*][49] results since, indeed, the finite conceptual content has become equivocal in the doxological act of its assertion about the eternal essence of God.[50] Since all theological statements about God have this structure it is impossible to derive theological connections

[47] *Ibid.*, p. 22.
[48] *Ibid.*, p. 41.
[49] [This type of fallacy occurs when the middle term of a syllogism is ambiguous or equivocal. It is a strictly verbal fallacy and may occur even where the form of the syllogism is perfectly sound. It violates the general rule that a syllogism must contain three terms only. Analogical arguments frequently commit this fallacy. – Tr.]
[50] On this point, see my earlier exposition of the problem of analogy,

deductively from the concept of God. The connection of theological statements with each other is always to be conceived
from the opposite side, by deeper penetration into the event in
which God is revealed.

This set of problems connected with doxological statements
does not apply only to statements about God's essence and
attributes. All statements about an act of God in a specific event
have this characteristic insofar as they speak of an act of the
eternal God, and ascribe such things as "act" and "deed" to
his eternal essence itself.

The proleptic character of statements about God is closely
connected with the element of doxological structure in dogmatic statements. To speak about their proleptic character
means that dogmatic statements rest entirely on an anticipation
of the eschaton, that they have, so to speak, a prophetic
tendency. The foundation of the whole history of the transmission of tradition in primitive Christianity is, in fact, a vision
of the Easter event which telescopes it together with the eschatological event of the end of the world and resurrection of the
dead which is still outstanding for us. One can speak about Jesus
as Son of Man, Son of God, and Lord only within this tele-
scoping vision. Indeed, even the language about the resurrection of Jesus himself presupposes such a simultaneous vision of
the Easter-event and the end of history. At this point, all those
problems break out which have to do with the problem of the
"already" and "not yet": the question of the relation between
the event which "already" occurred in Jesus and the event of
his return for final judgment and the general resurrection of
the dead which have "not yet" arrived. Dogmatic statements –
especially those of Christology, but not only these – "include,"
in a certain way, the still outstanding event within the one that
has already taken place, especially the resurrection of Jesus.
Or, better, they allow themselves to be guided by the actual

"Möglichkeiten und Grenzen der Anwendung des Analogieprinzips in der
evangelischen Theologie," *Theologische Literaturzeitung* 85 (1960), cols. 225–
228.

pre-occurrence of the end of history in Jesus. Dogmatics speaks constantly of something that will fully appear only in a future which is inconceivable for us, but which has already happened in Jesus at a specific time. And it speaks of this in a language that necessarily lags infinitely behind the future reality of the resurrection life because this new reality is precisely what we have not experienced, something which we can speak of only in a provisional and symbolic way on the basis of our quite different sort of experience of reality. Resurrection of the dead is, in truth, an image [*Vorstellung*] built up by analogy with rising or being awakened from sleep. It belongs to the sobriety of dogmatic speech that it be critically conscious of this problem and with it of the provisional character of all theological formulations.

The elements of proleptic and doxological structure in dogmatic statements are interrelated, since both of them express their universal character, each in its own peculiar way. Dogmatic statements have a proleptic tendency in that they have all of reality, history as a whole, in view, since in Christ, the consummation of history, the future of us all, has already begun. Only this proleptic conception of the whole of reality, whose wholeness was first constituted by the Christ-event, establishes the possibility of speaking of an act of God in this event (and then, retrospectively, in the history of Israel, too) and, on top of that, of specific properties of God's essence. Thus, the doxological element in the dogmatic statement is founded upon the proleptic, and both are interrelated through the universal meaning that inheres in this particular event.

7. DOCTRINE AND TRADITION

Everything that has been said so far may be summed up once again in this sentence: Dogmatics is essentially doctrine. Schlink, in his essay mentioned above, pointed out that dogmatics has its roots in doctrine [*Lehre*], and not primarily in confession [*Bekenntnis*], as is the case with dogma.[51] To be sure,

[51] Schlink, *The Coming Christ*, pp. 36f.

there is a didactic element in confession, too, insofar as it deals with a very specific event in history in which God is revealed. In confession, the believer confesses to the Jesus who appeared in Palestine "at that time" in a specific past age, and whom God raised from the dead and exalted to participation in his power. The task of doctrine is the transmission of what took place at that time, which is presupposed in confession. To this extent, doctrine and tradition are very closely related to each other.[52] But even the confession itself becomes once again the content of tradition and thereby also an object of dogmatics.

Dogmatic teaching lives in the tradition and itself has the task of passing on that which has been transmitted in the tradition. What is meant here, in the first instance, is the *de facto* tradition, not primarily a special, ecclesiastically sanctioned one. Dogmatic teaching is not a sterile passing on of what had been previously handed down, no matter how much it might preserve the tradition. The passing on accomplished by dogmatics is associated with personal advocacy of the truth of what was handed down and thus involves an element of personal witness. This advocacy of the truth of the content of the tradition is possible only in connection with reflection upon its basis and with critical testing of its truth claims. Such testing as we saw, must always reach back for the inherent meaning of the Christ-event itself in order to measure the contents of tradition by this standard. Admittedly, the way in which one inquires into the Christ-event is always determined to a large extent by the tradition in which one lives and by one's actual relationship to this. Nevertheless, one must not fail to recognize the significance of the constantly new situation, or of the creative power of the imagination. It is the imagination, however, which likewise can only develop itself within the realm of a spiritual tradition, always according to the degree to which that tradition is differentiated. Thus, in fact, the questions and hypotheses raised in relation to the history of Jesus are determined by the life of the interpreter on the basis of his tradition. But these notions, questions, and hypotheses are always to be

[52] *Ibid.*, pp. 25f.

tested against everything that can provide us with evidence, clues to the reality of the past event of Jesus. In the first instance, this is, of course, the primitive Christian tradition concerning Jesus, which is to be investigated as a historical source. To this extent, Scripture can in fact be designated as an "instrument of doctrine" (*instrumentum doctrinae*). The ideas and hypotheses about Jesus arising from the spiritual tradition – be it ecclesiastical, or quite another, even anti-Christian – in which those who are inquiring about Jesus live, need testing and confirmation by Scripture. Such hypotheses, no matter what their lineage, can claim historical truth only when they have been confirmed in this way. Naturally, the tradition from which they originate cannot reappear as an argument in the methodical procedure by which they are tested. Rather, these postulations – regardless of their background – are to be tested as to the extent to which they satisfy the available data on the history of Jesus. Nevertheless, it will always prove to be the case – thanks to the clarity of Scripture which exerts itself through the process of historical-critical discussion – that no arbitrary hypothesis can find confirmation in Scripture, but only those which have grown out of the true and living Christian proclamation. In any event, the tradition of the church will always be required, by outside factors, too, to prove in this process that it is truly alive.

Advocacy of the truth of the tradition includes its confirmation by the experience of reality of every successive present. In this way, too, dogmatic teaching brings about a new explication of the universal meaning of the transmitted events. Thus, on the one hand, it establishes the basis of doxological statements about God's eternal essence and his revelation in Jesus Christ and, on the other, it leads to the development of dogmatic statements about man the world in the light of the revelatory event. The form in which it is possible to express the universal truth of the Christ-event in this way changes with the times and with the general cultural situation to such a degree that what was justifiable at one time can stand in formal contradiction to what needs to be said today. Even Catholic theology, in the spirit of Johannes E. Kuhn, can agree with this.[53] However, the changes in the form of the tradition always occur in critical distancing from its own earlier forms. A criticism of the achievement of earlier theologies relative to their own cultural situation will become possible on the basis of the current, though time-bound, historical-dogmatic knowledge of the Christ-event. Such criticism of even ecclesiastical and biblical formulations is necessary if we are to be free for our own task of stating the universal meaning of the Christ-event in a contemporaneously possible form of truth.

One might want to ask whether such emphasis on the critical task of dogmatics does not sacrifice the continuity of the tradition. In no case may this be allowed to happen. Dogmatics has an obligation to the history of the church: a responsibility for the maintenance of continuity with the tradition. The maintenance of this continuity has to do with protecting the unity of the church throughout time. This aspect of the church's unity is no less urgent and obligatory than the task of the unity of all Christians in any given generation. And precisely the universality of the dogmatic statement also makes it indispensable for preserving the continuity of the tradition – a point that should be plain enough and needs no further justification.

But the unity of tradition does not mean the irreformability of a doctrinal concept which was once regarded as valid, any more than that the unity of the church in each new age must come about by accepting one and the same formula. It "can also consist in the mutual recognition of different dogmatic formulas."[54] In the same way, the unity of the tradition can exist despite different dogmatic formulations and in spite of many criticisms of the dogmatic formulations of past times. The unity of the tradition is grounded in the common relation of different theologians of different ages to the norm of one and the same Christ-event. It is the history of Jesus in its unity with the

[53] Cf. the work of Geiselmann, cited on p. 186, n. 16, where Kuhn's appropriation of the Hegelian dialectic for understanding the process of tradition is expounded.

[54] Schlink, *The Coming Christ*, p. 80.

eschatological future that induces the unity of the tradition, just as it already provided the basis for the unity of Scripture over and above the differences between the individual witnesses. Where theology is carried on in subordination to the Christ-event and as an explication of its inherent meaning,[55] there, in spite of all defects, all the needed criticisms, and all other differences, it is united in faith with all similarly ordered theology. This is just as true as the fact that faith does not cling to its own form of knowledge, but abandons itself to the event from which it lives, though always by means of the knowledge through which it holds fast to this event. Again, this does not mean any curtailment of the necessity of theological work. Rather, it is the consequence of knowledge of the eschatological limitation of all theological knowledge and formulation.

8. DOGMA AS AN ESCHATOLOGICAL QUANTITY AND ITS PROVISIONAL FORM

These last considerations provide an opportunity to raise the question with which I will conclude this presentation. If dogmatic formulations always have a fundamentally proleptic structure and, thus, always remain burdened with inadequacy in comparison with the eschatological truth; if, furthermore, the understanding of reality in which the universal meaning of the Christ-event is expressed is subject to ceaseless change – even this is a sign of the "not yet" in which we have to undertake doing theology! – then is not dogma reserved for the eschaton, and everything belonging to the present age dissolved in relativity?

Karl Barth, indeed, termed dogma an "eschatological concept."[56] According to Barth, we can never go beyond *asking* about the agreement between the church's proclamation and the revelation attested in Scripture. The possibility of "a

---

[55] Only where such acknowledgment is no longer possible does the boundary between the church and heresy arise.

[56] *CD* I/1, p. 309.

manifestation of dogma, or of the Word of God itself, can only be that of the great illusions and prolepses."[57]

One must say, in opposition to this, that it is precisely the Christ-event itself that is the great prolepsis of the eschaton. For this reason dogma already has a provisional, historical form in the church's confession. But the church's dogma, which is still on the way, cannot itself be the eschatological form of revealed truth. It always remains under the eschatological proviso, the sign of the "not yet," which characterizes all Christian life and thought, and operates within history in the revision of time-bound confessional formulations coined at some particular time.

It follows from this that the dogmatic authority of ecclesiastical confessions cannot mean that they are withdrawn from all criticism and are open only to fresh exposition in new, future situations. Rather, the authority of an ecclesiastical confession is to be seen precisely in the fact that its formulations, like those of every member of the church, are submittted to testing by the superordinated revelation attested by Scripture. Where it is a matter of understanding the Scripture, there is in the first instance, the confession of the church to be tested before all other theological hypotheses, as to whether and to what extent it appropriately states the meaning of revelation. The peculiar authority of the church's confession, its priority over other theological formulations, can consist only in that.

[57] *Ibid.*

7

ANALOGY AND DOXOLOGY

First appeared in *Dogma und Denkstrukturen; Festschrift für Edmund Schlink,*
ed. by W. Joest and W. Pannenberg (Göttingen, 1963), pp. 96–115.

A CRUCIAL, if not *the* most basic question of all theology is the
question about the right way to speak of God. In one way or
another, all theological efforts are involved in responsibility for
this problem. The most pressing consideration, here, is one's
viewpoint about the place where the reality of God may be
encountered: in the constancies of events, or in the problematic
character of human existence; in specific experiences in the
present, or in things that have happened in history which reach
us only through tradition. However, the question as to where
the reality of God is to be encountered already presupposes an
answer to the question about the meaning of the word "God."
Furthermore, it presupposes a decision as to whether the reality
so designated appears directly in the world of our experience –
whether alongside the reality of the men and things with which
we associate daily, gods also appear on the scene – or whether
the reality of God manifests itself in the world only indirectly,
through the mediation of other beings and things.

The biblical writings exhibit both viewpoints, albeit not in
simple juxtaposition. The older traditions of Israel know of
immediate interventions of God himself in the course of earthly
events. After the period of Solomon, however, God, because he
is understood as the Creator, is thought of as working mediately
through everything created by him, and therefore as no longer
having to appear directly in order to bring about specific
effects. Only when this point has been reached, at which God
or the gods no longer manifest themselves in the world by

becoming directly perceptible, but instead only intimate their reality indirectly through the existence of everything that makes up the world, does the problem arise with which the doctrine of analogy is concerned, and in which doxology is also involved: if the divine reality is not directly experienceable, then it can be spoken of only in an indirect manner, viz., by speaking about whatever worldly being it is through which the reality of God manifests itself. Thus, one speaks of God by speaking about something else, but in such a way that this other being is viewed in its relation to the reality of God. And the reality of God is spoken of only to the extent that it comes into view through some specific form of experience of the world. It will be shown later that in these two sentences we are not dealing simply with the same indirectness, but with a double indirectness in our speech about God. At this point we need only grasp the fact that the indirectness of our speech about God already means that we can only speak of him analogically, i.e., only by means of transferring the meaning of words that were formed in other contexts. Even the meaning of the word "God" can be expressed only by such analogical statements,[1] regardless of how it might be understood in detail.

The analogous nature of language about God is also independent of the question about where the divine reality is to be met, whether in nature or in history, whether in the totality of all occurrences or equally in every event or in certain special

[1] To be sure, the formation of the very idea of God is not a metaphorical act. Otherwise God would only be a metaphor for something else! The formation of the concept of God can, of course, only be understood from the side of some other reality – the world or (in modern times) man – but in this sense, that man himself is to be understood in no other way than as the question about the unknown, about the counterpart that lies beyond the given world horizon and which we call God. Metaphors are already involved in the formation of this concept, e.g., in the use of the term "counterpart" [*Gegenüber*] to refer to that which lies beyond the world; and even more so in the use of the term "God" in contrast to "deity," insofar as its use means the divine is already conceived as person (see vol. II, forthcoming). However, the idea itself is not metaphorical, insofar as it relates to the character of man's being infinitely directed toward something beyond itself, to man's ultimate concern, or, to speak with Luther, to the goal of man's (ultimate) trust.

events. The constitutive factor behind the assertion that all speech about God is analogical and involves a transference of meaning is simply the indirectness of the divine disclosure. Even the question whether such analogous traits belong to the divine being in and for itself or whether they apply to it only within our perspective, since we have no other way of speaking about the divine reality than by analogical transference, still remains open at this point in the argument.

In what is usually regarded as the classic theory of the analogy between God and the world, as it was developed by the Christian Scholasticism of the thirteenth century, this last question was answered by saying that the reality of God as such stands in an analogical relationship to the world, not only in our speech, but also *per se*. More precisely, the world of creaturely reality is analogous to God, whereas the reversal of this relationship, which occurs in our speaking about God insofar as this is accomplished by making him analogous to our experience of the world, already shows up the inadequacy of our knowledge of God.[2] Nevertheless, our knowledge is not simply inappropriate to the divine reality, for an analogy between God and the world does in fact exist. In this analogy, however, the world falls short of its divine archetype, so that the reverse transference back to God of what is read off of the world is no longer able to attain the purity of the divine archetypes. This conception originated in Neoplatonism, specifically, in the Neoplatonic idea of emanation according to which the emanated realities always constitute a lower level of being than their

[2] Thomas Aquinas, *Summa Theologiae*, pt. I, quest. 13, art. 6. In my (as yet unpublished) inaugural dissertation, "Analogie und Offenbarung" (Heidelberg, 1955), pp. 114–40, I have demonstrated that the solution presented here in the *Summa* to the problem of analogy represents the endpoint of the development of Aquinas' thought on this subject. If this solution were thought of as "paronymy" (see below, pp. 224, n. 22, and 227, n. 26) rather than as "analogy", one might find here a fruitful point of departure in the direction of the state of the matter expounded here. [Paronymous words are words derived from the same root which are related to each other as the substantive, adjective, verb, etc. formed from that root, e.g., just, justly, justice. It cannot be assumed, however, that there is a precisely corresponding meaning between these forms. – Tr. note].

source, so that the universe exhibits itself as a gradated structure. Within this structure, however, the motive power is always
transmitted from above to below,[3] both in the production of
the emanated forms and (by illumination) in their return to
their source, since the lower level in any given instance is unable
by its own power to attain the next higher one.[4] Nevertheless,
here, as well as in Scholasticism, analogizing speech about the
divine Origin is characterized by the effort to grasp God's
name (in keeping with the ancient Greek maxim about knowing
the unknown through the known[5]), even if the Origin, by virtue
of its superiority with respect to being, can always be only
approximately characterized by an analogical transference of
meaning based on the effects produced by this Origin. In
Christian Scholasticism greater emphasis had to be placed on the
positive significance of analogical knowledge than was the case
in Neoplatonism since, in the latter, mystical union with the
Origin could afford a certainty prior to all rational knowledge,
whereas for Christian Scholasticism, because of its concern for
the primordial difference between the Creator and the creature,

[3] Such a view of analogy, which grounds analogy both ontologically and
noetically from God's side (as proposed recently by G. Söhngen in particular), has led Karl Barth to suspend his criticism of the analogy of being
[*analogia entis*] (*CD*, II/1, pp. 81f.). In fact, the roots of his own doctrine of
analogy, which are expressed with particular clarity in his anthropology
(*CD*, III/2, pp. 205ff., 220f., 320ff.), are to be found here (cf. also, however,
CD, II/1, pp. 227ff.). The Thomistic doctrine of analogy is nevertheless
probably right in holding that, in fact, all analogizing proceeds from below
to above, and begins with some experience of the world. We have already
emphasized that according to Thomas it is precisely this point that is the
root of the inadequacy of all human knowledge of God.
[4] On this characteristic, see pp. 47–66 of my work mentioned above in n.
2. The fundamental significance of the Neoplatonic doctrine of analogy for
Scholasticism, especially for Thomas, has been worked out by Hampus
Lyttkens, *The Analogy Between God and the World: An Investigation of Its Background and Interpretation of Its Use by Thomas of Aquinas* (Uppsala, 1952). See
also my review of this work in *Verkündigung und Forschung* (1956/57), pp.
136–42.
[5] Anaxagoras frag. 21a: *opsis tōn adēlōn ta phainomena* [visible existences are
a sight of the unseen; translation from Kathleen Freeman, *Ancilla to the
Pre-Socratic Philosophers: A Complete Translation of the Fragments in Diels, "Frag-
mente der Vorsokratiker"* (Oxford: Basil Blackwell, 1962), p. 86. – Tr.].

it was essential to maintain that analogical knowledge of God was the necessary starting-point even for the union of the soul with God.

According to the doctrine of analogy, the effects produced by God are the basis of what is said about God himself, following the maxim about knowing the unknown by analogy with the known. At first sight, one might suppose this structure is also present in biblical statements about God. It is true that even the biblical writings speak about God by transferring to him words whose meaning is established in other contexts. Indeed, they do so with an often astonishing abandon and picturesqueness. For the most part, these are pictures that designate the uniqueness of a specific divine action. Such is the case, for example, in the talk about Yahweh's arm or hand, or of his voice and scolding. The verbs, especially, with which the deeds of Yahweh are described, often have a rough and unpolished ring to them. On the basis of his deeds, however, statements are also made about God which, on the basis of the attributes of his actions, designate God himself. Predominant among these attributes are those which derive their perspicuity from the realm of human conduct, as in statements which praise God's mercy, grace, love, justice, patience and faithfulness. Such statements describe the reality of God by analogy with a human act. The very idea of a divine act already exhibits such an analogy. Nevertheless, it is not the intention of such words to provide theoretical definitions of the being of God, in the sense of knowing the unknown through the known. Rather, they are characterized throughout by what Schlink has termed a "doxological" structure.[6] They express adoration of God on the basis of his works. All biblical speech about God, to the extent that its intention is to designate something beyond a

[6] Edmund Schlink, *The Coming Christ and the Coming Church* (Philadelphia: Fortress Press, 1968), pp. 16–84, esp. pp. 19ff., 41f. In his essay, "Der theologische Syllogismus als Problem der Prädestinationslehre" (in *Einsicht und Glaube; Festschrift für G. Söhngen*, ed. Joseph Ratzinger and Heinrich Fries [Freiburg, 1963], pp. 299–320; see p. 319) Schlink enters especially sharp criticism against the theoretical possibility of defining God which is implicit in the doctrine of analogy.

particular deed, namely, God himself and what he is from eternity to eternity, is rooted in adoration and is in this sense doxological.[7] Only if one keeps in mind that theological statements about God are rooted in adoration can the doctrine of God be protected against false conclusions.

Speaking of God in adoration on the basis of his works differs in intention from the enterprise of inferring the attributes of the divine origin from his effects by means of analogy. It is decisive for the analogical inference from the creation back to the divine origin that despite all dissimilarity between God and the realm of finitude, there nevertheless still exists a common logos which permits the attributes in question in any given instance to be ascribed to God himself. In the act of adoration, by contrast, the one who brings his praise sacrifices his "I" and thereby, at the same time, the conceptual univocity of his speech. This is already intimated in an external way by the fact that in the adoring glorification of God, the ego of the worshiper is not named.[8] The worshiper focuses his attention entirely upon God and away from himself, even if in his speaking he must inevitably use human words whose general meaning is already accessible from other contexts. In the act of adoration, in contrast to analogical inference from effect to cause, this continuity matters little. For in doxological statements, the otherwise usual sense of the human word is surrendered in its being used to praise God. To be sure, we speak of God's righteousness. But we thereby release this word from the manipulation of our thought, and must learn ever anew from the reality of God what the word "righteousness" properly means. In the act of

[7] Elsewhere I have pointed out that Schlink's concept of the doxological does not coincide with the form-critical literary genre of doxology. Schlink's concept is both broader and, in another respect, narrower than the form-critical concept: "narrower, because doxology in the form-critical sense can be found in accounts of the acts of God which contain no explicit mention of his eternal essence . . . more general because the doxological structure set forth here can be found elsewhere than in statements that fit the form-critical classifications, namely, in all faith statements about God himself. In any case, this structure appears in an exemplary way in the form of doxology" (see above, pp. 202f.).

[8] E. Schlink, *The Coming Christ*, pp. 22f.

adoration, our words are transferred to the sublime infinity of God. They are thereby set in contrast to their ordinary meaning. They become mysterious, and this can even have a reflexive, renovating influence upon everyday linguistic usage.

Speech about God in worship contains an analogy, to be sure, but only of the kind that subsists between the everyday meaning of the word and its theological use, not, on the contrary, between the everyday sense of the word and the being of God in and for itself. In any case, there is a relationship that justifies the choice of a particular word for the praise of God. This point will be dealt with again later. No matter how its use may be justified, however, the word used in the act of adoration is nevertheless released from our disposal and is handed over to God himself, except that it is impossible for us to survey the extent of the change its content thus undergoes and to point out a common logos as the basis of an analogicity between our speech and the essence of God itself.[9] Rather, the word is sacrificed by the adoration of God, and only the association of

[9] For this reason it is impossible to draw conclusions from doxological statements without further ado. It is required of the middle term joining the two extremes of a syllogism that it have strictly the same meaning in both premises. Just this univocity is what is lost to every word insofar as it is used to speak of God. There is no univocal middle term embracing God and the creature, and therefore one cannot conclude from the meaning something has among men, e.g., righteousness, something about the disposition of God. Duns Scotus had already seen that analogous concepts could be of use as middle terms in syllogisms only on the condition that they possess a univocal core (*Ord.* I, d. 3 = Ed. Vat. III [1954], n. 26). [An English translation of this passage, which, although it is based on the Vatican edition deviates from this where the translator thought the text was "obviously at fault," may be found in *Duns Scotus: Philosophical Writings*, ed. and tr. Allan B. Wolter (New York: Thomas Nelson and Sons, 1962), pp. 4ff. – Tr.]. In any case, he was of the opinion, contrary to ours, that it was possible to draw conclusions about God himself and, thus, that the univocal value of certain concepts for God and the creature was also to be postulated. Kant, on the contrary, rejected conclusions about God drawn from analogy. He believed "that while, in the ascent from the sensible to the supersensible, it is indeed allowable to *schematize* (that is, to render a concept intelligible by the help of an analogy to something sensible), it is on no account permitted to us to *infer* (and thus to *extend* our concept) by this analogy (so that what holds for the former must also be attributed to the latter)" (*Religion Within the Limits*

the worshiper with God, the experience of further concrete acts
of God, serves to show – always in a merely provisional way –
what has become of our words in this connection.

Thus, talk about God rooted in adoration does indeed intend
to speak about God's eternal reality by analogical transfer of
meaning, but it does not intend to accomplish this as an
analogue, but rather by opening itself unreservedly to the
infinity of God. Its form is closer to the Kantian than to the
Scholastic doctrine of analogy. When the doxological analogy
was designated above as one of linguistic usage and not of being,
this was reminiscent of Kant's distinction between dogmatic
and symbolic anthropomorphism. In the latter case, according
to Kant, we do not

attribute to the supreme being any of the properties in themselves, by which

---

of Reason Alone, tr. Theodore M. Greene and Hoyt W. Hudson [New York:
Harper Torchbooks, 1960], p. 59). For between the relation "of a schema to
its concept and the relation of this same schema of a concept to the objective
fact itself there is no analogy, but a mighty chasm, the overleaping of which
. . . leads at once to anthropomorphism" (*ibid.*). This remark of Kant's
applies also to conclusions drawn from the ordinary verbal sense of doxological statements about God's conduct, although these statements not only
schematize or illustrate the idea of God but give it its original concrete
delineation. Only if doxological statements are taken *as* doxological, i.e., as
statements of the man offering praise, can conclusions be drawn from them
without falling into the logical fallacy of four terms [*quaternio terminorum*; see
above, p. 203, n. 49]. It is self-evident that no conclusions about the essence
of God result from this, but only such as apply to the worshiper in the light
of his worship. An example of this structure is the challenge in 1. John 4. 19:
"let us love; because he first loved us" [tr. from author's text – Tr.] (cf. v. 8:
"He who does not love does not know God; for God is love" [RSV]); or
Matt. 5. 48: "You, therefore, must be perfect, as your heavenly Father is
perfect" [RSV]. Man's likeness to God is also to be understood in this sense
as functional unity with God: man ought to be lord over the world as God is
and as God's representative.

In addition to such conclusions about man's conduct, doxological statements also permit conclusions leading to other doxological statements – but
caution is demanded here. Fundamentally, every statement about God is to
be grounded in a historical experience of God's activity. Concluding from
one predicate of God to another can only have the meaning of furthering
understanding of the connection between various doxological statements
each of which has been obtained in its own way.

we represent objects of experience, and thereby avoid dogmatic anthropo-morphism; but we attribute them to his relation to the world, and allow ourselves a symbolical anthropomorphism, which in fact concerns language only, and not the object itself.[10]

Still, to be sure, there remains an obvious difference between doxological speech about God and the Kantian doctrine of analogy, since in the act of adoration specific attributes are ascribed to God "in himself," but only in such a way that they are handed over to him and thereby undergo a change in their meaning which is no longer determinable by us. Thus, speech rooted in the adoration of God, as distinct from the Kantian type of analogy, continually makes assertions about God him-self, about his eternal essence. Nevertheless, as in the Kantian conception, the analogy exists only in the language, not between the language and God himself. The only analogy that can be exhibited is between the theological and extratheological linguistic usage, while the reference of our words to the divine reality itself is withdrawn from our purview by the very act of adoration. In scholastic terminology, such a conception, like Kant's, would sooner be called "equivocation" than "analogy" with regard to the relationship of our words to the divine reality. In the very act of adoration, our words, since they are trans-ferred to God, become equivocal in relationship to their ordinary meaning, no matter how well founded and free from arbitrary derivation this use of words may be.

Hegel's concept of meditation [*Andacht*] expresses better than Kant the reference to God himself which is peculiar to doxo-logical speech precisely in the fact that the worshiper surrenders this and, with it, his own "I" as a sacrifice of praise to God.[11]

[10] Kant's *Prolegomena to Any Future Metaphysics*, ed. Paul Carus (Chicago: Open Court Publishing Co., 1949), p. 129; cf. *Critique of Pure Reason*, tr. J. M. D. Meikeljohn (London: George Bell and Sons, 1884), pp. 318f., 374f. (= *Kritik der reinen Vernunft*, A, pp. 566, 674); *Critique of Judgment*, tr. J. H. Bernard, The Hafner Library of Classics 14 (New York: Hafner Publishing Co., 1951), pp. 257f. (= *Kritik der Urteilskraft* 351, 353 passim); as well as the extensive observations in *Religion within the Limits of Reason Alone*, pp. 58ff.

[11] G. W. F. Hegel, *Vorlesungen über die Philosophie der Religion*, ed. Lasson, Philosophische Bibliothek 59/1 (Hamburg, 1966), p. 236 (cf. already pp. 141f.). In the Jubilee edition, edited by Marheineke, meditation is presented

According to Hegel, there takes place in meditation just that which is determinative for the structure of the cult, faith, and sacrifice, viz., the surrender of the finite ego to the absolute. The elevation to God which is constitutive for religion[12] is possible only in the surrender of one's own finitude. Thus, in meditation, too, the ego is utterly turned toward God since it offers its finitude to God in sacrifice. To this extent, Hegel's concept of meditation corresponds to Schlink's description of the "I's" self-offering as a sacrifice of praise to God in the act of adoration which underlies doxological statements. There remains an essential difference, however, in the fact that adoration and even true meditation do not succeed in attaining a concept of God, as happens in Hegel. Because of this, it seems that in Hegel the pathos of meditation – the self-sacrifice of the ego which is thinking the thoughts of God – is surpassed by the conceptualizing ego, for which the act of self-emptying before the limiting Other is only a transitional moment in order in the next moment to be totally self-possessed.[13] The act of meditation is not conceived radically enough so long as not it but a concept of the absolute has the last word. For in conceptualizing, the finite ego that is supposed to be sacrificed in meditation is once again precisely in itself and presides over the reality of God in its concept. This brings out an ambiguity that is characteristic of Hegel's thought as a whole. Nevertheless, his description of devotion itself corresponds to the structure of adoration as the

---

not as a part of the cult, but as the conclusion of the preceding section on the religious relation: as the elevation [*Aufhebung*] of the religious subject to God (*Lectures on the Philosophy of Religion*, tr. from the second German edition by E. B. Spiers and J. Burdon Sanderson, 3 vols. ([London: Kegan Paul, Trench, Trübner and Co., 1895], I, pp. 191f. On the fundamental significance of meditation for the concept of religion in Hegel's sense, cf. *ibid.*, pp. 18f.)

[12] This is the fundamental Hegelian determination of religion. Cf. *Lectures on the Philosophy of Religion*, I, p. 54 ("consciousness must . . . have already raised itself above all that is finite"); p. 166 (religious knowledge as "elevation to God"); p. 171 (the meaning of the proofs for the existence of God is "rising up to the infinite").

[13] Ego is the pure Notion [*Begriff*] itself which as Notion has reached existence" (*The Science of Logic*, tr. W. H. Johnston and L. G. Struthers [London: George Allen and Unwin, 1929], I, p. 217).

sacrifice of the ego. Thus, the fundamental doxological feature that belongs to all speech about God can also be indicated by referring to its character as an act of meditation. The concept of meditation points to an understanding of God which does not allow him to be comprehended in concepts, as is the case with Hegel's God, but which instead, like the Kantian doctrine of analogy, remains attentive to the infinite sublimity of God and, in spite of this, does not fall back again into abstract self-reflection, as happens in the Kantian way of talking about God, but is utterly turned toward God in the act of adoration.

By means of the element of the self-sacrifice of the ego, meditation and adoration transcend the scholastic concept of the analogy between God and creatures. It is true that the divine transcendence was not alien to the scholastic doctrine of analogy, which in fact was developed in the thirteenth century precisely in order to protect the otherness of God over against the world. At the very beginning of its development there stands the formulation of the Fourth Lateran Council of 1215 that there can be no similarity between God and creatures which is not surrounded by a greater dissimilarity.[14] In our day, Erich Przywara in particular repeatedly referred to this formulation of the Fourth Lateran Council and developed his own concept of analogy from it under the motto of "reduction to mystery" [*reductio in mysterium*], viz., the mystery of the God who is ever always greater. For him, "analogy of being" [*analogia entis*] meant that in every "similarity, no matter how great," the "ever-present greater dissimilarity" is the decisive factor. It expresses, as it were, "dynamic transcendence," i.e., God's ever-beyondness [*Je-über-Hinaus*] transcending "everything that

---

[14] *The Church Teaches*, tr. and ed. J. F. Clarkson *et al.* (London and St. Louis: B. Herder, 1955), No. 307: "Creator and creature are to be perfect, each in his own way, because between them no similarity can be found so great but that the dissimilarity is greater" [= Denzinger, *Enchiridion Symbolorum*, 432: *inter creatorem et creaturam non potest tanta similitudo notari, quin inter eos maior sit dissimilitudo notanda*]. The original intention of this formula consists in the denial of the attempt of Gilbert of La Poree to understand the trinitarian unity according to the analogy of the union of believers with Christ.

exists or can be thought of apart from God himself."[15] Przywara claims, not without justification, that this was the intention of the "negative theology" of the Greek fathers, which was also a vital part of Augustine's thought. The negative theology of Pseudo-Dionysius, for instance, was undoubtedly still concerned with the God who is always-still-greater-yet.[16] And without doubt Thomas Aquinas' doctrine of analogy, too, likewise sought to preserve the formula of the Fourth Lateran Council regarding the incomprehensibility of the divine essence.[17] In his *Quaestiones de veritate*, Aquinas in passing viewed the four-membered mathematical form of proportionality as the most appropriate form of analogy in speaking about God's essence on the basis of our experience of the world because such an analogy is still conceivable despite the infinite difference in magnitude that maintains between God and creatures.[18] On

[15] Erich Przywara, *In und Gegen; Stellungnahme zur Zeit* (Nürnberg, 1955), p. 278.

[16] [Correcting the German text, which omitted a line containing the first part of this sentence. – Tr.]

[17] Aquinas explicitly states in the *Summa Theologiae* (pt. I, quest. 2, art. 2, reply obj. 3; quest. 12, art. 4) that the essence of God is inaccessible to our intellect. The supernatural "light of glory" [*lumen gloriae*] first makes it possible to see the divine essence (*ibid.*, pt. I, quest. 12, art. 2), but even the blessed will not comprehend God in a strict sense because this is ruled out by his infinity (*ibid.*, pt. I, quest 12, art. 7). Normally, we are referred to his effects among creatures for our knowledge of God, although this is unable to attain to the divine Cause in its essence (*ibid.*, pt. I, quest. 12, art. 12). Every word that we ascribe to God "leaves the thing signified as uncomprehended and as exceeding the signification of the name" (pt. I, quest. 13, art. 5) [*relinquit rem significatam ut incomprehensam et excedentem nominis significationem*; translation taken from *Basic Writings of St. Thomas Aquinas*, ed. Anton C. Pegis (2 vols.; New York: Random House, 1945), I, p. 120]. Therefore these words are not applied univocally.

[18] *Truth*, tr. from the Leonine text by Robert W. Mulligan, S. J., 3 vols. (Chicago: Henry Regnery Co., 1952), I, p. 113 (= *De veritate*, quest. 2, art. 11). In connection with the repudiation of the analogy of proportion [*analogia proportionis*], it is explicitly stated here that "no creature has such a relation to God that it could determine the divine perfection" [*quia nulla creatura habet talem habitudinem ad Deum per quam possit divina perfectio determinari*]. However, Thomas seems here to have overlooked the fact that precisely the four-membered proportionality is constituted by a univocal logos which is common to the two relations being compared. He himself offers mathematical examples without sufficiently relativizing them. In the

this basis, it appears as if Aquinas' intention was to give expression to the infinity of God precisely by means of the doctrine of analogy. This intention is very closely related to the sacrifice of praise in adoration, for here, too, the stated word is transferred to God's essence in full consciousness of the fact that it is realized in God in another way that is completely beyond our comprehension.[19] In spite of this fact, however, this intention was only partially upheld among the Scholastics because they thought that not only their language about God but also God himself was analogous to the world of human experience. This was a consequence of the fact that they understood God primarily as the cause of the world.[20]

Summa Theologiae, he expresses himself more cautiously and explicitly denies a quantitative interpretation of the analogy between God and creatures. In pt. I, quest. 12, art. 1, reply obj. 4, he rejects analogy in the sense of "a certain relation of one quantity to another" [*certa habitudo unius quantitatis ad alterum*] in favor of, "in another sense," a "relation of one thing to another . . . inasmuch as it is related (to Him) as the effect to its cause, and as potentiality to act" [*quaelibet habitudo unius ad alterum . . . ut effectus ad causam, et ut potentia ad actum*: translation from *Basic Writings of St. Thomas Aquinas*, I, p. 93]. Significantly, the analogy of proper proportionality [*analogia proportionalitatis*] is no longer mentioned here.

[19] Thomas Aquinas, *Summa Theologiae*, pt. I, quest. 13, art. 3 and *ibid.*, reply obj. 3. In any case, Aquinas felt he was in a position to give a more exact account of the mode in which the perfections ascribed to God exist in him. It is the mode of the divine simplicity (*ibid.*, reply obj. 4). Only because we conceive of these perfections in isolation and in their plurality, instead of in the unity of the divine simplicity, do our words fail to be synonymous when applied to him. Thus, Thomas apparently did not reckon with a substantive transformation of what was stated in its being applied to God.

[20] That an analogical knowledge of God is still possible, despite what was mentioned in n. 17, p. 222, about the incomprehensibility of God, is grounded, for Thomas, in the fact that the creatures of God are similar to him as every effect resembles its cause; for "the effect must in some way resemble the form of the agent" (*Summa Theologiae*, pt. I, quest. 4, art. 3) [*necesse est quod in effectu sit similitudo formae agentis*; tr. from *Basic Writings of St. Thomas Aquinas*, I, 40]. Thomas relies heavily upon the causal relationship as the basis for speaking about God (so *Summa Theologiae*, pt. I, quest. 12, art. 12; and quest. 13, art. 5). Just as in the place last mentioned, he also explains the analogy of creatures to God by means of the relationship of effects to causes in pt. I, quest. 12, art. 1, reply obj. 4. But can the causal relationship itself – even if we concede that the form of the agent [*formae agentis*] in the effect must be knowable, a point which is by no means beyond

In the inference from effects back to their cause, the structure of the idea of analogy as a determination of the unknown by the known is at work. This heuristic power of analogy depends, as the Pre-Socratics and Plato, in particular, already knew, upon the same logos holding sway in the unknown as in the already known, if analogous traits are to be found there as well as here.[21] The cognitive power of analogy depends upon this presupposition of an identical logos. But precisely this point also makes clear the spiritual violence that occurs in analogizing which incorporates the unknown within the confines of the already known – an attitude that is certainly inappropriate with respect to God, and which in any case is opposed to the sacrifice of praise that occurs in adoration. Scholasticism could easily deceive itself about this essential characteristic of analogy because in the thirteenth century one started out from the opinion of Averroes that analogy is a mean between univocity and equivocity, and not in actuality a mere mixture of these extremes but an independent third, in opposition to the characteristic mentioned above, viz., that analogy always presupposes an identical logos which first makes the analogates analogous.[22]

---

all doubt – be uncritically transferred to the relationship between God and creatures? Does not the question arise here already whether God may be designated as a cause in the same sense as other causal agencies? But if the question of analogy already arises at this point, then the interpretation of analogical statements about God as involving similarity with the being of God itself can hardly be established by appealing to the causal relationship between the Creator and creatures.

[21] Cf. on this point my inaugural dissertation (above, n. 2), pp. 20ff., 24ff., 29ff.

[22] I have demonstrated this and the following assertions in detail in chapters V and VI of my inaugural dissertation (see especially pp. 94f.). The criticism pointed out in what follows is aimed in the first instance at the old concept of analogy oriented toward mathematical proportion, the scholastic analogy of proper proportionality [*analogia proportionalitatis*]. (In the interests of terminological clarity, one should, in general, speak of analogy only in this sense.) This criticism, however, is also pertinent to the scholastic "analogy of attribution" ("of many to one" [*ad unum*], or "of one to another" [*ab uno*]), which either (in a more Neoplatonic manner) depends on the cause giving to its effects a share in its being (see above, n. 20), or presupposes (in a more Aristotelian manner) an ontological medium common to the different categories, viz., the being of substance. In every case, the

The whole thirteenth century strove repeatedly to develop new lines of argument to prove the Averroistic principle of analogy as a mean between univocity and equivocity, not so much because knowledge of God did not appear as mental coordination of God into the world of man's experience,[23] but rather in order to escape the dilemma that arises here for the realist position on universals, viz., the dilemma between pantheism (if one claims that universal concepts are applied to God in a univocal sense) and agnosticism (if one completely accepts equivocal signification). Nevertheless, these attempts at proving analogy to be a mean broke down. For by the end of the thirteenth century, Duns Scotus and, later, William of Ockham recognized that analogy itself presupposes a univocal element.

Because of its presupposition of analogy as an independent third between univocity and equivocity, the thought of the thirteenth century was able to remain oblivious to the structure of spiritual assault in the concept of analogy, even though this remained a potent factor in the systems of the medieval thinkers, doubtless against their own intentions. For there can be no doubt that by emphasizing the merely (!) analogous sense of all human statements about God, they intended to respect his transcendence and incomprehensibility. Nevertheless, in that moment in which one recognizes the true nature of analogy, viz., that in fact it is able to assimilate the unknown to the known by means of its presupposition of a common logos between them, it is no longer possible to overlook its contradiction to the intention of adoration and devotion which is alone appropriate for a legitimate knowledge of God. Therefore, one must say that Przywara's formula of a "reduction to mystery"

---

members designated as analogous are bound together by an identical element common to each of them.

Johannes Hirschberger showed, in his significant essay, "Paronymie und Analogie bei Aristotles", *Philosophisches Jahrbuch* 68 (1960), pp. 191–203, that the paronymous relationship of attribution ("of many to one" [*ad unum*] or "of one to another" [*ab uno*]) was connected, by way of metaphor, with genuine analogy as early as the Greek commentators on Aristotle. [On the notion of paronymous words, see the translator's note above, p. 213.]

[23] Cf., however, Thomas' argument for the rejection of univocity in *de veritate*, 2, quest. art. 11 (cited above, n. 18).

[*reductio in mysterium*], by attending to the ever greater dissimilarity of God bursts the intention of analogy (which aims at uncovering the common logos) since, conversely, this tendency toward coordinating the unknown into the known which is at work in the concept of analogy, is diametrically opposed to a reduction to mystery. It is true that since human thinking cannot be carried on except by means of analogical steps, analogy may also be present as a subordinate element in a devotional mode of thought which aims at the praise of the ever greater God. But the intention of such thought and speech transcends the structure of analogy. Analogy would be used, but not intended as analogy. In this case, however, the relationship of the element of analogous transference to the actual intention of thought and speech directed toward the ever greater God will become questionable.

This problem leads us back to the theme of the basis of doxological statements, which was previously bracketed out. Our rejection of an analogy between our statements and God himself has given heightened urgency to the problem of demonstrating how a specific doxological statement, which cannot be exchanged at will with another, arises out of a specific situation. If there were an analogy of the sort that has been rejected, then it would be immediately evident why God would be more appropriately designated as spirit, life, or love, for example, rather than as a stone or a bull. If, however, no analogy between our words and the divine being itself is presupposed, then the question arises as to how specific statements about God are to be supported at all. Thomas Aquinas reiterated this question in opposition to the position of Rabbi Moses Maimonides which allows our concepts to become equivocal when applied to God.[24] Answering this objection would mean at the same time

---

[24] So in the *Summa Theologiae*, pt. I, quest. 13, art. 2: ". . . because in neither of them could a reason be assigned why some names more than others should be applied to God" [. . . *secundum neutram harum positionum posset assignari ratio, quare quaedam nomina magis de Deo dicerentur quam alia* (tr. from *Basic Writings of St. Thomas Aquinas*, p. 115)]. Similarly, in *De veritate*, quest. 2, art. 11; if our words were applied to God only in an equivocal manner, then we could obtain knowledge of God by means of created things: "nor from

being able to explain why the equivocation that is introduced in the transfer of our words to God does not leave the door open for an arbitrary use of language. With Boethius, we say that what is involved here is not an "equivocation by accident" [*aequivocatio a casu*] but a "deliberate equivocation" [*aequivocatio a consilio*],[25] a use of the same word for specific reasons, even if for another content. Although Boethius, among others, also introduced the idea of proportion here, this "deliberate equivocation" is, nevertheless, by no means to be equated with the assertion of an analogy between the words and the thing they designate, as has commonly happened since the period of high Scholasticism.[26] It will be shown that a "deliberate equivocation" [*aequivocatio a consilio*] takes place in doxological statements, although no analogy between the ordinary meaning of our words and the being of God is intended; or, better, the

---

among the names devised for creatures could we apply one to him more than another; for in equivocal predication it makes no difference what name is used, since the word does not signify any real agreement" [*nec nominum quae creaturis aptantur, unum magis de eo dicendum esset quam aliud; quia ex aequivocis non differt quodcumque nomen imponatur, ex quo nulla rei convenienta attenditur* (*Truth*, I, p. 112)].

[25] Boethius, *In cat. Arist.*, lib. 1 (J. P. Migne, *Patrologie cursus completus, Series Latina*, 221 vols. [Paris, 1844–1902], 64, 166B).

[26] Explicit explanations on this point are rare. Still, Henry of Ghent, for example, has a detailed discussion of the relationship of the doctrine of analogy to the Boethian "deliberate equivocation" [*aequivocatio a consilio*] (*Summa Quaestionum ordinarium*, Paris [1520], fol. 270r). He summarizes his exposition with this sentence: "And such an equivocation as is in these four modes (proportion, relation, likeness, and fitness) is properly called analogy, because the term is applied to many things by priority and posteriority, and signifies by priority and posteriority" [*Et vocatur talis aequivocatio, quae est in istis quatuor modis (= proportio, relatio, similitudo, decensus), proprie analogia, quia nomen per prius et posterius dicitur de pluribus, et per prius et posterius significat illa*; tr. mine – Tr.]. On closer examination, important differences can be detected between the various Boethian species of "deliberate equivocation": qualitative similarity [*similitudo*] and analogy [*proportio*] constitute *mixtures* of univocal and equivocal components; only paronymy presents a genuine "deliberate equivocation" – a difference which, in any event, is overlooked if from the outset one construes it metaphysically as "participation" (so Hirschberger, "Paronymie und Analogie bei Aristotles," p. 196, with Olympiodorus).

analogy posited in the statement is transcended in the act of adoration.

Every metaphorical use of language requires that its basis be shown by reference to a state of affairs that occasions this metaphorical use of the word in question. The state of affairs must have some sort of relation to the comparatively original, genuine sense of the word in question in order for there to be sufficient cause for its metaphorical use. If one understands speech about God only in the sense of causal analogy, then the proximate occasion for this is in reflection upon the causal structure of the universe, or in looking at the place of this or that perfection in the system of the universe. That which occasions such reflection is, for its part, no longer important for the structure of the analogical transfer. In contrast to this, the occasion for doxological speech about God is a specific experience of a divine act.[27] On the basis of his deeds, God is praised as he who is eternally good, righteous, and faithful. But how do things stand with the possibility of experiencing an act of God? Would not such experience presuppose that one already possesses a specific idea of God which he brings with him to the experience? And can this idea, on its part, arise in any other way than by analogical transfer (if, in fact, the reality of God is supposed to be only indirectly experienceable and representable)? We now note that the indirectness of experience and speech about God that formed the basis of our discussion is itself complex. This must now be studied more closely.

One speaks of an act of God in reference to a concrete event that nevertheless can always be described in another way without having recourse to God. Perhaps it would then be described less appropriately or more superficially in that case. Otherwise talk about a divine act would be completely dispensable for an understanding of the event. But if one concedes that specific circumstances – or rather, actually, all events, only not with the same degree of clarity in every case – can be understood in their full significance only when they are seen as acts of God, it still holds that one can describe the same events even if their

[27] E. Schlink, *The Coming Christ*, pp. 20f.

dimension of depth is obscured. Such obscuration is characteristic of our everyday experience, so that our speaking of an act
of God in the circumstances of our experience seems to be
something appended to them which has nothing to do with the
things that are experienced. Above all, the experience of a
divine action in an event does not permit of the same indispensability being imputed of another as the perception of the event
itself which is in question. It may, therefore, seem as if speaking
of a divine act were a merely subjective way of construing the
event in question. But it is this appearance which is deceptive;
and such deception can arise out of a lack of understanding of
the inner basis of speech about God generally. Namely, in the
moment in which we grasp, by means of a single event, the
totality of the reality in which we live and around which our
lives circulate, there we experience a work of God in the individual event.[28] This happens when and to the extent that we are
able to think of the unity of all reality and of our own existence
only on the basis of a presupposition that transcends everything
we find before us or within us, and which we name God or the
divine – still prior to any distinction between monotheism and
polytheism, or between personal or impersonal conceptions of
God. As opposed to this, atheism either does not understand
the scope of the word "God" and only fights against the scare-
crow of a specific theistic world view – then it would itself speak

[28] Gerhard Ebeling also, rightly, saw that speaking about God is connected with becoming aware of the whole of reality. However, this is not
primarily a phenomenon of conscience, but, initially, of a rational experience of reality as it is, whereby it is well to note, in any case, that reality is
always more than it allows to be discovered. Only what is experienced as
reality – and this certainly does not occur in a way that bypasses reason – can
place the conscience under obligation. Cf. "Theological Reflections on Conscience," in *Word and Faith,* tr. James Leitch (London: SCM Press and
Philadelphia: Fortress Press, 1960), pp. 407-33, esp. p. 412. See also
Ebeling's way of determining the relationship between reason and conscience
in RGG[3], VI, col. 822, according to which both have "ultimately *one* origin,"
although for all that "rationally governed thought participates in that abstraction from real human existence which distinguishes reason from conscience." But is not reason in its unconditionedness, in the question about
the totality of reality, concerned in the last analysis with precisely the
determination of men, of real human existence?

of God, only under another name – or else it clings to the details of events and does not press on far enough to run into the question of the totality of reality beyond everything given.

The indirectness of speech about God has to do, first of all, with the difference between the current, concrete event and the totality of reality experienced therein.[29] In this connection something occurs which we cannot pursue any further at this point, viz., the current understanding of the totality of reality and also of God are influenced by concrete experience, but, conversely, the individual experience appears in a strange, new light when viewed from the standpoint of the understanding of God and of the earlier experiences that have gone into this. Therefore, in order to fulfill the task of describing the individual experience in its relationship to the totality of reality and to the origin of this, in other words, to the current understanding of God that already developed in history, another language is required than that by means of which we express these individual experiences in themselves or in relation to other contents. That is the second aspect of the indirectness of our speech about God. Not only is God never directly experienced in an unmediated confrontation, but the finite reality that is distinct from God, and which is capable of mediating experience of God in the way indicated, requires, in order to be able to assert this event as act of God, another way of speaking than the ordinary language which names this particular event as taken by itself. This, again, is related to the fact that the depth dimension of all events is usually overlooked because it is screened out by the orientation of our experience toward domination over the world. Therefore, a special language is necessary which speaks of this or that event as an act of God. The expression "act of God" itself already belongs to this religious language. And analogical transference occurs precisely at this point.

We saw earlier that this involves the use, as a designation for

[29] Naturally God is not interchangeable with the totality of all reality, but is indeed its origin. For this reason, it is significant that without the idea of God even that of a whole of reality is without support.

God, of a term that is at home in our experience of the world. The tradition posed the problem of analogy in this way. What it failed to see, as far as I know, is the circumstance that the word transferred to God does not stem from that experience which is thereby understood as an act of God. When the unmolested transit of the Israelites through the Red Sea and the subsequent drowning of the Egyptian pursuers are understood and designated as an act of God, then a word appears that really has nothing to do with the description of the circumstances at the Red Sea. That a sea is there; that waters were driven back by the wind; that a column of men succeeded in crossing the ford; that others followed who were drowned in the returning water; all this lies on another plane than the description of this event as the act of a person. But that is precisely what happens when this event is related to the divine power which determines its total horizon.[30] This power is now thought of as an acting person, analogous to man. And since the event in question, whose improbability made awareness of the operation of this power possible, allowed the Israelites (or proto-Israelites) involved to see salvation coming to them in a situation of dire need, this event thus comes to be understood as a redemptive, merciful act of God.

We must pause here for a moment. The analogies which serve to express the depth dimension of the event, its reference to the totality of reality and to its divine ground, are taken from the realm of human behavior in these cases, and obviously not in these cases only. They are anthropomorphisms. How can we account for the fact that the experience of divine power in an

[30] The circumstantial formulation is intended to express the fact that an unqualified monotheistic conception of deity must not be thought of in this context. The form of a god always has a relationship to the totality of reality, even when a plurality of gods are reverenced and only a partial aspect of reality is dealt with in a given instance. Cf. W. F. Otto's statement: "The god, however he may be named and distinguished from the rest of his kind, is never a single power, but always the whole being of the world to which his revelation belongs. We call those powers demons or spirits to whom a limited sphere of influence is assigned. But that one of these ever developed into a god is an empty assertion of evolutionary theory" (*Theophaneia; Der Geist der Altgreichischen Religion* [Hamburg, 1956], pp. 22).

event is repeatedly described by means of analogies to human behavior? How does it happen that gods, whether conceived as a multiplicity of gods or as the one God, are so often represented in precisely human form?

This brings us to the problem in the phenomenology of religion of the so-called personification of the divine power. I have elsewhere[31] expressed the opinion that the personification of the divine power is connected with the conviction of its essential (not merely situationally conditioned) non-manipulability. Whatever permits of being manipulated – if not at the moment, then still in principle – becomes a thing. Only that is a person which has a hidden, inner side and is not completely transparent to thought, so that it confronts one as an independent being. Thus, even today the experience of the child tends toward personification of the forms of its environment, which for us adults are mere things. This goes on until his acculturation into our modern objectified [*versachlichte*] everyday world gives rise to the conviction that, in principle, everything is at our disposal with the exception – as we still believe – of other men, whom we therefore respect as persons. If this conjecture illuminates the basis of religious personification,[32] then it is possible to understand why the divine power experienced in a particular event was understood to be that of an acting person. Whether we can also understand the divine ground of the totality of reality as a person is another question. Its solution depends upon whether for us this totality, as it expresses itself in individual events, is in principle manipulable or not. The later would be the case if we understood the totality of reality as a history of ever new events, as the Israelites tried to do: the God

[31] RGG[3], V, article on "Person," cols. 232f.

[32] Of course, the problem is far from solved by the above remarks. One would have to inquire further, for example, whether the personification of deity is not connected with a deeper level of this phenomenon, viz., that man asks about God when he asks about himself and vice versa. The question about God and that about man can only be answered together, although the one may not be used to dissolve the other, as Feuerbach worked it out. But perhaps the incarnation of God is to be understood as the fulfillment of this coinherence and thus, also, of the phenomenon of personification.

of history is essentially person because events occur at his initiative in unforseeable ways.[33] If, on the contrary, the totality of reality is conceived primarily under the idea of law, then the ground of all events can hardly be understood as Creator and thus as person. This is shown by the depersonalization of the divine in the history of Greek religion, a process which surely is connected with the Greek passion for the normal and the rational.

Thus, it is clear that speaking of an act already presupposes a specific understanding of reality which expresses itself in the manner in which individual events are experienced. It involves an analogizing transfer which must be grounded in a total understanding of reality and which on its part already has the same structure as doxological speech about God. It is distinguished from the latter only by the fact that usually God is not spoken of in a generality such as acting person – this would be a doxological statement, as is found, for instance, in the idea of omnipotence – but rather designates a specific event as an act of God. Only this intention toward a specific event distinguishes kerygmatic from doxological statements. Thus, kerygmatic speech about a specific divine act already presupposes a doxological element, viz., that God is an acting person. On the other hand, the experienced divine action which underlies the kerygmatic formulations provides the basis for further knowledge of God insofar as he is the one who acts just that way and not another. That he chose Israel – did that not happen by his mercy? That he gave this people a land – was that not an expression of his goodness and grace? By fulfilling what had been foretold he proved his faithfulness, and by maintaining his covenant, even in "wrath" against its violators, he proved himself righteous. All these statements rediscover in God features of a human disposition. Their transfer to God is meaningful, generally speaking, once the divine power has been

---

[33] The real core of personal life is not yet reached by this remark, viz., being in relation to another, which finds its fulfillment in love. But the presupposition for such a mode of being, the freedom to produce an effect, is included in the concept of act.

understood as an acting person. In every specific case, however, such a transfer needs to be supported by the peculiar character of the particular event which is experienced and proclaimed as an act of God. By means of such doxological statements, Israel built up something like a characterological picture of its God, based on the cumulative experience of how this God had shown himself to be through his dealings with Israel. Thus, "attributes" accrued to him from the mouths of his worshipers, to which nevertheless he was not bound as to a law.[34] The tension between the attributes themselves kept alive an awareness of the provisionality of all speech about God, a provisionality which is grounded in the character of all such speech as analogous transference in the worshipful glorification of God's sublimity.

Is such provisionality the last word about all human speech about God? It seems that the idea of the revelation of God goes beyond this, provided that revelation means an ultimate self-disclosure and thus a self-commitment, a final self-demonstration of God. When occasion arises for speaking about a self-revelation of God, then and only then is our speech about God, in all its provisionality, nevertheless carried beyond this provisionality "in all its provisionality," because speaking of God as a self-revealing person is itself doxologically fashioned and open to the infinity of the freedom of God. How, in spite of this, revelation in the sense of an ultimate self-disclosure, can still be possible is barely conceivable. But in the history of Jesus there was a more differentiated and convincing event than any previous thought had conceived or could have imagined. Therefore, the concern to give conceptual development to what revelation really is can do no better than to reflect upon the history of Jesus.

The ultimacy of the self-demonstration of God through Jesus is grounded, on the one hand, in Jesus' own claim to possess

[34] In this connection it is important to note that the "attributes" of the human disposition, virtues as well as vices, have the structure of law. They are not the causes of a particular behavior in a specific situation, but they regulate human behavior in a way similar to laws which become effective when a given occasion presents itself. Cf. Gilbert Ryle, *The Concept of Mind* (London: Hutchinson and New York: Barnes and Noble, 1949), pp. 85ff.

full authority to execute the ultimate will of God over every man who encountered him. The resurrection of Jesus from the dead brought about for the first time a confirmation of his claim by God himself. Provided that an event can at all be understood as an act of God, then this event and its meaning cannot be understood as anything else than the vindication of the earthly ministry of Jesus against his judges. Both together, the claim of Jesus and the confirmation he experienced, provide the basis for Christian speech about the revelation of God in Jesus. By means of the event of the resurrection of Jesus, God himself attested to the ultimacy of his public ministry, and this very ultimacy entails revelation. If this is true, then God can henceforth no longer be present in any other way than as he was proclaimed by Jesus, namely, as the Father who wants all men to be his children and who makes them his children by his forgiving love, and moves them to community among each other. The metaphorical character of our speech about God, which Jesus also shared when he spoke of God as father, is at the same time taken up by God himself, insofar as he raised Jesus and thus gave his acknowledgment to him.

In any case, the metaphorical character of our speech about God is not thereby overcome. Only it is one thing whether our speech about God leads to emptiness, and quite another if God himself acknowledges the metaphors of our devotional speech about him – even if this statement again has a metaphorical character. Even the revelation of God in Jesus does not yet empower us with final knowledge of God. Although it itself has ultimate validity, we cannot grasp its full content. This limitation is rooted in the peculiar proleptic character of the resurrection of Jesus, viz., that the final salvation or judgment which for us still belongs to the undecided future has already befallen him and, indeed, for the sake of salvation, so that thereby the way to salvation is open to the rest of us through faith in Jesus.[35] The resurrection of Jesus is the ultimate revelation of the glory of God only to the extent that the ultimate salvation corresponding to the ultimacy of Jesus' claim has actually happened

[35] For a fuller discussion of this matter, see above, pp. 204ff.

in him. Only to that extent is Jesus' claim to absolute authority *unqualifiedly* confirmed by his resurrection. However, it may be said that in the resurrection of Jesus, the final future of man has already occurred in him and has been decided in favor of salvation, only because this event in the past is viewed in union with the future that is still outstanding from our point of view. For this reason, only in that future will we be able to know as we have been known: that is to say, only then will we be able to know the full reality of what has already happened in the resurrection of Jesus, which as yet we can speak of only in a metaphorical manner.[36] But because we can speak of the revelation of God in Jesus only in fore-conception of the universal end of history, even our speech about God on the basis of his revelation in Jesus still remains provisional. This applies to knowledge of the love of God in Jesus just as much as to the confession of his unity with God, which is presupposed in the ultimacy of Jesus' authority. This provisionality does not prevent our doxological statements from being well founded, however. But it opens up room for a plurality of formulations of what happened in Jesus Christ – a consequence of fundamental importance for the ecumenical life of Christians, as Edmund Schlink has repeatedly emphasized.[37]

The adoring speech about God himself which is contained in doxology always points ahead to God's revelation. When, on the basis of individual experiences, statements are made about God himself as he is from eternity to eternity – viz., almighty, gracious, just – an ultimacy is claimed that can be justified only by the revelation of the deity of God. And only the humility of adoration protects it against becoming the overweening pride

---

[36] This metaphorical character of our language differs in intention from that of doxological language. For the latter pertains to the eternal reality of God, whereas the former deals with the future expected and hoped for by men. Nevertheless, both are closely related because only in that final future can God be known by us as he has revealed himself. And in both cases it is a matter of "absolute" metaphors, i.e., such that can no longer be displaced and outbid by concepts in the strict sense of that term. On this expression, see H. Blumenberg, *Paradigmen zu einer Metaphorologie* (Bonn, 1960), pp. 84f.

[37] *The Coming Christ*, pp. 78ff.

of having comprehended the eternal truth of God by means of human words, as if one henceforth knew which attitude befitted God and which did not. The moment of ultimacy that is included in doxological statements about God makes it possible to say that even the Old Testament speech about God himself, based on his actions, anticipates in its essential content the Christ-event in which God himself is for the first time revealed with the ultimacy presupposed by doxological speech. And, as we saw, even the Christ-event is only a prolepsis of the consummated revelation of God which will occur only in the future, with the return of Christ. From this standpoint, light is shed on the substantive legitimacy of designating worshipful speech as "doxology." For the appearance of the *doxa*, the glory of God, at the end of all history is nothing else than his definitive revelation. The expression "doxology" thus contains a reference to the fact that all worshipful speech about God anticipates his ultimate revelation.

We have hereby completed a circuit of the question of how speech about God rooted in adoration can be true, even though it contains only an analogy between uses of language – between the theological and the ordinary use of language – but not an analogy of the language used to God himself. At the place where the old doctrine of analogy asserted a correspondence of the word used to name God with God himself, there stands, in our view, the concept of revelation. This is connected with the opposition between the Greek understanding of the divine as the ground of the present world, and the biblical conviction that the creation is still underway to its proper reality and that the essences of all things will finally be decided simultaneously with the final end by which God will be definitively revealed. The creation occurs from the side of the end. For this reason, God is not – as it were, "naturelike" [*naturhaft*] – in analogy to our speech about him, but rather – once again, metaphorically speaking – he makes our metaphorical speech his own through his revelation, and thereby for the first time gives our words of praise their ultimately valid content. The correspondence of our words to God himself has not already been decided, but is yet to be decided. This temporal difference between our speech about God and its fulfillment by God himself cannot be expressed by means of the concept of analogy. Judged from our standpoint, the concepts by which we praise God's essence become equivocal in the act of the sacrifice of praise. At the same time, however, we utter them in the hope of a fulfillment which by far overcomes the distance fixed in the analogy.

Date Due